Flash + After Effects

Flash + After Effects

Chris Jackson

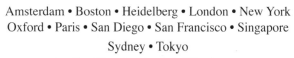

Amsterdam • Boston • Heidelberg • London • New York
Oxford • Paris • San Diego • San Francisco • Singapore
Sydney • Tokyo
Focal Press is an imprint of Elsevier

ELSEVIER

Acquisitions Editor: Paul Temme
Publishing Services Manager: George Morrison
Project Manager: Andre A. Cuello
Assistant Editor: Chris Simpson
Marketing Manager: Rebecca Pease
Cover Design: Chris Jackson

Focal Press is an imprint of Elsevier
30 Corporate Drive, Suite 400, Burlington, MA 01803, USA
Linacre House, Jordan Hill, Oxford OX2 8DP, UK

∞ Recognizing the importance of preserving what has been written, Elsevier prints its books
on acid-free paper whenever possible.

Library of Congress Cataloging-in-Publication Data
Application submitted

British Library Cataloguing-in-Publication Data
A catalogue record for this book is available from the British Library.

ISBN: 978-0-240-81031-7

For information on all Focal Press publications visit our website at www.books.elsevier.com

08 09 10 11 12   5 4 3 2 1

Printed in the China

Table of Contents

Chapter 4: Alpha Channels

Chapter 5: Type in Motion

Chapter 6: The Third Dimension

Chapter 7: Character Animation

Chapter 8: Visual Effects

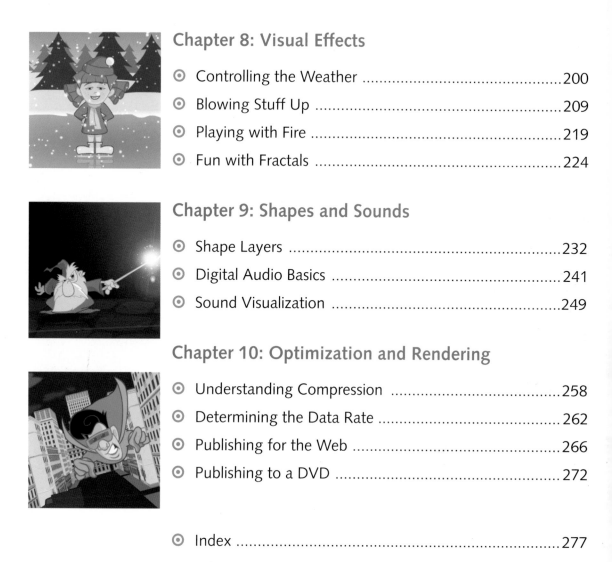

Chapter 9: Shapes and Sounds

Chapter 10: Optimization and Rendering

Introduction

Flash Designers: Take your projects to the next level with After Effects' robust toolset. You are about to take a journey that combines these two powerhouse applications. Enter the world of Adobe After Effects. Welcome aboard.

What Is This Book About?

This book will help Flash animators and designers understand how After Effects integrates with Flash. Now that Adobe owns both Flash and After Effects, the two programs are becoming tightly interwoven together with every product update. Flash provides a creative web tool for animation and interactivity. After Effects provides an easy-to-use application for creating visual effects and motion graphics. With the ever increasing presence of video on the Web, Flash animators and designers are jumping on the bandwagon and integrating After Effects into their projects.

Why would someone who uses Flash care about After Effects? After Effects provides many features and effects that not only can enhance Flash projects but save on development time because of how these two applications are integrated. After Effects implements a variety of ways to create video with alpha, animate graphics in 2D or 3D space, and then export the animation with a transparent background, as well as apply a variety of effects and presets that help differentiate a Flash designer's work.

For Flash animators, After Effects takes their project to the next level in 2D animation. It provides Flash animators with an assortment of visual effects that are rather difficult or next to impossible to achieve in Flash. Within After Effects, these complex effects can be applied through a simple drag-and-drop interaction. After Effects incorporates character animation tools (parenting and puppets) that easily hinge and animate multilayered artwork. After Effects also incorporates a 3D engine, allowing animators to add depth to their backgrounds.

After Effects is an excellent tool to prepare your Flash animation for broadcast. This book covers the technical requirements you need to be aware of in video production. You will explore the world of broadcast design and learn the basics in setting proper frame size and frame rates, pixel aspect ratios, title and action safe areas, and color management.

Digital video no longer has to be linear. Flash designers can use ActionScript to control video playback. Cue points can be added to the video that allow users to jump to certain frames (similar to DVD chapters). These cue points can also trigger other events or animations in the published Flash file. Flash supports alpha channels in digital video. This feature can enhance Flash games and instructional content.

All a Flash user needs to do is know more about After Effects, its features, and what they can do with them to enhance their Flash projects. That is what this book addresses. The book's objective is to bridge the two applications together and clearly demonstrate how Flash and After Effects can be integrated to produce enriched content for the Web, CD/DVD, and broadcast.

Who Is This Book For?

The primary audience for this book is Flash animators and designers. These Flash users can be professionals in the workforce, students, or anyone interested in creatively enhancing their Flash projects. This book assumes that readers have prior Flash experience. They should have a working knowledge of the Flash workspace and an understanding of animation concepts and basic ActionScript.

The book provides an introduction to After Effects, its workspace, and tools. The book does not necessarily show the reader what all the tools do; rather, it shows how to use them to enrich Flash animation and interactive projects. Flash is everywhere and with the enhanced video capabilities present in the new versions of Flash Player, showcasing After Effects content using Flash is the best way to go.

Regardless of how a reader approaches this book, using After Effects to enhance Flash content is growing in popularity. This book teaches readers how to think creatively and get excited about animation and visual effects in their Flash projects. It clearly illustrates how these two applications complement each other and help raise the design bar for Web, CD/DVD, and broadcast.

Book Structure and Layout Conventions

Flash + After Effects is designed to walk the reader through project-based exercises that effectively use Flash and After Effects. To use this book, you need to install both Flash CS3 and After Effects CS3 on either your Macintosh or Windows computer. If you do not have a licensed copy, you can download fully functional time-limited trial versions on Adobe's website **(www.adobe.com)**.

The book's structure falls into two sections. The first section discusses how the two applications can work together in unison. Chapter 1 introduces you to After Effects, its workspace and workflow. As you build a typical After Effects project, comparisons are made between Flash and After Effects. Chapters 2 and 3 illustrate how to seamlessly import and export raster and vector animation from each application. A video primer is provided as you journey into broadcast design.

The second section of the book explores visual effects and animation techniques involved in using both applications together. You will learn about using alpha channels for keying and enhancing interactivity. Chapter 5 puts vector animation to work using Text layers and animation presets. In chapter 6 you will create 3D backgrounds with cameras and lights. Chapter 7 provides a lot of fun animating characters with Parenting, Expressions, and the Puppet Tool.

After Effects is the industry standard when it comes to visual effects. You will see why this is true in chapter 8. You must not forget audio. It plays an important role in your Flash animation and chapter 9. The last chapter, chapter 10, discusses optimization and publishing.

Chapter exercises consist of practical applications as well as experimental projects. Each exercise provides step-by-step instructions and tips for the reader to use in conceptualizing and visualizing creative solutions to their own Flash and After Effects projects. Videos used have been created in the NTSC format.

To help you get the most out of this book, let's look at the layout conventions used in the chapters.

- **Words in bold** refer to names of files, folders, layers, or compositions
- Menu selections are presented like this: **Effect > Simulation > Shatter**
- Code blocks in Flash are separated from the text like this:

```
// import Flash packages
import fl.video.*;
import fl.controls.ProgressBarMode;
```

- Icons are used throughout the book. Here is a brief explanation of what they are and what they mean.

 DVD: Reference to files on the accompanying DVD-ROM

 Note: Supplemental information to the text that sheds a light on a procedure or offers miscellaneous options available to you

 Caution: Warnings that you need to read

All of the footage, source code, and files are provided on the accompanying DVD-ROM found in the back of the book. Each chapter has its own folder. Inside each folder you will find the material needed to complete each exercise. Competed versions for every exercise are provided in a **Completed** folder in each chapter folder. As you work through the chapter's exercises, you can choose to manually build the project or review the finished example.

All of the material inside this book and on the DVD-ROM is copyright protected. They are included only for your learning and experimentation. Please respect the copyrights. I encourage you to use your own artwork and experiment with each exercise. This is not an exact science. The specific values given in this book are suggestions. The ActionScript is used to provide a solution. If you know of a different method, by all means, use it. There are many ways to perform the same task for both applications.

About the Author

Chris Jackson is a computer graphics designer and professor at Rochester Institute of Technology (RIT). He teaches a variety of graduate-level courses including 2D Computer Animation, 3D Computer Graphics, Instructional Multimedia, and Motion Graphics. Before joining the RIT faculty, Chris was a new media designer with Eastman KODAK Company, creating and delivering online instructional training via the Web and CD-ROM.

Chris' professional work has received over 25 distinguished national and international awards for online communication. His areas of research include user's experience design, 2D character animation, digital storytelling, and interactive design for children. Chris continues to publish and present his research and professional work at ACM SIGGRAPH and the Society for Technical Communication (STC). Chris is co-author of *Flash 3D: Animation, Interactivity and Games* (Focal Press, October 2006).

He continues to be a Flash animator, designer, developer, and consultant for worldwide corporations. He lectures and conducts workshops relating to interactive design and Flash animation.

Acknowledgements

This book is dedicated to my wife, Justine. Thank you for all your unconditional love and the constant support. I love you with all my heart.

This book is for my parents, Roger and Glenda. Thank you for your inspiration and encouragement for me to become an artist. You made it possible for me to fulfill my dreams. I love you both.

This book has taken many months to write with a lot of time and effort put into making the examples. I owe a debt of gratitude to all at Focal Press, but especially Paul Temme, Dennis McGonagle, and Chris Simpson. Thank you for all your support and advice in enabling me to bring this book to print.

Special thanks goes to my Computer Graphics Design students at the Rochester Institute of Technology, especially Darryl Marshall, Scott Bessey, Steve Gallo, Itai Shperber, and Wail Al Hamid. Thank you for finding the time from all of your assignments and thesis projects to help me with this book.

Some of the images and stock footage used in this book are from the following royalty-free sources: www.istockphoto.com and Artbeats (www.artbeats.com). Special thanks to Kevin Poll of iStock International Inc., and Julie Hill of Artbeats for assisting me in acquiring footage to use in this book.

For Instructors

Flash + After Effects provides hands-on exercises that demonstrate core features in Flash and After Effects. As an instructor, I know you appreciate the hard work and effort that goes into creating lessons and examples for your courses. I hope you find the information and exercises useful and can adapt it for your own classes.

All that I ask is for your help and cooperation in protecting the copyrights of this book. If an instructor or student distributes copies of the source files to anyone who has not purchased the book, that violates the copyright protection. Reproducing pages from this book or duplicating any part of the DVD-ROM is also a copyright infringement. If you own the book, you can adapt the exercises using your own footage and artwork without infringing copyright.

Thank you for your cooperation!

Credits

The following stock images were provided for this book:

- ▶ **Portrait of Red Haired Girl**, photo courtesy of iStockphoto, Nadezhda Kulagina, Image #4367558
- ▶ **Window of Opportunity**, photo courtesy of iStockphoto, Paul Kline, Image #3013679
- ▶ **Pirate's Secret**, photo courtesy of iStockphoto, Joshua Blake, Image #2961897
- ▶ **Big City**, illustration courtesy of iStockphoto, Boris Zaytsev, Image #2749388

The following stock footage was provided for this book:

- ▶ **ReelExplosions 2**, footage courtesy of Artbeats, #RE222
- ▶ **ReelFire 1**, footage courtesy of Artbeats, #RF107
- ▶ **ReelFire 2**, footage courtesy of Artbeats, #RF215

CHAPTER 1

Getting Started in After Effects

As your journey towards integrating Flash and After Effects begins, you first need to understand the similarities and differences between the two applications. This chapter introduces After Effects and compares its project workflow to Flash.

Project Workflow

Flash and After Effects follow a similar project workflow (Figure 1.1). You start a project by defining what the end product will be. Once you have a clear goal in mind, storyboard and create your assets. Next, you import and arrange the media elements on layers within a timeline. Once everything is in place, you add complexity to the project through either animation or programming. After previewing and refining the project to meet its output goals, you publish the project for its intended destination.

1. Define the End Product   **2.** Storyboard   **3.** Design and Layout

4. Animate and Program   **5.** Preview Project   **6.** Publish Final Product

Figure 1.1: *A project workflow that can be applied to either Flash or After Effects.*

Both Flash and After Effects allow you to import and layer raster and vector images, digital video and sound. However, when it comes to adding complexity to a project, the two applications differ. Some of these differences are dramatic while others may not seem so obvious.

One major difference is interactivity. Flash has its own native scripting language called ActionScript. ActionScript allows you to create nonlinear interactive content for DVD, CD-ROM, or the Web. After Effects provides a JavaScript-based scripting language used for automating animation, not interactivity. It can only render out linear content in the form of a Flash animation, image sequence, digital video, or sound.

Another difference between Flash and After Effects is output. Typically a Flash project is vector-based and is published for the Web. Vector art uses math to store and create an image. This makes the artwork resolution-independent. It can be scaled without losing any detail. As a result, vector-based artwork produces rather small file sizes that are ideal for Web delivery.

After Effects focuses primarily on pixels, not vectors. These tiny units of color are grouped together to form an image (Figure 1.2). The resulting images tend to be photorealistic and larger in file size. A pixel-based, or raster, image is resolution-dependent. If scaled too large, the pixel grid becomes noticeable. A project in After Effects is usually designed to render out large video files destined for film or broadcast television.

Figure 1.2: *Vector art versus raster art.*

Over the past few years, there has been an exciting evolution in Flash and in the way it handles video content. With each new release, Flash is incorporating more and more video playback options and controls. After Effects has also evolved to add cross-compatibility with Flash. After Effects includes the ability to import SWF files with transparent backgrounds and export Flash Video (FLV) and SWF file formats.

Flash and After Effects users are slowly discovering the creative potential in combining these two powerhouse applications. I say slowly because this integration still remains relatively uncharted. It is truly exciting to explore and unlock the artistic possibilities that both applications offer each other. That is what this book is about. You are the explorer and the book provides a road map. It opens the door for you, the Flash designer, to explore and unleash your Flash creativity by learning about After Effects.

So as Flash designers, where does one start in After Effects? You begin by exploring the structure of its user interface, referred to as the workspace. So let's dive in and get an overview of how After Effects works.

Creating a Project

In this chapter, you will build a typical After Effects project. The exercises are broken into four steps: creating a new composition using imported media, animating layer properties, applying effects, and rendering out your final composition. As you proceed through each exercise, comparisons will be made between Flash and After Effects.

 Locate the Chapter_01 folder on the DVD. Copy this folder to your hard drive. The folder contains all the files needed to complete the chapter exercises.

To see what you will build, locate and play the **DeepBlueTitle.mov** in the Completed folder inside Chapter_01. The goal of this project is to provide an overview on how to assemble a project in After Effects. It is a step-by-step tutorial that introduces you to After Effects, its workspace and workflow.

Figure 1.3: *The finished project is a title sequence in After Effects.*

Exercise 1: Creating a New Project

All your work in After Effects begins with a project file. This file references the imported files and holds the compositions created using those files. When you finish this first exercise, you should know what the Project, Composition, and Timeline panels are and how they work together. In addition to that, you'll know how to import media elements and save your project.

1. Launch **Adobe After Effects**. It opens an empty project by default.

> *Whereas Flash can open multiple movies, only one project in After Effects can be opened at a time. This is a key concept to understand. If you try to open another project or create a new project within After Effects, After Effects will close down the current project you are working on.*

2. The graphical user interface, referred to as the Workspace, can be configured in many ways. To make sure that you are using the same configuration as the book, locate the Workspace popup menu in the upper right corner. Select **Standard**. "Reset Standard" restores the Workspace to its original arrangement.

The Workspace

The Workspace is divided into several regions called frames. The frames consist of docked panels to reduce screen clutter. Most of the work done in After Effects revolves around three panels: the Project, Composition, and Timeline panel. If you were to compare these three panels to Flash's workspace, they are similar to the Library, Stage, and Timeline respectively.

Figure 1.4: *The project's Workspace should be set to Standard to be consistent with exercises in this book.*

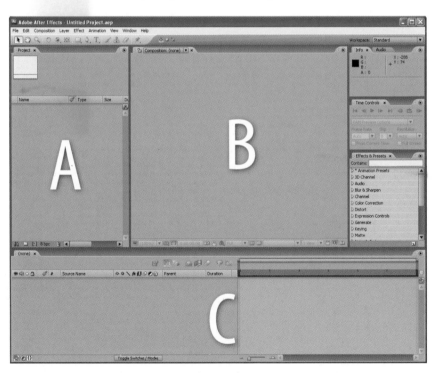

Figure 1.5: *The Workspace in After Effects consists of three primary panels. They are: A = Project panel, B = Composition panel, C = Timeline panel.*

If you are familiar with other Adobe products, this interface should look slightly familiar. Adobe has adopted a consistent graphical user interface across all their software. Some of the frame functionality such as expanding and collapsing panels should be familiar to you as Flash users.

Projects are made up of compositions. You create compositions from various imported files referred to as **footage**. Footage can be still images, image sequences, Flash SWF files, digital video clips and audio.

3. To import footage into After Effects, double-click inside the Project panel. This opens the Import File dialog box.

There are many ways to import footage into After Effects. You can select the File menu and choose Import. The keyboard shortcut is Command + i (Mac) or Control + i (Windows). You can also use Adobe Bridge or drag files from the desktop into After Effects.

4. From within the Import File dialog box, locate the **01_Footage** folder inside the Chapter_01 folder you copied to your hard drive. Select the folder. Click on **Import Folder**.

Figure 1.6:
When importing files, a timesaver is to double-click inside the Project panel.

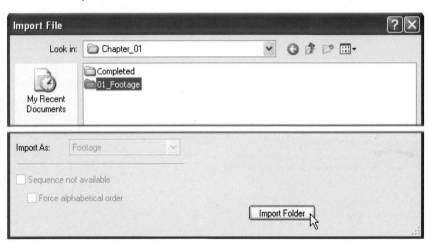

Figure 1.7: *Import the 01_Footage folder.*

5. In the DeepBlueScene.psd dialog box that appears, choose **Import Kind > Composition**. Click **OK**.

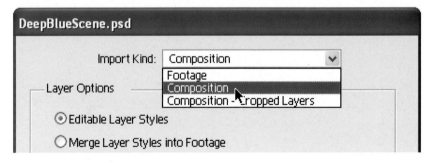

Figure 1.8: *After Effects will detect if a Photoshop or Illustrator file contains multiple layers. If detected, a dialog box appears requesting additional input on how you want the file to be imported. This setting imports the layered Photoshop file as a composition. Each Photoshop layer is imported as a separate piece of footage.*

6. In the DeepBlueTitle.ai dialog box that appears, choose **Import Kind >
Composition**. Click **OK**.

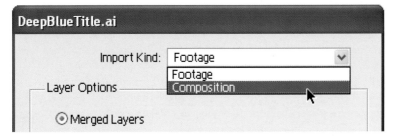

Figure 1.9: *This setting imports the layered Illustrator file as a composition.
Each Illustrator layer is imported as a separate piece of footage.*

The Project Panel

A folder appears inside the Project panel. It is labeled 01_Footage, the same
name as the folder you imported. Double-click on the folder to reveal its
contents. After Effects supports a wide range of file formats including Illustrator,
Photoshop, QuickTime, and even Flash SWF files.

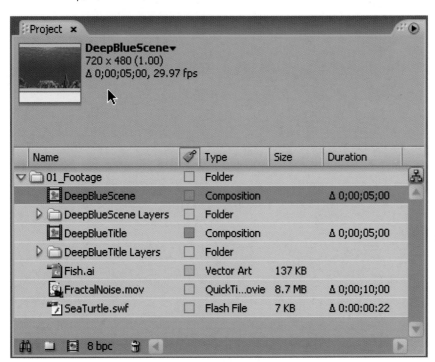

Figure 1.10: *The Project panel (left) is similar to the Library in Flash (right).*   **Flash Library**

The Project panel in After Effects acts a lot like the Library in Flash. It displays
imported footage and stores the compositions created with these files. When
you select an item, a thumbnail image appears at the top of the Project panel
along with information about the selected footage. Buttons along the bottom

of the panel allow you to search for footage, organize files into folders, create new compositions, and delete selected items.

 Unlike Flash, footage imported into After Effects is NOT embedded within the project. These files are always linked to the folder they were imported from. If you delete, rename, or change the location of your files after they were imported, After Effects will lose the link and not be able to properly display the footage.

7. Good organizational skills are essential to creating projects in After Effects. Let's organize the Project panel a little better by creating a new "Comps" folder that will only contain compositions. To do this:

   ▸ Deselect any selected item in the Project panel by clicking on the gray area under the footage.

   ▸ Click on the **New Folder** icon at the bottom of the Project panel.

   ▸ Rename the new folder to Comps. You can rename any folder at any time by selecting it and pressing the Return/Enter key on the keyboard. This highlights the name and allows you to rename the item.

Figure 1.11: *Create a new folder and name it Comps.*

8. Click and drag the two compositions (DeepBlueScene and DeepBlueTitle) from the 01_Footage folder to the new Comps folder.

Name		Type	Size	Duration	
▽ 📁 01_Footage	☐	Folder			
▷ 📁 DeepBlueScene Layers	☐	Folder			
▷ 📁 DeepBlueTitle Layers	☐	Folder			
📄 Fish.ai	☐	Vector Art	137 KB		
📄 FractalNoise.mov	☐	QuickTi...ovie	8.7 MB	Δ 0;00;10;00	
📄 SeaTurtle.swf	☐	Flash File	7 KB	Δ 0:00:00:22	
▽ 📁 Comps	☐	Folder			
📄 DeepBlueScene	☐	Composition		Δ 0;00;05;00	
📄 DeepBlueTitle	☐	Composition		Δ 0;00;05;00	

Figure 1.12: *Move the two compositions from 01_Footage to the Comps folder.*

ℹ️ *As projects become more complex, the Project panel can get quite cluttered. It is not uncommon to have hundreds of footage files. Get into the habit of organizing your footage into separate folders.*

Chapter 1: Getting Started in After Effects

Figure 1.13: *Composition Settings specify the size and duration of the composition.*

To animate or apply an effect to the footage, you first must create a new **composition**. A composition is a container that holds layers of footage. These layers are manipulated within the space and time defined by the composition.

 Think of compositions as movie clips in Flash. Compositions are independent timelines. You can have as many compositions as you want within an After Effects project. Each composition contains its own unique timeline just like movie clips in Flash.

9. Select the Comps folder in the Project panel. Select **Composition > New Composition**. Make the following settings in the dialog box that appears:

   ▶ Composition Name: **DeepBlue_FINAL**
   ▶ Width: **720**
   ▶ Height: **480**
   ▶ Pixel Aspect Ratio: **Square Pixels**
   ▶ Frame Rate: **29.97**
   ▶ Resolution: **Full**
   ▶ Duration: **0:00:05:00**

   Click **OK**. The new composition opens with a black screen in the Composition panel. The Timeline opens a tab. These two panels work closely together.

The Composition Panel

The Composition panel acts like the Stage in Flash. You use it to compose, preview, and edit your project. Buttons along the bottom of the Composition panel include controls for magnification, viewing color channels, displaying the current frame, and adjusting the resolution. As you resize your panels, you may want to set the magnification to **Fit up to 100%**.

Figure 1.14: *The Composition panel is similar to the Stage in Flash. A popular magnification setting is Fit up to 100%.*

The Timeline Panel

The Timeline shows how the structure of your composition is built. The panel is divided into two sections. The right section is the actual Timeline where each layer's starting and stopping points, duration, and keyframes are displayed. The left section of the Timeline panel is broken up into a series of columns and switches. These affect how the layers are composited together.

Figure 1.15: *The Timeline panel is divided into two sections. Controls and switches for layer compositing are on the left. The actual Timeline is on the right.*

As the Timeline becomes more populated and complex, you may want to zoom in or out. Use the Zoom slider at the bottom of the Timeline panel to do this.

Figure 1.16: *The Zoom slider allows you to control the view of the time graph. The Zoom In and Zoom Out buttons next to the slider provide incremental zooming.*

10. Click and drag the **DeepBlueScene Layers** folder from the Project panel to the left side of the Timeline. Release the mouse. Three layers appear in the Timeline and the Composition panel displays the underwater scene (Figure 1.15).

11. Click and drag the **DeepBlueTitle Layers** folder from the Project panel to the Timeline. Position it above the **grass/DeepBlueScene** layer. Release the mouse. Two Illustrator layers are added to the TImeline. The Deep Blue title appears in the center of the Composition panel.

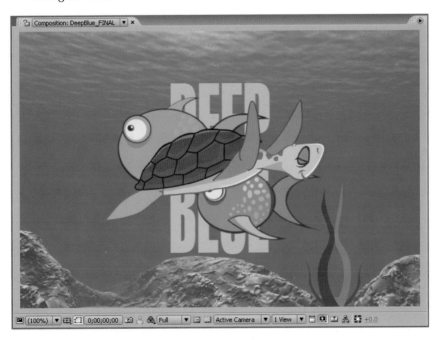

Figure 1.17: *Add the Illustrator layers to the Timeline.*

12. Click and drag the **Fish.ai** file from the Project panel to the Timeline. Position it at the top of the layers in the Timeline.

13. Click and drag the **SeaTurtle.swf** file from the Project panel to the Timeline. Position it at the top of the Timeline. Your Composition panel should look like Figure 1.18.

Figure 1.18: *Add the fish and sea turtle artwork to the Composition.*

14. Your first project is well on its way. Before you do anything else, save your project. Select **File > Save.** The keyboard shortcut is **Command + s** (Mac) or **Control + s** (Windows). This opens the Save As dialog box.

15. Name your file **01_DeepBlueTitle** and save it in your Chapter_01 folder on your hard drive. Click **Save**. The file has an **.aep** file extension. This stands for After Effects Project (AEP). The saved file is not meant to be a standalone file such as a Flash projector. An AEP file is only read by After Effects.

Figure 1.19: *Save your project to the Chapter_01 folder.*

Let's do a quick review. The three primary panels you used in this exercise include the Project, Composition, and Timeline. You created a new project, imported footage into the Project panel, and built a new composition using the imported items. Now it's time to learn how to bring this project to life.

After you create a composition, the remaining amount of work takes place in both the Composition and Timeline panels. The Composition panel works in conjunction with the Timeline panel. Any changes made to layers within the Timeline will be reflected visually within the Composition panel.

You will continue to build on this project using the Composition panel to position and move your artwork around. The next exercise focuses heavily on the Timeline panel, where you will set keyframes for your animation and navigate through time. The animation process in After Effects is rather different than animating in Flash. This is where the fun really begins.

Setting Keyframes

Although Flash and After Effects allow you to create keyframe animation, each application handles time rather differently. Flash is a frame-based application, whereas After Effects is time-based. This is an important difference you need to understand as you proceed through this book. As a Flash designer, it may take some time getting used to animating in After Effects. To visualize this difference, take a quick comparative look at each application's Timeline.

Figure 1.20: *Flash creates frame-based animation.*

Flash works with objects and frames. Figure 1.20 shows the Flash Timeline that has one layer named Object. The layer contains an instance of a movie clip. Keyframes have been set for the object as a whole. This means that any changes made on the Timeline will affect the entire movie clip instance.

The actual Timeline is divided into cells and the unit of measurement is frames. As we see in the Timeline, the Flash movie is set to 30 frames per second. A keyframe at frame marker 30 indicates that this is a one-second animation.

Figure 1.21: *After Effects creates time-based animation.*

After Effects deals with properties and time rather than objects and frames. Figure 1.21 shows the Timeline in After Effects. Here we have a similar object layer with only the position property keyframed. Each layer in After Effects has transform properties associated with it. These include Anchor Point, Position, Scale, Rotation, and Opacity.

The Timeline displays no individual cells and the unit of measurement indicates seconds. The output delivered is referred to as time-based media. This means that the media content changes with respect to time.

Exercise 2: Setting Keyframes

Unless you are familiar with nonlinear editing programs such as Final Cut Pro or Premiere, the Timeline panel in After Effects can be a little intimidating and overwhelming at first. Fear not, this exercise will help demystify this panel.

In the first exercise you created layers in the Timeline. After Effects stacks layers in the same order as Flash. Layers that are higher in the Timeline panel will appear in front of lower layers in the Composition panel. Just like Flash, you can place or move a layer anywhere in the stacking order.

1. Select the **Fish.ai** layer in the Timeline panel. Drag it underneath the grass/ DeepBlueScene layer. Release the mouse.

A black horizontal line appears to indicate where the layer will be positioned after you release the mouse.

Figure 1.22: *Change the stacking order in the Timeline.*

2. Let's compose a couple of items in the Composition panel. Click and drag the **Fish** artwork in the Composition panel down to the bottom right corner. Notice that the fish are behind the seaweed (Figure 1.23).

3. Click and drag the **Sea Turtle** in the Composition panel to the upper left corner.

   Similar to Flash symbols, you can reuse footage in After Effects as many times as you want without adding to the project's file size. Remember, footage files are linked, not embedded, within a project.

   You can drag the footage to the Composition panel. This allows you to place it in the Comp Window where you want. You can also drag the footage to the Timeline where it automatically centers in the Composition panel.

Notice one important difference between the Composition panel and the Flash Stage. After Effects will only display pixel information for footage contained within the Composition image area, referred to as the Comp Window. Any item that falls outside the Comp Window is displayed as an outlined bounding box.

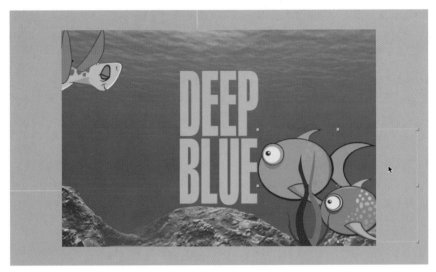

Figure 1.23: *Reposition footage items in the Composition panel.*

4. Before you start setting keyframes, lock the grass, rocks, and water layers in the Timeline panel. This will prevent you from accidentally moving them when animating other layers. The first grouping of switches in the Timeline panel are the A/V Features (Figure 1.24).

   ▶ Click on the empty box in the fourth column next to each layer you need to lock. These switches should look familiar to Photoshop users. They are toggle switches; they are either on or off.

Video: *turns on or off visibility*

Audio: *turns on or off audio layers*

Solo: *reveals only the selected layer in the Comp Window*

Lock: *locks layer*

Figure 1.24: *A/V Features hide or show layers and turn any audio layers on or off.*

5. To create an animation, you keyframe transform properties inherent to a layer. In the Timeline, click the **twirler** ▷ to the left of the **Fish.ai** layer. This will reveal the word Transform. Each layer has its own transform properties.

6. Click the Transform twirler to reveal five properties, the values of which you can adjust on a frame-by-frame basis. The transform properties are Anchor Point, Position, Scale, Rotation, and Opacity.

Transform properties

You adjust the transform properties of a layer in the Timeline to change its appearance in the Comp Window. Each property has a numeric value associated with it that you can manipulate. Let's start with the Scale property.

There are two ways to adjust the Scale. One way is to click and drag on any of the layer's four corner points in the Comp Window. If you hold down the Shift key, the scaling is constrained proportionally. The other method involves the Scale property in the Timeline.

There are two numeric values linked to scale — X (horizontal dimension) and Y (vertical dimension). The chain link icon in front of the numbers constrains the vertical and horizontal proportions equally. By default, the chain is active to prevent the layer from distorting as you change the values.

7. Click in the first number of the Scale field (100%) and drag the pointer to the right and left while watching the results in the Comp Window.

   ▸ Once you understand how this function works, set the value to **30%**.

   ▸ This act of clicking and dragging to change a value is known as **scrubbing**.

Figure 1.25: *Scrub through the Scale value and set it to 30%.*

8. Now that the fish are scaled to fit their environment, it is time to have them swim across the Comp Window. Every keyframe animation must contain at least two keyframes. If you change the position of a layer your first keyframe needs to record a starting position.

   ▸ Click and drag the **Fish** artwork off the right side of the Comp Window. This will be the starting position for the fish.

Figure 1.26: *Position the fish artwork off the right side of the Comp Window.*

If you don't set a keyframe, the current position of the fish will remain constant for the duration of the composition. You would never see them because they are outside the Comp Window. So how do you set a keyframe in After Effects?

Chapter 1: Getting Started in After Effects

9. In the Timeline panel, click on the **stopwatch** icon ⏱ next to the Position property. This enables the Position property for keyframing. A keyframe in the form of a yellow diamond ◈ appears in the Timeline at the current time.

Figure 1.27: *The Stopwatch activates keyframes for animation.*

10. Change the position of the Fish.ai layer at a different point in time.

   ▸ Press the **End** key on the keyboard. This moves the **Current Time Indicator** (CTI) to the end of the Timeline. The CTI is the red vertical bar that shows where you are in time.

Figure 1.28: *The Current Time Indicator shows where you are in time.*

   ▸ Click and drag the fish off the left edge of the Comp Window (Figure 1.29).

Figure 1.29: *Position the fish artwork off the left side of the Comp Window.*

A **motion path** appears in the Comp Window. This dotted line traces the path of animation from start to finish. Each dot represents the position of the fish at each frame in the Timeline.

The Time Controls panel is a secondary panel located to the right of the Composition panel. It contains buttons similar to VCR/DVD controls. You use this panel to perform RAM previews of your composition. Let's preview the animation you just created.

Figure 1.30: *Click on RAM Preview to play back the animation.*

11. Click on the **RAM Preview** button. There are two parts to a RAM preview. First, the Current Time Indicator moves across the Timeline loading the content at each point in time. A green bar appears under the time ruler indicating what has been loaded into RAM. After the first pass is complete, After Effects does its best to play back the animation in real time.

> *The keyboard shortcut for a RAM preview is the 0 key on the numeric keypad. Depending on the complexity of the composition and the amount of RAM installed on your computer, the RAM preview may not be able to store every frame in memory. Once full, the preview will start dropping from memory the first frames stored.*

12. Let's add more movement to the motion path. Move the Current Time Indicator (CTI) to one second (01:00) in the Timeline.

Figure 1.31: *Move the CTI to a new point in time (01:00).*

13. In the Comp Window click on the fish and move them up slightly. Since you are changing their position at a different point in time, a new keyframe is automatically generated. The path contains **Bezier** handles next to each keyframe. These allow you to fine-tune the curve of the motion path.

Figure 1.32: *Move the fish in the Comp Window to generate a new keyframe.*

14. Let's repeat those steps to create a wavelike motion for the fish.

   ▶ Move the Current Time Indicator (CTI) to two seconds (02:00) in the Timeline.

   ▶ In the Comp Window click on the fish and move them down slightly.

   ▶ Move the Current Time Indicator (CTI) to three seconds (03:00).

   ▶ In the Comp Window click on the fish and move them up slightly.

   ▶ Move the Current Time Indicator (CTI) to four seconds (04:00).

   ▶ In the Comp Window click on the fish and move them down slightly. Your Comp Window and Timeline should look similar to Figure 1.33.

Figure 1.33: *Add more position keyframes to alter the motion path.*

15. Click on the **RAM Preview** button. Save your project.

Tweening versus Interpolation

As you may have noticed, animation in After Effects is a lot different than animating in Flash. Flash creates animation through the use of a **tween**. Flash has two types of tweens: shape and motion. A shape tween can only be applied to shapes drawn directly on the Stage. A motion tween works only with symbol instances or grouped objects. Either tween has to be applied manually.

After Effects uses **interpolation** to fill in the transitional frames between two keyframes. Interpolation is the same as tweening. Once keyframes have been activated by clicking on a property's stopwatch icon, interpolation occurs automatically as changes are made at different points in time.

Creating and controlling complex motion in After Effects is much simpler than it is in Flash. After Effects uses **spatial** keyframes visualized as a motion path with Bezier handles. Spatial refers to how a layer moves in the composition's space. In Flash, you need to create a separate motion guide layer and link a drawn path to an object layer. Let's continue to work with keyframes.

16. Press the **Home** key on the keyboard. This moves the Current Time Indicator to the beginning of the composition (00:00).

17. Select the **SeaTurtle.swf** layer in the Timeline. Type **S** on the keyboard to show only the Scale property. Each transform property has a keyboard shortcut that will reveal only that property. This helps reduce clutter in the Timeline panel.

    ▸ Scrub through the numeric value and set it to **60%**.

Figure 1.34: *Scrub through the Scale value and set it to 60%.*

18. You are going to animate the sea turtle; however, there is a problem. The duration of the SWF file is shorter than the duration of the composition. Luckily, the Flash animation is a complete cycle and can be looped in After Effects. To loop the animation:

    ▸ Go to the Project panel and single-click on the **SeaTurtle.swf** footage.

    ▸ Select **File > Interpret Footage > Main**. This opens the Interpret Footage dialog box.

    ▸ In the Other Options section, enter **10** for the number of loops.

    ▸ Click **OK**.

Figure 1.35: *The Interpret Footage dialog box allows you to modify how After Effects interprets specific footage in the Project panel.*

19. After you have looped the SWF animation, a ghosted bar now extends to the end of the composition in the Timeline. Re-trim its Out Point by clicking and dragging it to the end of the composition. Now it is time to set keyframes.

Figure 1.36: *Re-trim the Out Point to extend to the end of the composition.*

20. Press the **Home** key on the keyboard just to make sure you are at the beginning of the composition (00:00).

21. Click and drag the **sea turtle** artwork off the left side of the Comp Window. This will be its starting position.

22. Make sure the **SeaTurtle.swf** layer is still selected. Press **Shift + P**. Shift keeps the Scale property visible and P reveals the Position property.

23. Click on the **stopwatch** icon next to Position to activate keyframes.

24. Press the **End** key to move the CTI to the end of the Timeline.

25. Click and drag the sea turtle off the bottom right edge of the Comp Window. This will be its ending position.

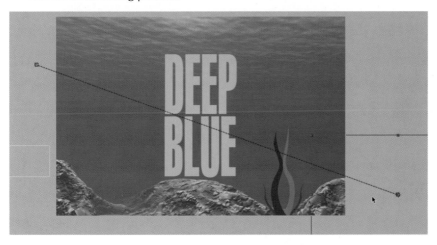

Figure 1.37: *Set the end position for the sea turtle in the Comp Window.*

26. Now that you have established the starting and stopping positions, let's add some more keyframes to the motion path. Click and drag the Current Time Indicator to around 01:20 in the Timeline.

0;00;01;20

27. Move the sea turtle up slightly in the Comp Window. Changing the sea turtle's position at a different point in time generates a new keyframe.

Figure 1.38: *Move the sea turtle in the Comp Window to generate a new keyframe.*

28. Click and drag the Current Time Indicator to around 03:10 in the Timeline.

29. Move the sea turtle down slightly in the Comp Window.

Figure 1.39: *Move the sea turtle in the Comp Window to generate a new keyframe.*

30. Just like Flash, you can easily rotate the layer to follow the path by selecting **Layer > Transform > Auto-Orient**. In the Auto-Orientation dialog box, select the option Orient Along Path. Click **OK**.

31. Click on the **RAM Preview** button. The sea turtle rotates to follow the motion path. Save your project.

Spatial and Temporal Interpolation

After Effects interpolates both space (spatial) and time (temporal). It bases its interpolation methods on the Bezier interpolation method. Directional handles are provided for you to control the transition between keyframes.

Spatial interpolation is viewed in the Composition panel as a motion path. The default interpolation used is **Auto Bezier**. This creates a smooth rate of change from one keyframe to the next.

There is also interpolation happening between the keyframes in the Timeline. **Temporal** interpolation refers to the change in value between keyframes with regards to time. You can determine whether the value stays at a constant rate, accelerates or decelerates. The default temporal interpolation used in the Timeline is **Linear**. That means the value changes at a constant rate.

You can view the temporal interpolation through the Graph Editor in After Effects. This visually displays the change in value between keyframes in the form of a graph. You can select keyframes and adjust their Bezier handles to affect the rate of change or speed. It is important to understand both methods of interpolation in order to fine-tune your animation.

Chapter 1: Getting Started in After Effects

32. Select the Position property for the **SeaTurtle.swf** layer. This highlights all of its keyframes in the Timeline.

33. With the layer still selected, click on the **Graph Editor** icon along the top of the Timeline. The keyframes are replaced with a graph showing the change in position over time. The graph shows an example of a linear interpolation.

   ▶ Linear interpolation sets a constant rate of change and is defined in the Graph Editor as a straight line.

   ▶ As you previewed your sea turtle animation, you may have noticed abrupt directional changes at each keyframe. The line shows that instant change.

Figure 1.40:
Turn on the Graph Editor.

Figure 1.41: *The Graph Editor shows the current Linear interpolation.*

34. Select the Position property again for the **SeaTurtle.swf** layer. This highlights all of its keyframes in the graph. They are the yellow squares.

35. Select **Animation > Keyframe Interpolation**. In the dialog box that appears change the Temporal Interpolation from Linear to **Auto Bezier**. Click **OK**.

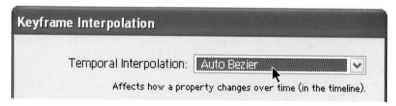

Figure 1.42: *Change the Temporal interpolation from Linear to Auto Bezier.*

36. The graph line changes to a more smooth curved line. Preview your animation. Notice the fluid movement in the sea turtle.

Figure 1.43: *The Graph Editor shows the Auto Bezier interpolation.*

37. Click on the **Graph Editor** icon again to hide the graph. Notice that the keyframes have changed from diamonds to circles. This is just a brief overview of the Graph Editor. We will devote more time to this tool later in the book.

38. The last set of keyframes you need to set are for the title. Typically in title sequences, the title doesn't appear on the first frame. Move the Current Time Indicator (CTI) to one second (01:00).

39. Click and drag the **Deep/DeepBlueTitle.ai** bar's Set In Point to align with the Current Time Indicator. Changing the layer's In or Out point is referred to as **trimming.** The word "Deep" will now appear at the one second mark.

40. Move the Current Time Indicator (CTI) to two seconds (02:00).

41. Click and drag the **Blue/DeepBlueTitle.ai** bar's Set In Point to align with the Current Time Indicator.

Figure 1.44: *Trim each title's Set In Point in the Timeline.*

42. Move the Current Time Indicator (CTI) back to one second (01:00).

43. Select the **Deep/DeepBlueTitle.ai** layer in the Timeline. Type **S** on the keyboard to show only the Scale property. Scrub through the numeric value and set it to **0%**. The word "Deep" disappears in the Comp Window.

44. Instead of the layer's Position, you will set keyframes for the Scale. Click on the **stopwatch** icon next to Scale to activate keyframes.

45. Move the Current Time Indicator (CTI) to two seconds (02:00).

46. Scrub through the Scale numeric value and set it back to **100%**. A keyframe is automatically generated.

Figure 1.45: *Set keyframes to the Scale property.*

47. Click on the **RAM Preview** button. The word "Deep" scales up from 0 to 100%.

48. Now let's set keyframes for the word "Blue." Move the Current Time Indicator (CTI) to two seconds (02:00).

49. For this animation, you will keyframe the layer's Position. Select the **Blue/DeepBlueTitle.ai** layer in the Timeline. Type **P** on the keyboard to show only the Position property.

Chapter 1: Getting Started in After Effects

50. Click on the **stopwatch** icon next to Position to activate keyframes.

51. Currently, the word "Blue" is in its final position. Let's record that as well. Move the Current Time Indicator (CTI) to three seconds (03:00).

52. Click on the gray diamond to the left of the word Position. This adds a keyframe at the current time. The two arrows allow you to jump to either the previous or next keyframe in the Timeline.

 Do NOT click on the stopwatch icon again. This button toggles keyframes on or off. If you turn off the keyframes, you lose all of them. If you want to delete a specific keyframe, click on it in the Timeline and press the Delete key.

Figure 1.46: *Add a keyframe at the current time.*

53. Move the Current Time Indicator (CTI) back to the first keyframe you set at two seconds (02:00). Hold the Shift key while you drag the CTI and it will snap to that keyframe.

54. Click and drag the word "Blue" off the bottom of the Comp Window. This will be the starting position for the word. The interpolation automatically recalculates the transitional frames in between the two keyframes.

55. Click on the **RAM Preview** button. Save your project.

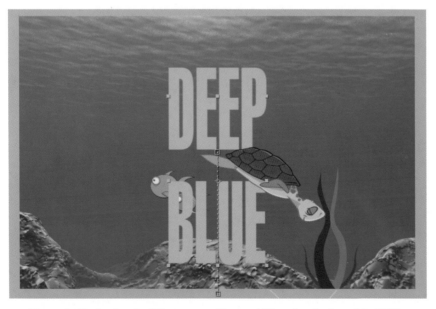

Figure 1.47: *Preview the title sequence. The word "Deep" scales from 0 to 100% and the word "Blue" moves up from the bottom of the Comp Window.*

Easing in After Effects

Before you finish this exercise, there is one more topic to cover: **keyframe assistants**. You already used the Graph Editor to view and manually control temporal interpolation between keyframes. Keyframe assistants automate the task of easing the speed into and out of keyframes.

Easing provides more realistic movement to objects since nothing in real life moves at a constant speed. In Flash, you apply easing through the Properties panel. A slider allows you to ease the speed in or out of a tween.

After Effects provides keyframe assistants. There are three assistants: Easy Ease, Easy Ease In, and Easy Ease Out. The last two work similar to Flash. Easy Ease smooths both the keyframe's incoming and outgoing interpolation.

56. Let's apply a keyframe assistant to our title animation. Select the Position property in the **Blue/DeepBlueTitle.ai** layer. This selects all the keyframes.

57. Hold down the Shift key and select the Scale property in the **Deep/DeepBlueTitle.ai** layer. This adds all of its keyframes to the previous selection.

58. Select **Animation > Keyframe Assistant > Easy Ease**. The keyframes change from diamonds to hour glass shapes in the Timeline.

Figure 1.48: *Apply the keyframe assistant, Easy Ease, to the title keyframes.*

59. Click on the **RAM Preview** button. The text animates in more smoothly. Save your project.

Your project has now come to life. Animation in After Effects is quite different from creating tweened animation in Flash. Complex motion paths can be easily created and tweaked in After Effects. You also have more control over specific layer properties such as Scale and Position.

Let's quickly review the basic process for setting keyframes. Each layer has transform properties inherent to it. These include Scale, Position, and Rotation. You set keyframes for each transform property by clicking on its stopwatch icon. This icon activates the keyframes. After Effects automatically records new keyframes for changes made at different points in time.

The next exercise focuses on applying visual effects to your project. This is what After Effects is known for. Effects allow you to enhance, transform, and distort both video and audio layers. The possibilities are endless.

Applying Effects

This is where After Effects truly shines. Once you see how easy it is to apply effects, you'll never want to stop. There are hundreds of effects that ship with the program. You can add any combination of effects and modify properties contained within each effect. It's insane! The only limitation is your creativity.

So let's start with the Effects & Presets panel. It is located to the right of the Composition panel. All effects are stored in a Plug-Ins folder inside the After Effects application folder. The Effects & Presets panel categorizes effects according to their function.

Figure 1.49: *The Effects & Presets panel organizes and categorizes effects.*

Flash provides very basic visual effects. These are called filters and can only be applied to movie clip instances. These effects include drop shadow, blur, glow, and bevel. That's it. You need to create all other effects either through tweened animation or ActionScript.

Figure 1.50: *Flash provides filters that add visual effects to movie clips.*

Exercise 3: Applying Effects

Effects are used to enhance a project in After Effects. These effects range from very simple drop shadows to complex 3D particle systems. In this exercise you will apply two visual effects: a 3D particle generator and a distortion effect. These effects will add the finishing touches to your project.

1. Make sure the Timeline panel is highlighted. Select **Layer > New > Solid**. The Solid Settings dialog box appears. A **solid** layer is just that, an area of color.
   - ▶ Enter **Bubbles** for the solid name.
   - ▶ Click on the **Make Comp Size** button.
   - ▶ Click **OK**. The color of the solid layer doesn't matter.

ℹ️ *All solid layers are stored in a Solids folder in the Project panel. This folder is automatically generated when you create your first solid layer. Any new layers you create will also be stored in the Solids folder.*

Figure 1.51: *Solid Settings dialog box.*

2. A solid layer of color appears at the top of the Timeline and in the Composition panel. Go to the Effects & Presets panel. Enter **Foam** into the Contains field. The item in the effects list that matches is displayed.

3. To apply the Foam effect to the solid layer, click and drag the effect to either the layer in the Comp Window or the Timeline panel. A red box with an X highlights the layer that will receive the effect. Release the mouse.

4. The effect is applied automatically. Notice that the solid color disappears and is replaced with a red circle in the center of the Comp Window. Click on the **RAM Preview** button to see the Foam effect.

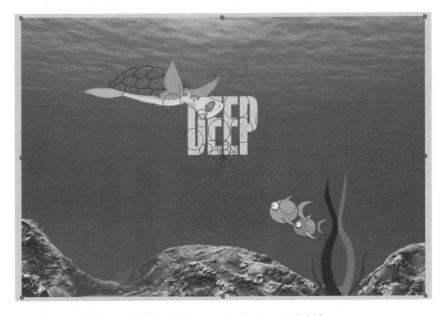

Figure 1.52: *Foam is a 3D particle generator that creates bubbles.*

Blue outlines of bubbles come out of the red circle in the center of the Comp Window. That is what Foam does. It generates bubbles that flow, stick together, and eventually pop. You can control exactly how the particles interact with each other and with their environment. When you apply an effect, the Effect Controls panel opens as a new tab in front of the Project panel (Figure 1.53). It contains a list of properties associated with the effect.

5. Click on the twirler to the left of **Producer**. This controls where the bubbles originate from. Make the following change:

   ▸ Producer Point: 360, **480**. This lowers the vertical position of the producer point to the bottom of the Comp Window.

6. Click on the twirler to the left of **Bubbles**. This controls the size and lifespan of the bubbles. Make the following change:

   ▸ Size: **0.200**. This makes the bubbles smaller.

7. Click on the twirler to the left of **Physics**. This controls how fast the bubbles move and how close they stick together. Make the following changes:

   ▸ Initial Speed: **5.000**

   ▸ Wind Speed: **1.000**

   ▸ Wind Direction: **0 x 0.0**

   ▸ Viscosity: **1.000**

   ▸ Stickiness: **1.000**

   ▸ These changes increase the speed and force the direction of the bubbles upward. Viscosity and stickiness keep the bubbles stuck together.

8. Click on the twirler to the left of **Rendering**. This controls the visual look of the bubbles. Make the following change:

   ▸ Bubble Texture: Change from **Default Bubble** to **Spit**.

9. To see the finished results, select **Rendered** from the View popup menu at the top of the Effect Controls panel. There is so much more that you can do with Foam that we will come back to this effect in a later chapter.

Figure 1.53: *Effect Controls panel*

Figure 1.54: *Change the view from Draft to Rendered to see a better representation of the bubbles in the Comp Window.*

10. Click on the **RAM Preview** button to see the final Foam effect. Save your work.

The last effect you will apply is a distortion effect. It will simulate the bending of light seen underwater. The effect you will use is called a **Displacement Map**. This effect distorts a layer by displacing pixels horizontally and vertically based on the color values of pixels in another layer. Here is how it works:

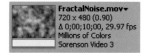

11. Go to the Project panel and double-click on the **FractalNoise.mov** footage file. This opens a preview window for the QuickTime movie. Play it. When you are done, close the preview window.

    To Photoshop users, this movie looks like an animated version of rendered clouds. That is exactly what it is. A Displacement Map can use the grayscale information to distort pixels within a layer. Areas of light grays will displace pixels up and to the right. Darker grays do just the opposite. Since this grayscale information is constantly changing in this movie, the displacement will also animate over time.

12. In order to apply a Displacement Map, you need to add the FractalNoise.mov file to the Timeline. Click and drag the footage item to the bottom of the layers. It will be hidden underneath the water layer. That is OK since the effect only needs to access the changing grayscale information.

Figure 1.55: *Add the FractalNoise.mov file to the Timeline. Position it at the bottom.*

13. Make sure the Timeline panel is still highlighted. Select **Layer > New > Adjustment Layer**. An adjustment layer is added at the top of the Timeline. The footage item is also stored inside the Solids folder in the Projects panel.

    Adjustment layers in After Effects work just like they do in Photoshop. This type of layer holds effects, not footage. Any effect applied to an adjustment layer is also applied to all the layers below it.

14. Go to the Effects & Presets panel. Enter **Displacement** into the Contains field. Two matched items appear: Displacement Map and Time Displacement. You will use the Displacement Map.

15. To apply the Displacement Map effect to the adjustment layer, click and drag the effect to **Adjustment Layer 1** in the Timeline panel. Release the mouse. The Effect Controls panel opens to display the effect's properties.

16. In the Effect Controls panel make the following changes as seen in Figure 1.56.

Figure 1.56: *Displacement Map settings.*

17. Click on the **RAM Preview** button to see the effect. The Displacement Map gives the illusion of being underwater. It pushes and pulls pixels based on changes in luminosity (brightness and darkness) occurring in the Fractal Noise movie.

18. There is one small problem. The edges of the water layer are also distorting. As a result, the black color underneath is being revealed. To correct this, unlock the **water/DeepBlueScene.psd** layer.

19. Select the **water/DeepBlueScene.psd** layer.

20. Type **S** on the keyboard to show only the Scale property. Scrub through the numeric value and set it to **110%**. Now the edge distortion occurs outside the Comp Window.

21. Let's rearrange the stacking order of the layers. Reposition the **Bubbles** and **Blue/DeepBlueTitle.ai** layers to go between the rocks and water layers.

Figure 1.57: *Rearrange the stacking order so that the bubbles and blue title go behind the rocks in the Composition panel.*

22. Click on the **RAM Preview** button to see the final animation. Congratulations. You have finished your first project in After Effects. The final step in the workflow is to render the composition. Before you do that, save your work.

Rendering a Project

Your composition has been built and the layers are in place. Several of these layers animate in the Comp Window. Visual effects have been applied. Now it is time to see all of your hard work saved to a movie. This exercise focuses on rendering your composition to a movie file.

After Effects renders compositions within a project. There are many file formats that the composition can be rendered out to. These include QuickTime, SWF, or an FLV file. It is a fairly simple process.

Exercise 4: Rendering a Project

1. Make sure the **DeepBlue_FINAL** comp is still open in the Timeline panel.

2. Select **Composition > Make Movie**. This opens the Render Queue. It is a new tab that sits on top of the Timeline panel. You may need to drag this frame larger to see all the options in the Render Queue.

3. In the Output To dialog box select the Chapter_01 folder on your hard drive as the final destination for the rendered movie. If this dialog box does not appear, click on **DeepBlue_FINAL.mov** next to Output To.

4. Click on **Based on Lossless** next to Output Module. This opens the Output Module Settings dialog box. Here you can change the file format and compression settings.

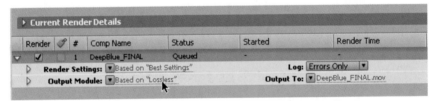

Figure 1.58: *Click on "Based on Lossless" to launch the Output Module Settings.*

5. Set the format to **QuickTime** movie. Under Format Options, set the compression setting to **MPEG-4 Video**. MPEG-4 offers a very good trade-off on file size versus quality for digital television, animated graphics, and Web pages.

6. One of the nice features in After Effects is the ability to render out multiple formats at one time. Since we are dealing with the integration of Flash and After Effects, let's render out another movie file in the FLV format. To do this, click on the words **Output Module** to select it.

Figure 1.59: *Click on "Output Module" to select it.*

Chapter 1: Getting Started in After Effects

7. Select **Edit > Duplicate**. This creates a copy of the selected Output Module.

8. Click on **Based on Lossless** next to the duplicate Output Module.

9. In the Output Module Settings dialog box, change the format from QuickTime Movie to **Adobe Flash Video**.

Figure 1.60: *Change the format to Adobe Flash Video.*

10. The Adobe Flash Video dialog box appears. If it doesn't, click on the Format Options button. Uncheck the Export Audio checkbox. Click **OK**.

Figure 1.61: *Uncheck the Export Audio checkbox.*

11. In the Output Module Settings dialog box, click on the Stretch checkbox to activate it. Uncheck the Lock Aspect Ratio checkbox. Enter **360 x 240** for the Stretch To dimensions. Click **OK**.

Figure 1.62: *Stretch the rendered FLV movie to a standard Web video size.*

12. Click the **Render** button. Your composition will start to render. The Render Queue provides feedback such as which frame is currently being rendered and approximately how much time is left.

DeepBlue_FINAL

13. When the render is done, go to the Chapter_01 folder on your hard drive. You will find the two rendered files. Launch the QuickTime movie in the QuickTime player.

DeepBlue_FINAL_1

Figure 1.63: *The final QuickTime movie.*

DeepBlueFLASH

To see an example of the FLV file in action, launch the **DeepBlueFLASH.swf** in the Completed folder inside Chapter_01. Flash makes it so easy to add video to your project. The FLV format has revolutionized online video almost overnight. From You Tube to personal Blogs, Flash Video is the perfect choice for deploying video content online. Let's take a quick peek at how easy it is to add video to Flash. The DeepBlueFLASH FLA file is provided for you to view.

Video can be imported into Flash in a couple of ways. It can be embedded as a frame-by-frame sequence on the Timeline. You have to be careful with file size if you choose to import video this way. Video is notorious for large files sizes.

One way to help keep your Flash file size manageable is to reduce the dimensions of the video file before you import it. These smaller videos are typically used to add visual effects to buttons or other elements on the Stage. Video that is longer in duration and larger in size should be kept external.

Chapter 1: Getting Started in After Effects

The most popular method used for Flash Video is to keep the video file external and play it through a video component. Flash comes with a number of prebuilt movie clip symbols called components. For this example, the FLVPlayback video component was used. It was added to the Flash Stage. The parameters were modified to link the appropriate source file and display a set of controls referred to as a skin. Once published, the SWF plays back the FLV video when launched.

Figure 1.64: *The final FLV file was imported into Flash using the FLVPlayback video component. The component provides button controls for the user.*

As you may have noticed, even though the FLV is external from the Flash SWF file, its dimensions are much smaller than the QuickTime's height and width. Common dimensions for Flash Video are 320 x 240, 240 x 180, and 120 x 90. Frame rate is also an important factor to consider. Common frame rates are 7, 15, 24, and 30 frames per second. The higher the number, the smoother the playback and the larger the file size.

Now that you are developing video for Flash, you need to know how to deal with the technical issues surrounding video formats. If you don't, you run the risk of watching all your hard work go down the drain when rendering your final project. The next chapter focuses specifically on these technical issues. These include frame size and frame rate, pixel aspect ratios, title and action safe areas, and color management. They are all important video concepts to understand before you start your Flash movie.

Summary

Your journey has begun. This chapter introduced you to After Effects. Each of the four exercises discussed the steps it takes to create a typical project. Although Flash and After Effects share a common project workflow, the two applications differ when it comes to animation and visual effects. Throughout the chapter comparisons were made to Flash, its workspace and workflow. These tables summarize the key similarities and differences.

Table 1.1: *After Effects and Flash Workspace*

After Effects Workspace	Similarities to Flash	Differences from Flash
Project Panel	It is similar to the Library in Flash. It displays the imported footage and stores compositions.	It provides more information about the imported footage files within the panel itself. A search feature allows you to quickly locate footage nested within folders.
Composition Panel	It is similar to the Stage in Flash. It is used to compose, preview, and edit a project.	In addition to magnification, there are more controls available. The workspace outside the Comp Window's image area does not render pixels, only a bounding box.
Timeline Panel	It shows the structure of your project's composition. Footage layers are stacked in a similar order. Keyframes are displayed over time.	You can access individual Transform properties for a layer. Adjustment layers can be added to effect other layers.

Table 1.2: *After Effects and Flash Project Workflow*

After Effects Workflow	Similarities to Flash	Differences from Flash
Creating a Project	The project file is similar to a Flash file. It references imported files and stores the animation for publishing.	Only one project file can be open at one time. Flash can open multiple files at the same time.
Importing Footage Files	These imported files are used to compose the project.	The files are NOT embedded within the project.
Setting Keyframes	Interpolation is the same as tweening in Flash — filling in the transitional frames between two keyframes.	After Effects interpolates both space and time. Bezier handles give you more control over a motion path.
Applying Effects	Enhances items on the Stage.	After Effects provides hundreds of effects and an unlimited number of ways to combine them.
Rendering a Project	This is similar to publishing a file in Flash.	You have more output options available.

CHAPTER 2

From Flash to After Effects

Video production presents technical requirements and limitations that can't be ignored. This chapter explores the world of broadcast design and offers a basic guide to exporting Flash files to After Effects.

Flash to Broadcast Video

Say you have just finished the world's greatest Flash animation and want to watch it on TV. What do you do? Similar to the Web standards you follow when publishing your Flash file online, there are video standards you need to be aware of when creating a Flash file destined for video.

This chapter guides you through these technical issues surrounding broadcast design. These include frame and pixel aspect ratio, frame rate, title safe and action safe areas, and color management. A good place to start is at the beginning by determining the proper frame size to use.

Setting the Stage

Before you start any Flash project, you first determine the dimensions of the document's Stage. In video, this is referred to as the **frame aspect ratio**. It is the relationship between the width and height of an image. Standard television has a 4:3 frame aspect ratio (Figure 2.1). Where did this ratio come from?

Figure 2.1: *For every four units of width there are three units of height.*

Motion pictures through the early 1950s had roughly the same aspect ratio. This became known as Academy Standard and had an aspect ratio of 1.37:1. Television adopted the Academy Standard to a 1.33:1 aspect ratio. This is the recognized video standard commonly referred to as a 4:3 frame aspect ratio.

In 1953 Hollywood introduced the widescreen format for motion pictures in an effort to pry audiences away from their television sets. Today, widescreen film has two standardized ratios: Academy Flat (1.85:1) and Anamorphic Scope (2.35:1). High-definition (HD) television adopted Academy Flat and has an aspect ratio of 1.78:1. This is referred to as a 16:9 aspect ratio (Figure 2.2).

Figure 2.2: *For every sixteen units of width there are nine units of height.*

There are three popular video format standards used throughout the world. NTSC, which stands for National Television Standards Committee, is the video format used in the United States, Canada, Japan, and the Philippines. Phase Alternating Line, or PAL, is the format of choice in most European countries. France uses SECAM, which stands for Séquential Couleur Avec Memoire. All three standard video formats use a 4:3 frame aspect ratio.

As previously mentioned, HDTV displays a 16:9 frame aspect ratio. It is a digital television broadcasting system that provides higher resolution than the standard video formats — NTSC, PAL, and SECAM. How does all this affect Flash and its Stage size when Flash movies can be resolution independent?

If you use only vector art, the published Flash movie can be scaled as big or small as you want without any loss in quality. Even though the movie size may not be important, designing for the correct aspect ratio is. If you don't, image distortion will occur going from Flash to video or DVD. So what dimensions should you set the Flash Stage to?

Square versus Non-square Pixels

Before you adjust the Stage width and height, you need to be aware of the **pixel aspect ratio**. This refers to the width and height of each pixel that makes up an image. Computer screens display square pixels. Every pixel has an aspect ratio of 1:1. Video uses non-square rectangular pixels, actually scan lines.

To make matters even more complicated, the pixel aspect ratio is not consistent between video formats. NTSC video uses a non-square pixel that is taller than it is wide. It has a pixel aspect ratio of 1:0.906. PAL is just the opposite. Its pixels are wider than they are tall with a pixel aspect ratio of 1:1.06.

Computer Screen	**NTSC DV or D1**	**PAL DV or D1**
(square pixels)	(non-square pixels)	(non-square pixels)

Figure 2.3: *The pixel aspect ratio can produce undesirable image distortion if you do not compensate for the difference between square and non-square pixels.*

Flash only works in square pixels on your computer screen. As the Flash file migrates to video, the pixel aspect ratio changes from square to non-square. The end result will produce a slightly stretched image on your television screen. On NTSC, round objects will appear flattened. PAL stretches objects making them appear skinny. The solution is to adjust the dimensions of the Flash Stage.

A common Flash Stage size used for NTSC video is 720 x 540 which is slightly taller than its video size of 720 x 486 (D1). For PAL, set the Stage size to 768 x 576. This is wider than its video size of 720 x 576. The published movie can be rescaled in After Effects to fit the correct dimensions. Even though the image may look distorted on the computer screen, it will appear correct on video. Table 2.1 shows the correct Stage size needed for each video format.

Table 2.1: *Flash Stage Size Settings for Different Video Formats*

Video Format	Frame Ratio	Pixel Ratio	Video Size	Flash Stage
NTSC DV	4:3	non-square	720 x 480	720 x 534
NTSC D1	4:3	non-square	720 x 486	720 x 540
PAL DV/D1	4:3	non-square	720 x 576	768 x 576
NTSC DV	16:9	non-square	720 x 480	864 x 480
NTSC D1	16:9	non-square	720 x 486	864 x 486
PAL	16:9	non-square	720 x 576	1024 x 576
HDTV 720p	16:9	square	1280 x 720	1280 x 720
HDTV 1080i	16:9	square	1920 x 1080	1920 x 1080

There is some good news with high-definition (HD) television. HD uses square pixels. This means that depending on the HD format you choose, either 720p or 1080i, your Flash Stage dimensions are the same as the video size. We'll discuss other methods of adapting a 720 x 540 Stage size to HDTV's wider aspect ratio later in the chapter. Let's focus on setting the proper frame rate.

Chapter 2: From Flash to After Effects

Frame Rates

Video is measured in units called frames. Frame rate is the speed at which video plays back its frames. The default frame rate in Flash is 12 frames-per-second (fps). This works fine for Web animation but not for video.

NTSC has a frame rate of 29.97 fps. Why not 30 fps? When black and white television became popular in the early 1950s, the broadcasts ran at 30 fps. When the color signal was added to the broadcast, the video frame rate had to be slowed to 29.97 due to technical issues. Video engineers were forced to allocate a certain amount of time each second for the transmission of the color information. PAL and SECAM operate at 25 fps.

Flash movies cannot be set to 29.97 fps. If your Flash movie is intended for NTSC video, use a frame rate of either 15 or 30 fps. After Effects can conform the different frame rate to match 29.97 fps. Just remember that lower frame rates will not play back smoothly after being converted. If your Flash movie is migrating to PAL or SECAM video, use 25 fps. Use 24 fps for film output.

Interlaced versus Progressive Video

Have you ever gotten really close to your television screen? Each frame of video is split into two sets of scan lines. Interlaced video draws each set of scan lines in an alternating fashion. The scan lines are held in two fields: the odd field consists of the odd-numbered lines and the even field consists of the even-numbered lines. Two fields equal one frame of image (Figure 2.4).

Field 1	Field 2	Interlaced Frame

Figure 2.4: *Interlaced video is made up of two sets of scan lines, or fields.*

In the United States, interlaced video refreshes the screen 60 times per second in order to create 30 frames of images per second. First the even lines appear on the screen, then the odd lines appear. All analog televisions use an interlaced display. High-definition video can be either interlaced or progressively scanned.

Your computer screen uses progressive video. The video is scanned from side to side, top to bottom to create a frame. Every pixel on the screen is refreshed in order. The result is a higher perceived resolution and a lack of "jitters" that can make the edges in your artwork or patterns appear to move or shimmer.

Your artwork in Flash can be severely impacted by the alternating scan lines used in interlaced video. Avoid using thin lines or small text in your Flash file. A horizontal line 1 point thick or less will flicker on video. It is visible when the first set of scan lines appear, then disappears as the second field is displayed.

To have your Flash artwork and text display properly on video, a general rule is to set all horizontal lines to 2 points thick or greater. All screen text should be at least 18 points in size. Use bold san serif typefaces. Avoid typefaces with very thin lines or serifs. These will tend to flicker on a television screen.

Title Safe and Action Safe Areas

If you look at the edge of your computer screen, you see every pixel in the displayed image. Television screens do not show the entire video picture. This problem is known as **overscan**. An average of 10% of the image around the edges of the screen is not visible to the viewer. This percentage can be smaller or larger and varies due to the television's make and model.

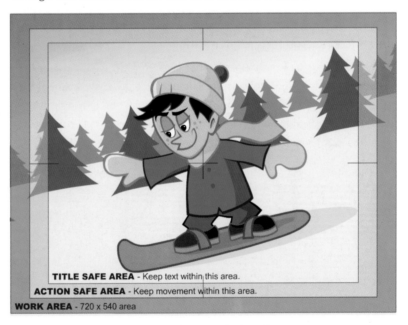

Figure 2.5: *Title Safe and Action Safe areas solve broadcast overscan.*

To solve this problem, television producers defined the Title Safe and Action Safe areas. The Title Safe area is a space, roughly 20% in from the edges of the screen, where text will not be cut off when broadcast. The Action Safe area is a larger area that represents where a typical TV set cuts the image off.

What about high-definition? HDTV also overscans the image so that older programming will be framed as intended to be viewed. Some broadcasters crop, magnify, or stretch the original video based on the picture's aspect ratios.

You can easily adapt your 720 x 540 Flash file to accommodate the wider HDTV aspect ratio. One method is to keep the Stage height at 540 pixels. The Stage width needs to be increased to 961 pixels. Where did that number come from? HDTV has an aspect ratio of 1.78:1. Multiply the height (540) by 1.78 and the result is 961. This size is smaller than the HDTV dimensions so you will need to increase the resolution of the QuickTime movie when you export the Flash file.

Figure 2.6: *Two solutions for creating an HDTV Flash template using the 720 x 540 Stage size as a starting point.*

If you want to maintain a 4:3 Stage size but have a widescreen image, you need to set up a new layer that masks, or letterboxes, the HDTV aspect ratio (Figure 2.6). Increase the resolution of the QuickTime movie when you export your file from Flash (Figure 2.7). After Effects allows you to resize or crop your published Flash movie to the proper HDTV dimensions.

Figure 2.7: *Export your Flash movie at a higher resolution.*

Color Issues

Computer screens display RGB colors. Video uses a YUV color space. While computers provide millions of colors to choose from, video has a limited range of colors it can display. So it is possible to use RGB colors on a computer monitor that cannot be reproduced on a television screen.

NTSC video makes life even more complicated. It uses the YIQ color space, which has an even smaller color range than YUV. NTSC is not as consistent at reproducing colors as PAL. If Flash designers are not careful with their color choices, their movie will not display properly on NTSC video.

This results in the colors bleeding, or spilling into neighboring colors. It produces a visible muddiness to the overall image. Warm, saturated colors such as red tend to bleed the most, making them a bad choice for fine detail or text. Blues translate quite well from RGB to video and make good background colors.

One solution is to apply the Broadcast Colors effect inside After Effects to the imported Flash movie (Figure 2.8). This effect forces the RGB colors to conform to the color space of NTSC or PAL. Keep in mind that if you are using the standard color palette in Flash, any reds, greens, and yellows could dramatically shift to an undesirable color.

Figure 2.8: *After Effects provides a Broadcast Colors filter to conform the RGB colors to the color space used in NTSC or PAL video.*

The best way to avoid any color shifts or bleeding is to create original art using only broadcast-safe colors. The full range of RGB color values is represented numerically from 0 to 255. The color value for black is 0-0-0 (red, green, blue). The color value for white is 255-255-255. To create safe broadcast colors, limit the R, G, and B values between 16 and 235.

In Flash, go to the Color panel and select the black swatch. Make sure you are using the RGB color mixer. Change the R, G, and B values to 16. Add the color to the swatches. Next, select the white swatch. Change the R, G, and B values to 235 and add the swatch. A general rule to follow is that all colors should have a saturation value lower than 236, especially the color red (Figure 2.9).

Figure 2.9: *Limit the RGB color values between 16 and 235 for broadcast video.*

You can also replace the default color palette in Flash by importing an existing color palette or even a GIF file. Warren Fuller at www.animonger.com provides a NTSC color palette that you can download for free. It is included on the DVD.

Chapter 2: From Flash to After Effects

Publishing SWF Files for After Effects

As you can see, there are a lot of technical issues surrounding video that you need to be aware of before creating your Flash movie. Let's apply what you have just learned by exploring how to migrate Flash movies to After Effects. There are several ways to do this. Let's start with a SWF file published in Flash.

Flash can export content to a SWF file, QuickTime movie, and an image sequence. All of these formats can be imported into After Effects. After Effects is one of the few applications that supports a wide variety of file types. SWF files are imported into After Effects as flattened, continuously rasterized layers. This means they can be scaled without losing detail or quality.

 Locate the Chapter_02 folder on the DVD. Copy this folder to your hard drive. The folder contains all the files needed to complete the chapter exercises.

The first exercise provides a step-by-step tutorial on importing a SWF file into After Effects. To see what you will build, locate and play the **BikeRide.mov** in the Completed folder inside the 01_SWF folder (Figure 2.10). When you finish this exercise you will be able to set up a Flash animation that will import correctly into After Effects, and create a seamless scrolling background.

Figure 2.10: *The finished SWF file in After Effects.*

1. Launch **Adobe Flash**. Locate and open **Cycling.fla** in the 01_SWF folder inside Chapter_02. The file contains a looping animation of the cyclist.

    ▸ The Stage dimensions are set for NTSC D1 video at 720 x 540 (square) pixels.

    ▸ The frame rate is set to 30 fps.

    ▸ The background color is not important. After Effects imports SWF files with their alpha channel preserved.

2. The root Timeline consists of one animated graphic symbol that occupies the first 15 frames. Scrub through the Timeline to see the animation. Double-click on the graphic symbol to open its Timeline (Figure 2.11).

Figure 2.11: *The cyclist animation is made up of several layers.*

The looping animation consists of several layers of artwork. Motion tweens are applied to nested graphic symbols that only change in position over time. These include the head, sneakers, and bicycle wheels. The legs, arms, and shirt are vector shapes that morph over time. Shape tweens and shape hints are used to create the desired movement.

3. Return to the root Timeline by clicking on Scene 1. Why use a graphic symbol instead of a movie clip? Movie clips are the most popular type of symbol used in interactive projects. Unfortunately for this exercise, the movie clip is useless.

If you change the symbol type from a graphic to a movie clip and publish the SWF file it will play back correctly in the Flash Player. However, once imported into After Effects, the symbol will just sit there on its first frame and do nothing else. Avoid using movie clips when saving a Web-based animation to video. Convert all existing movie clips to graphic symbols (Figure 2.12).

Figure 2.12: *Use graphic symbols when converting Flash animation to video.*

4. Test the movie to see the animation. A SWF file has already been published and saved to the 01_Footage folder in the 01_SWF folder inside Chapter_02. There is one other footage file you will use to complete this exercise. Double-click on **Forest.psd** inside the Footage folder to launch the file in Adobe Photoshop. This artwork will be used for the scrolling background.

Cycling

Forest

   ▸ The image height is 540 pixels which matches the height of the Flash Stage. It is also the correct square pixel height to use for NTSC D1 video.

   ▸ To create a seamless scroll the image was duplicated and flipped horizontally so that the edges align (Figure 2.13).

Figure 2.13: *Duplicate and flip the image horizontally to create a seamless image.*

5. Launch **Adobe After Effects**. It opens an empty project by default.

6. Import the footage files. Double-click inside the Project panel. This opens the Import File dialog box. Locate the 01_Footage folder inside the 01_SWF folder you copied to your hard drive. Select the folder. Click on **Import Folder**.

Figure 2.14: *Import the 01_Footage folder into the Project panel.*

7. Deselect the 01_Footage folder in the Project panel by clicking on the gray area under the footage. Click on the **New Folder** icon at the bottom of the Project panel. Rename the new folder to **Comps**.

8. Select **Composition > New Composition**. Enter **BikeRide** as the Composition Name. Select **NTSC D1** from the Preset popup menu. Set the duration to **0:00:05:00**. Click **OK** to create the new composition.

9. Selecting a video preset in After Effects automatically configures the correct frame rate and pixel aspect ratio for the composition. The new composition has a frame rate of 29.97 fps. The SWF footage has a different frame rate of 30 fps. To conform its frame rate to match the composition's:

   ▸ Twirl open the **01_Footage** folder to reveal its contents in the Project panel. Single-click on the Cycling.swf footage to select it.

   ▸ Select **File > Interpret Footage > Main**.

   ▸ In the Frame Rate section, select **Conform to frame rate** and enter **29.97**.

   ▸ In the Other Options section, enter **10** for the number of loops.

   ▸ Click **OK**. Conforming the frame rate does not affect the original file, only the linked footage in the Project panel. After Effects changes the internal duration of frames but not the frame content.

Figure 2.15: *The Interpret Footage dialog box allows you to conform frame rates.*

10. Click and drag the **01_Footage** folder from the Project panel to the left side of the Timeline. Release the mouse. Two layers appear in the Timeline and the Composition panel displays the artwork.

Figure 2.16: *Add the layers to the Timeline.*

11. The artwork is larger than the Comp Window. Remember that the footage was created using square pixels. To compensate for non-square pixels in video, you need to rescale the layers to fit the dimensions of the Comp Window. In the Timeline panel, deselect both layers by clicking on the gray area underneath.

12. Select only the **Cycling.swf** layer. Then select **Layer > Transform > Fit to Comp**. The width and height of the layer snap to the dimensions of the Comp Window. The bicycle wheels will look slightly flattened but will appear as circles on video.

Figure 2.17: *Round objects will appear stretched on the computer screen which is displaying only square pixels. On video, these shapes will appear normal.*

13. To see how the image will look on video click on the **Toggle Pixel Aspect Ratio Correction** button in the bottom right corner of the Composition panel (Figure 2.18). Click on the toggle button again to view in square pixels.

   This function does not affect the final rendering, however, it does distort the layers displayed in the Comp Window. This distortion can produce unwanted jagged images. Turn this toggle button on only to preview the image. Turn it off while you are building the project to view the full anti-aliased images.

Figure 2.18: *The Toggle Pixel Aspect Ratio Correction button provides a preview of how the image will look in a non-square pixel aspect ratio.*

14. Click on the **RAM Preview** button. The cyclist is going nowhere. The final step is to create the scrolling background. Before you do that, save your project.

15. Let's focus on the background image. Only the height of the **Forest.psd** layer needs to conform to the height of the Comp Window. Select the **Forest.psd** layer. Then select **Layer > Transform > Fit to Comp Height**.

16. With the **Forest.psd** layer still highlighted in the Timeline, select **Effect > Distort > Offset**. The Offset filter in After Effects is similar to Offset in Photoshop. It pans the image within a layer. Visual information pushed off one side of the image appears on the opposite side.

17. Press the **Home** key on the keyboard. This moves the Current Time Indicator to the beginning of the composition (00:00). You first need to record the layer's center point position. This position will animate over time.

18. Go to the Effect Controls panel. Click on the **stopwatch** icon next to **Shift Center To**. This generates a keyframe at the beginning of the composition.

19. Press the **End** key to move the CTI to the end of the Timeline (05:00).

20. Go to the Effect Controls panel. Change the first value to **6000** (Figure 2.19). The image's center point animates over time. Since the Photoshop file was designed to be seamless, the end result is a continuous scrolling background.

Figure 2.19: *Shift the horizontal center of the image to create the scrolling movement.*

21. Before you render the composition, let's make sure that the colors will display properly in NTSC video. Select **Layer > New > Adjustment Layer**.

22. Select **Effect > Color Correction > Broadcast Colors**. The effect is applied to all layers through the adjustment layer. It alters the pixel color values to keep the composition's color space within the range allowed for broadcast video.

Figure 2.20: *Apply the Broadcast Colors effect to an adjustment layer to keep the composition's color space within the color range allowed for NTSC and PAL video.*

23. Click on the **RAM Preview** button. Save your project.

24. Select **Composition > Make Movie**. This opens the Render Queue.

25. Click on **Lossless** next to Output Module. Set the Format to **QuickTime** movie. Click on **Format Options** and set the compression setting to **MPEG-4 Video**. Click on **Output To** and select the Chapter_02 folder on your hard drive as the final destination for the rendered movie.

26. Click the **Render** button. This completes the exercise. An important concept to remember is to use graphic symbols instead of movie clips when publishing Flash SWF files for After Effects. Also, the Offset effect is a quick way to create scrolling background images.

Using the QuickTime Exporter

Exporting SWF files for After Effects is quite simple as long as you remember to keep your artwork as vector shapes or stored in graphic symbols. What happens if the animation is driven by ActionScript? Welcome to the QuickTime Exporter.

The QuickTime Exporter in Flash allows you to save your movies as a QuickTime, Windows AVI, or an image sequence. There are two methods in which you can export your Flash file. The first method renders on a frame-by-frame basis all content placed directly on the Flash Timeline. The second option allows you to export dynamic content over a period of time. This includes ActionScript-driven animation that uses movie clips. Let's explore each method in detail.

This exercise provides a step-by-step tutorial on using the Flash QuickTime Exporter to save content on the Timeline to a fixed-frame video format. Unlike the SWF file in the first exercise, movie clips are supported using this first method. The artwork can be a movie clip, a graphic symbol or vector shape.

scene_01

scene_02

Figure 2.21: *It is better to break scenes from a large Flash animation into separate FLA files. Use After Effects to edit the exported clips back together into one movie.*

1. Open the **02_QuickTimeExporter** folder inside the Chapter_02 folder. When creating animation for video, save each scene as a separate Flash FLA file (Figure 2.21). Even though Flash can store multiple scenes in one large movie, having smaller individual files provides easier editing capabilities in After Effects. It also reduces the risk of file corruption that could occur using longer timelines.

2. Double-click on **scene_01.fla** to open the file in Flash. The animation is made up of several layers. The artwork is either nested within a graphic symbol or a vector shape drawn on the Stage.

The top layer labeled SAFE AREA contains the Title Safe and Action Safe guides for NTSC D1 video. All titles and text are framed within the Title Safe area (Figure 2.22). Notice that it is a guide layer. It is visible in the Flash FLA file but will not be included in the exported movie.

 Title Safe and Action Safe templates are provided in the Chapter_02 folder for you to use in your projects. Simply copy the frame and paste it into your file.

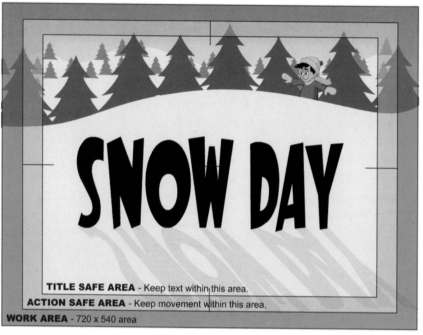

Figure 2.22: *The title is contained within the Title Safe area.*

Figure 2.23: *Only NTSC video safe colors were used to create the artwork.*

3. Unlike the previous exercise, the artwork in this Flash file uses only NTSC video safe colors. The default color swatches were replaced with the NTSC color palette provided by www.animonger.com (Figure 2.23).

4. Select **File > Export > Export Movie**. This opens the QuickTime Movie dialog box. Select the 02_QuickTimeExporter folder inside the Chapter_02 folder on your hard drive as the final destination for the rendered movie. Make sure the file format is set to QuickTime. Click **Save**.

Figure 2.24: *QuickTime Export Settings provides several options to choose from.*

5. The QuickTime Export Settings dialog box appears. Make sure the width and height are set to 720 and 540 respectively. The Stop Exporting area provides

the two exporting methods mentioned at the beginning of this exercise. Since this Flash movie is a frame-by-frame animation, you want to stop exporting when the last frame is reached. Click on **QuickTime Settings**.

6. The Movie Settings dialog box allows you to adjust the video and audio settings. There is no audio in this file. Turn off the audio export by unchecking the checkbox next to Sound (Figure 2.25).

7. Click on the **Settings** button under the Video area. This opens the Standard Video Compression Settings dialog box (Figure 2.26). Here you can adjust the compression settings. Animation compression works well for Flash movies. Leave the frame rate at 30 fps. You will conform it to 29.97 in After Effects. Click **OK** twice to return to the QuickTime Export Settings dialog box.

Figure 2.25: *Turn off the audio export. Audio can be added later in After Effects.*

Figure 2.26: *The QuickTime Exporter allows you to control the video compression.*

8. Quit out of all other applications so only Flash is open. Click **Export**. The QuickTime Exporter captures every frame as a SWF movie in the background to create the QuickTime movie. This can take a few minutes.

    You may need to lower the frame rate to prevent frames dropping. What does this mean? If the video size and fast frame rate are too much for the QuickTime Exporter, certain frames will be dropped as it renders the movie.

9. A dialog box will appear when the QuickTime movie is complete. Click **OK**.

10. Open **scene_02.fla**. This animation is set up similar to scene_01. Repeat the previous steps to export the file as a QuickTime movie. Once you've finished creating both QuickTime movies, it is time to import them into After Effects.

scene_01

scene_02

11. Launch **Adobe After Effects**. Import the two QuickTime movies into the Project panel. If the Interpret Footage dialog box appears, click on Ignore Alpha (Figure 2.27). Chapter 4 covers alpha channels in detail.

Figure 2.27: *The QuickTime movie does not need an alpha channel. Select Ignore.*

12. Conform the frame rate of both QuickTime footage files to 29.97 fps. To do this, select the footage item. Select **File > Interpret Footage > Main**. In the Frame Rate section, select **Conform to frame rate** and enter **29.97**. Click **OK**.

13. Deselect any selected footage items in the Project panel. Click on the **New Folder** icon at the bottom of the Project panel. Rename it to **Comps**.

14. Select **Composition > New Composition**. Enter **SnowDay** as the Composition Name. Select **NTSC D1** from the Preset popup menu. Set the duration to **0:00:10:00**. Click **OK** to create the new composition.

15. Click and drag both QuickTime footage files to the Timeline (Figure 2.28). With both layers highlighted select **Layer > Transform > Fit to Comp**.

Figure 2.28: *Add the layers to the Timeline.*

16. In the Timeline, click and drag **scene_02.mov's** colored bar. Align its starting point to the end point of **scene_01.mov's** colored bar (Figure 2.29).

Figure 2.29: *Align the layers to play back one after the other.*

17. Trim the Timeline's workspace to the end of **scene_02.mov**'s colored bar. To do this, click and drag the **Work Area End** handle to align with the end of the colored bar (Figure 2.29). The last step is to add some snow to the layer. Where this would require either ActionScript or a lot of layers in Flash, After Effects has an effect that automatically generates snowflakes. It's simple.

18. Make sure the **scene_02.mov** layer is selected. Select **Effect > Simulation > CC Snow**. The effect adds falling snow to the animation. You can control the amount of snow, its size, and rate of descent in the Effect Controls panel.

Figure 2.30: *The CC Snow effect automatically generates falling snow on a layer.*

19. After Effects has the Title Safe and Action Safe guides built into the Comp Window. To make them visible, click on the **Grid & Guides** button at the bottom left of the Composition panel. Select **Title/Action Safe** from the popup menu (Figure 2.31). The guidelines appear in the Comp Window.

Figure 2.31: *After Effects has the Title Safe and Action Safe guides built in.*

20. Select **Composition > Make Movie**.

21. Click on **Lossless** next to Output Module. Set the Format to **QuickTime** movie. Click on **Format Options** and set the compression setting to **MPEG-4 Video**. Click on **Output To** and select the Chapter_02 folder on your hard drive as the final destination for the rendered movie.

22. Click the **Render** button. Save your project. As you can see, rendering frame-based animation using the QuickTime Exporter in Flash is fairly straightforward. What's the benefit of using it over importing a SWF into After Effects? In this example, none. In some cases it is better to use the SWF file. So why use it? The next exercise clearly demonstrates the benefit of using the QuickTime Exporter.

Exporting ActionScript-driven Movies

Flash CS3 introduced the ability to export content over a period of time to a QuickTime file format. You define the amount of time and the QuickTime Exporter records the movement on the Stage whether it is frame-by-frame or ActionScript driven. This is a huge improvement and good news for Flash programmers who want to export their dynamically driven movies to video.

This final exercise provides a step-by-step tutorial on exporting an ActionScript-driven animation using the QuickTime Exporter. To see an example, locate and play the **SpaceWars.mov** in the Completed folder inside the 03_ActionScript folder (Figure 2.32). When you finish this exercise you will be able to export movie clips controlled by ActionScript to a video format.

Figure 2.32: *The finished QuickTime movie file uses ActionScript-driven content.*

The retro rocketship was created in Flash as a short, frame-by-frame animation stored in a movie clip. Through the use of ActionScript, the movie clip is duplicated six times and positioned off the left edge of the Stage. Over time, each duplicated ship moves across the Stage at a random speed.

1. Let's first deconstruct the Flash code. Open the **03_ActionScript** folder inside the Chapter_02 folder. Here is the breakdown of the files you will look at:

    ▸ **RocketshipCode.fla** is the Flash document that stores the retro rocketship movie clip in its Library.

    ▸ **rocketDocumentClass.as** is the Document Class that duplicates the ships and defines their initial position and speed.

    ▸ **AnimateShip.as** is an ActionScript file that positions and moves each ship.

2. Double-click on **RocketshipCode.fla** to open the file in Flash. The Stage is set to a customized size of 640 x 320 pixels. There is nothing on the Stage or in the Timeline. The Library stores the rocketship movie clip.

3. Select **Control > Test Movie** to preview the animation. Each time you test the movie, you will see six rocketships fly across the Stage at random speeds.

RocketshipCode

4. Close the SWF file and return to Flash. Go to the Properties panel. Notice that the Document class field contains **rocketDocumentClass**. This is the link to a separate ActionScript file that will set up the animation for this Flash document.

Size:	640 x 320 pixels	Background: ■	Frame rate: 30 fps
Publish:	Settings...	Player: 9	ActionScript: 3.0 Profile: Default

Document class: rocketDocumentClass

Figure 2.33: *Link to the Document Class file in the Properties panel.*

5. Select **File > Open**. Choose **rocketDocumentClass.as** in the 03_ActionScript folder. Click **Open**. The code duplicates the rocketship six times using a for loop. Each time through the loop a new movie clip object (AnimateShip) is created.

rocketDocumentClass

```
public function rocketDocumentClass() {
        for(var i:uint=0; i < 6; i++) {
            var ship:AnimateShip = new AnimateShip(Math.random()*640 - 700,
                        Math.random()*200 + 60, Math.random()*10 + 5);
            addChild(ship);
        }
    }
```

For each new object, a random horizontal and vertical position is created based on the dimensions of the Stage. It also generates a random speed value. These three random numbers are passed as parameters to the **AnimateShip.as** file. The last line of code (addChild) draws the movie clip instance on the Stage.

6. Select **File > Open**. Choose **AnimateShip.as** in the 03_ActionScript folder. Click **Open**. This code is linked to the movie clip in RocketshipCode.fla through the Linkage Properties panel in the Library (Figure 2.34).

Figure 2.34: *Link to the ActionScript file in the Linkage Properties panel.*

AnimateShip

7. Each time the Document Class creates an object, this AS file is attached to the new rocketship. Remember, this code is linked to the movie clip. The Action-Script basically tells the ship where to go and how to move across the Stage based on certain parameters sent by the Document Class.

```
public class AnimateShip extends MovieClip {
    // define variable to hold positive speed
    private var speedX:uint;
    // create constructor
    public function AnimateShip(x,y,dx) {
        // set scale, location, and speed
        this.scaleX = this.scaleY = .4;
        this.x = x;
        this.y = y;
        speedX = dx;
        // move the ship to the left each frame
        this.addEventListener(Event.ENTER_FRAME, moveShip);
    }
    // move according to speed set in DocumentClass
    public function moveShip(event:Event) {
        // move the ship to the left
        this.x += speedX;
    }
}
```

The code first creates a variable called **speedX**. This will be used to move the ship horizontally across the Stage. The Class Constructor is defined and the parameters from the Document Class are stored in **x**, **y**, and **dx**. The first two parameters are used to position the ship. The rocketship's scale is set to 40%.

An Event Listener "listens" for the playback head entering the frame. It calls an event handler that moves the ship. Since this file is continuously entering the same frame, this function is called repeatedly, creating the movement. The rate at which the ship animates is based on the value stored in **dx**.

8. Return to the **RocketshipCode.fla** file. Select **File > Export > Export Movie**. This opens the QuickTime Movie dialog box. Select the 03_ActionScript folder inside the Chapter_02 folder on your hard drive as the final destination for the rendered movie. Make sure the file format is set to QuickTime. Click **Save**.

9. The QuickTime Export Settings dialog box appears. Make sure the width and height are set to 640 and 320 respectively.

10. Check the checkbox to **Ignore Stage Color**. An alpha channel will be generated to use in After Effects.

11. In the Stop Exporting area select **After Time Elapsed** and enter **00:00:10**. Flash will record activity on the Stage for 10 seconds (Figure 2.35). This method includes movie clips in the captured frames. Click on **QuickTime Settings**.

Figure 2.35: *To export ActionScript-driven content, select After Time Elapsed and enter a value. Flash will record any activity on the Stage for the time entered.*

12. Click on the **Size** button under the Video area. This opens the Export Size Settings dialog box (Figure 2.36). Make sure the width and height are set to 640 and 320 respectively. Click **OK** twice to return to the QuickTime Export Settings dialog box.

Figure 2.36: *Make sure the Export Size matches the Stage dimensions.*

13. Quit out of all other applications so only Flash is running. Click **Export**. A dialog box will appear when the QuickTime movie is complete. Click **OK**.

14. Go to the 03_ActionScript folder on your hard drive where you will find the QuickTime movie. Launch the QuickTime movie in the QuickTime player. The ability to export ActionScript-driven content is a great improvement for Flash and opens the door wider in creating content for After Effects.

RocketshipCode

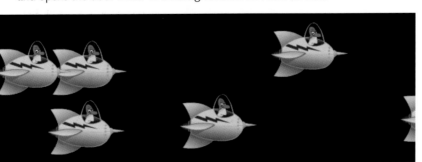

Figure 2.37: *The QuickTime Exporter recorded the code-driven animation.*

SpaceWars

15. To see how this Flash animation was used to create the Space Wars title sequence, open **SpaceWars.aep** in the Completed folder.

16. The Project panel contains the exported QuickTime movie as a footage item. Other footage includes two audio files, a sound effect and background music. A starfield was created in Photoshop. The title was created in Illustrator as a vector shape so that it can be scaled without losing detail (Figure 2.38).

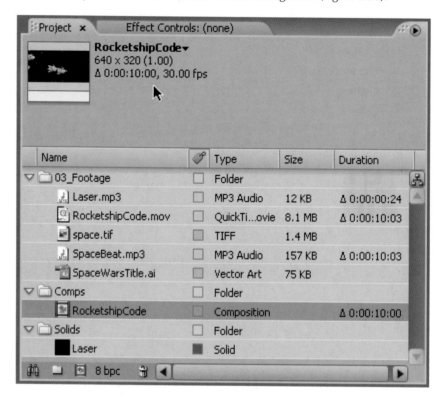

Figure 2.38: *The Project panel contains all the footage files used.*

17. Let's deconstruct how the final composition was created. It was set to the same duration and frame rate as the RocketshipCode.mov file. All of the footage items were added to the composition as layers:

   ▸ The **space.tif** layer's height is slightly larger than the composition's. Two Position keyframes animate in a downward movement, like a camera pan.

   ▸ The **RocketshipCode.mov** layer has no effects or keyframes applied. The alpha channel generated by the QuickTime Exporter makes compositing easy to do in After Effects. The layer reveals the starfield underneath it.

   ▸ The **SpaceWarsTitle.ai** layer contains the vector art. The Scale property is reduced from 4000% to 100%. An important note worth mentioning is the **Continuously Rasterize** switch that is available for all vector layers in the Timeline (Figure 2.39). Activate this switch to maintain the smooth detail in the vector artwork as the layer scales larger than its original size.

👁	🔊	○	🔒		✐	#	Layer Name		⚭ ✳ ↖ ƒⱷ ▤ ◯ ◯ ◯
👁				▷ ☐		16	🗋 [SpaceWarsTitle.ai]		⚭ ✳ ╱ ƒⱷ
👁				▷ ☐		17	🎞 [RocketshipCode.mov]		⚭ ╲ ╱
👁				▽ ☐		18	▣ [space.tif]		⚭ ╱
◁ ◠ ▷					⏱	Ⱶ	Position		320.0, 142.4

Figure 2.39: *The Continuously Rasterize button is used on vector layers to maintain their smoothness and detail as the layer is scaled larger than its original size.*

18. At the eight second mark (08:00) the title "Space Wars" begins to fade off the screen using a combination of scale, reducing opacity, and an applied effect. The effect used is located at **Effect > Generate > CC Light Burst 2.5**. It simulates rays of light emanating from the layer. To create the "warp speed" effect, two keyframes were set for the Ray Length value. The value was increased from 0 to 500 in the Effect Controls panel (Figure 2.40).

Figure 2.40: *The CC Light Burst 2.5 effect was applied to the title layer to produce the blurred special effect.*

19. A Solid layer was created to hold a laser beam that shoots out of a rocketship (Figure 2.41). To create the lasers, the Beam effect was used. This is located at **Effect > Generate > Beam**. This simple effect is used quite frequently to produce amateur light saber duels that you see online.

Figure 2.41: *The Beam effect was applied to a Solid layer to create the laser beams.*

In the Effect Controls panel, the beam's starting and ending points were set at the left edge and right edge of the Solid layer. Keyframes were set for the Time property. Its value changes from 0 to 100, creating the movement of the beam. This Solid layer was then duplicated six times and repositioned in the Timeline. A couple of layers were moved in the Comp Window to align the beam to the laser cannon at the end of the rocketship.

20. The audio files were added to the Timeline as separate layers. An audio layer can be positioned anywhere within the stack of layers. A good practice to adopt is either position all the audio at the top or the bottom of the layers to keep them out of the way while you work.

Figure 2.42: *Audio was added last in the Timeline.*

The sound effect, Laser.mp3, was duplicated six times and aligned to sync up with the animation. The background music spans the entire duration of the composition. The last step was rendering the final output.

SpaceWars
24,505 KB

SpaceWars
733 KB

21. The composition was rendered as a QuickTime movie and a Flash Video (FLV) file. Both files were rendered at the same size and frame rate. Notice the file size difference between the two formats. The FLV file was linked through the FLVPlayback video component in **SpaceWars.fla**. You can see the final results by double-clicking on the published file — **SpaceWars.swf**.

Summary

This completes the chapter. Some key concepts to remember include:

▶ Frame aspect ratio is the relationship between the width and height of an image. There are two common video aspect ratios — 4:3 and 16:9.

▶ Computers use square pixels and video does not. To compensate for this, adjust the dimensions of your square pixel art to properly display on video.

▶ Frame rate is the speed at which video plays back its frames. NTSC uses a frame rate of 29.97 fps. PAL and SECAM use 25 fps. Film is 24 fps.

▶ Computer screens use a progressive scan while television uses an interlaced scan. The interlaced scan is broken up into two fields of scan lines and can affect the display of thin lines and small text.

▶ Title Safe and Action Safe guides solve the problem of television overscan.

▶ When publishing a SWF file for After Effects, use graphic symbols and vector shapes. Movie clips within the SWF will not display properly in After Effects.

▶ To export movie clips to After Effects, use the QuickTime Exporter. It will export content on the Flash Stage over a set timespan to a QuickTime movie.

Chapter 2: From Flash to After Effects

CHAPTER 3

From After Effects to Flash

There are different techniques used for exporting movies from After Effects to Flash. This chapter explores each method, and when and why you should use After Effects to create Flash content.

Exporting Vector and Raster Objects

File size plays an important role when designing Web-based content. Flash is a great Web tool for producing animation and interactive projects with small file sizes. After Effects is the preferred choice for motion graphics, but it renders rather large video files. How can these two applications be integrated and still maintain a respectable file size for Web delivery?

Figure 3.1: *After Effects can export files to Flash SWF and Flash Video (FLV) files. These files are then imported into Flash and published for the Flash Player.*

After Effects can export compositions as Adobe Flash SWF files and Flash Video (FLV) files. The exported SWF file will play back immediately in the Flash Player or it can be imported into another Flash project. FLV files must be imported into Flash and published in SWF files in order to view them (Figure 3.1).

Flash publishes SWF files that are typically composed of vector graphics. Although After Effects can import and display vector art, it is pixel-oriented. When a composition is exported as a SWF file, After Effects tries to retain the vector art as much as possible. Some content may be rasterized which will generate a larger file size. So what does After Effects export as vectors?

Text is vector-based in After Effects. Static text layers and basic text animation export as vector objects. However, if the text layer is converted into a 3D layer, or an adjustment layer is applied, or any type of motion blur is used, the layer will be exported as a raster image (Figure 3.2).

Figure 3.2: *Basic text layers and animation (left image) will export as vector objects. Once a motion blur has been applied (right image), the layer exports as a raster image.*

Adobe Illustrator files imported into After Effects will export as vector objects. The Illustrator artwork needs to contain only solid strokes and fills using either RGB or CMYK color spaces. Any gradient fills will cause the layer to be exported as a raster image (Figure 3.3).

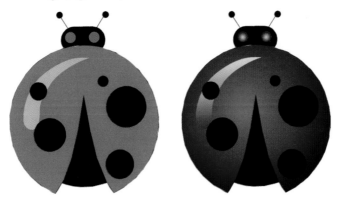

Figure 3.3: *Imported Adobe Illustrator files with solid strokes and fills (left) will export as vector objects. If gradients are used (right), the artwork exports as a raster image.*

Solid layers that have a mask applied to them will render out as vector objects. Masks in After Effects work similar to masks in Flash. There are also three effects that export as vectors for use in Flash: Path Text, Audio Waveform, and Audio Spectrum. What happens to the rest of the layers when After Effects exports a SWF file?

If After Effects encounters something it can't export as a vector object, it will do one of two things. Which one depends on what you select in the SWF Settings dialog box (Figure 3.4). The first option rasterizes at full quality any object that can't be exported as vector art. This results in a larger file size. The second option ignores any unsupported layer or effect. This is the default setting. It ensures that only vector objects end up in the exported SWF file. This option is the best to use when you only want vector-based art.

Figure 3.4: *After Effects allows you to choose how to export unsupported features to a Flash SWF file.*

Flash Video (FLV) contains only rasterized images, not vector art. FLV files can be output directly from the Render Queue in After Effects. Render settings allow you to specify size, compression, and other output options. The FLV file can then be imported into Flash and published in a SWF file, which can be played by the Flash Player.

FLV files can be imported into Flash using ActionScript or Flash components. Components provide additional control of the visual interface that surrounds the imported video. You can also add graphic layers on top of the FLV file for composite effects.

An alternative to saving a composition as a SWF and FLV file is to export it as an image sequence. After Effects renders each image file with a numerically sequential naming convention. Upon importing the first image, Flash recognizes the naming convention and prompts you to import the entire sequence (Figure 3.5). Image sequences should be imported into a movie clip or graphic symbol. This allows for more flexibility in your Flash project.

Figure 3.5: *After Effects can also export image sequences. It uses a sequential naming convention that Flash recognizes and allows you to import the entire sequence.*

Both applications include many tools that allow you to easily composite graphics and video. The previous chapter discussed how to save Flash content to After Effects. File size was not a concern since the final output was video. The exercises in this chapter focus on exporting After Effects content to Flash, with an emphasis on maintaining a respectable file size for Web delivery.

Exporting SWF Files

Let's start by exporting compositions in After Effects to Flash SWF files. The goal is to export only vector objects to maintain a small file size. Why use After Effects to create Flash content? After Effects provides effects and animation presets that go way beyond the capabilities that Flash provides. It can be a real production time saver. The first exercise illustrates this by creating a complex text animation in After Effects by applying only one effect.

Exercise 1: Export Text Animation as Flash SWF

Text animation is rather difficult to do and time consuming in Flash. Each letter in the animation needs to be either ActionScript-driven or keyframed by hand in the Timeline. Either way, creating a complex text animation can be a real nightmare to a Flash designer. Here comes After Effects to the rescue!

 Locate the Chapter_03 folder on the DVD. Copy this folder to your hard drive. The folder contains all the files needed to complete the chapter exercises.

After Effects provides many text animation presets that can be applied in one step. To see the text animation you will build, locate and play the **Vertigo.swf** file in the Completed folder inside the 01_SWF folder in Chapter_03 (Figure 3.6). When you finish this exercise you will be able to use the Text tool in After Effects to set up a text animation. You will export it as vectors for use in Flash.

Figure 3.6: *Title sequence uses text animation created in After Effects.*

1. Launch **Adobe After Effects**. It opens an empty project by default.

2. Select **Composition > New Composition**. You need to make the composition the same size as the Flash Stage you will be importing the text animation into. Make the following settings:

   ▶ Composition Name: **VertigoText**
   ▶ Width: **550**
   ▶ Height: **400**
   ▶ Pixel Aspect Ratio: **Square Pixels**
   ▶ Frame Rate: **15**
   ▶ Duration: **0:00:03:00**

   Click **OK**. The new composition opens with a black screen in the Composition panel. The Timeline opens a tab.

3. Click on the **Type** tool T at the top left of the screen. Go to the Comp Window and click inside to start typing. Type "Vertigo." A text layer is automatically created in the composition and appears in the Timeline.

4. This can be any font or size that you want. Use the Character panel that opens by default when a text layer is created. Arial Black was used for this exercise. When you are done, center the text in the Comp Window (Figure 3.7).

Figure 3.7: *The Type tool automatically generates a text layer and opens the Character panel that allows you to change the font, size, leading, etc.*

5. Click on the **Effects & Presets** tab to the left of the Character tab. This brings that panel forward. Twirl open the **Animation Presets** folder. Twirl open the **Text** folder. This contains all the different preset folders of text animation. Twirl open the **Animate In** folder and select **Center Spiral**. This effect rotates in each letter from the center of the text layer to form the word.

6. To apply the preset, click and drag the effect from the Effects & Presets panel to the text in the Comp Window. A red marquee box appears indicating the selected layer. Release the mouse and you will notice that the text disappears. This is because the text is at the beginning stage of the animation preset.

7. Click on the **RAM Preview** button. The letters spiral in to form the word "Vertigo" (Figure 3.8). That was easy. Imagine trying to keyframe the spiral movement by hand in Flash. Save your project.

Figure 3.8: *The text presets create complex text animation quickly and easily. When creating text, make sure you do not apply a stroke to it. This adds complexity to the animation and will increase the file size of the exported SWF file.*

Chapter 3: From After Effects to Flash

Wouldn't it be nice to see a preview of each text animation preset before you applied it? You can. Go to the Effects & Presets panel and click on the menu arrow ▶ in the top right corner. Select Browse Presets from the popup menu. This opens Adobe Bridge. Double-click on the Text folder. Open any preset folder and single-click on the effect you want to see. A thumbnail preview of how the effect works appears in the Preview panel on the right side (Figure 3.9).

Figure 3.9: *Adobe Bridge allows you to preview all preset effects before you apply.*

8. Press the **Home** key on the keyboard. This moves the Current Time Indicator to the beginning of the composition (00:00).

9. Select the **VERTIGO** text layer and press **S** on the keyboard to open the Scale property. Click on the **stopwatch** icon ⏱ next to Scale to generate a keyframe.

   ▸ Scrub through the numeric value and set it to **50%**.

Figure 3.10: *Scrub through the Scale value and set it to 50%.*

10. Move the Current Time Indicator to where the text stops rotating (02:08).

11. Scrub through the Scale numeric value and set the text layer back to **100%**. A keyframe is automatically generated. Now the text will slowly scale up from 50% to 100% as it spirals in.

12. Click on the **RAM Preview** button. Save your project. It is time to export the composition as a Flash SWF file.

13. Select **File > Export > Adobe Flash (SWF)**. This opens the Save File As dialog box. Save the SWF file to the 01_SWF folder in Chapter_03.

14. The SWF Settings dialog box appears. This is where you set up how the SWF will be exported. In the Images area, set After Effects to **Ignore Unsupported Features**. Anything that After Effects can't export as a vector object will be ignored and will not show up in the final SWF file. Since text in After Effects is vector-based, you don't need to worry about missing any letters.

Figure 3.11: *Set After Effects to ignore unsupported features when exporting vectors.*

15. There is no audio so leave that unchecked. Leave the rest of the settings as the default (unchecked). Click **OK**. After Effects creates a Flash SWF file.

Vertigo

16. Let's move to Flash. Double-click on **Vertigo.fla** in the 01_SWF folder to open the file in Flash. It contains two layers: spiralAnimation and eye. The spiral animation is a movie clip that contains a spiral graphic symbol that rotates counter-clockwise creating a vortex tunnel effect.

Figure 3.12: *The Flash file contains two layers. The animation consists of a movie clip that contains a spiral graphic rotating counter-clockwise.*

17. Select **Insert > New Symbol**. Enter **mcTextAnimation** for the name and make sure that the type is set to Movie Clip. Click **OK**.

18. The Timeline for the new movie clip appears. Highlight the first blank keyframe and select **File > Import > Import to Stage** to open the Import dialog box. Choose the SWF file you created in After Effects. Click **Open**.

Figure 3.13: *Import the SWF file created in After Effects into a movie clip in Flash.*

19. When the SWF file is imported into the movie clip, it appears as a series of keyframes. Scrub through the Timeline to see the animation. Go to the Library. There is a graphic symbol for each letter in the text animation. Double-click on a graphic symbol and you will see that the letter form is a vector shape.

Figure 3.14: *The imported SWF file appears as a series of keyframes in the Timeline and each letter appears as a graphic symbol in the Library.*

20. Let's add to this animation. First, insert a frame (F5) at frame 85 (Figure 3.15). This will hold the text on the screen long enough to read it.

Figure 3.15: *Insert a frame (F5) at frame 85. This will extend the text's time on the screen to allow the viewer to read it.*

21. Next, create a spiral-out sequence using the exact same keyframes just in reverse order. To do this:

   ▸ Select the keyframes from frames 1 to 45.
   ▸ Select **Edit > Timeline > Copy Frames**.
   ▸ Click on the empty cell at frame 86. Select **Edit > Timeline > Paste Frames**.
   ▸ Highlight the pasted keyframes. Select **Modify > Timeline > Reverse Frames**.

Figure 3.16: *Create a spiral-out sequence by copying and pasting the frames at the end of the Timeline. Then reverse the frame sequence.*

22. Close out of the movie clip and return to the root Timeline. Click on the **New Layer** icon at the bottom of the Timeline panel. Rename the layer to text.

23. Click and drag the **mcTextAnimation** symbol from the Library to the Stage.

24. Go to the Properties panel and set the X and Y position to **0** (Figure 3.17). This aligns the registration point to the upper left corner of the Stage. Since the composition in After Effects was set to the same dimensions as the Flash Stage, the text will be positioned in the center of the Flash movie.

Figure 3.17: *Set the X and Y positions to 0 to center the text on the Stage.*

Vertigo
Flash Movie
8 KB

VertigoText
Flash Movie
9 KB

25. Save and publish your movie. The text spirals in and then out. You may want to add a "stop" action on the last frame of the text movie clip. Note that the final file size for the SWF file is around 8 KB. That is even smaller than the text animation SWF file exported from After Effects (9 KB). Flash does provide better compression than After Effects when exporting SWF files.

Creating and exporting complex text animation as a SWF file is rather easy to do in After Effects. This exercise introduced you to text layers and animation presets. There is much more that you can do with these. In fact, Chapter 5 devotes itself entirely to creating and animating text in After Effects.

Exercise 2: Export Illustrator Animation as Flash SWF

Let's export one more SWF file from After Effects. For this exercise, you will use footage created in Adobe Illustrator to export a SWF file for the Flash Player. The final SWF file will only contain vector art, keeping the file size small.

1. Create a new project in **Adobe After Effects**.

2. Import the footage file. Double-click inside the Project panel. This opens the **Import File** dialog box. Locate the **SpringLogo.ai** file inside the **01_Footage** folder in 01_SWF/Chapter_03. Select the file.

Figure 3.18: *Import the Adobe Illustrator file into the Project panel.*

3. Before you import, choose **Composition – Cropped Layers** as the Import type in the Import dialog box. Each layer will import with their original dimensions. This will make it easier to animate in the Comp Window. Click **OK**.

4. Double-click on the SpringLogo composition in the Project panel to open it in the Timeline and Composition panels.

5. Select **Composition > Composition Settings**. Make sure the duration of the composition is set to five seconds (05:00). Click **OK**.

6. If you added more time to the original duration, you will need to zoom out the Timeline to view the entire composition. To do this, click and drag the Zoom slider at the bottom of the Timeline all the way to the left.

Figure 3.19: *Zoom out to view the entire composition's Timeline.*

7. Each layer's colored bar needs to extend to the end of the Timeline. Re-trim the Out Point for each layer by clicking and dragging it to the end (Figure 3.20).

Figure 3.20: *Re-trim each layer's Out Point to the end of the Timeline.*

8. Let's animate the ladybug. Go to the Comp Window and click and drag the ladybug to the lower left side of the Comp Window. This will be the starting point for its animation (Figure 3.21).

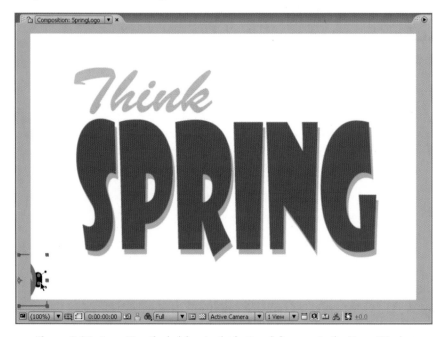

Figure 3.21: *Reposition the ladybug to the bottom left corner in the Comp Window.*

Motion Sketch

In addition to manually setting keyframes, After Effects provides a Motion Sketch tool that records a motion path as you draw in the Comp Window. This is another great time saver in terms of animation.

9. Select **Window > Motion Sketch**. This opens the Motion Sketch panel in the bottom right corner of the Workspace.

10. Set the Smoothing to **10**. This reduces the number of keyframes recorded and produces a much smoother motion path. The higher the number, the smoother the motion. Don't set this value too high or the tool will not accurately preserve the motion path drawn. Ten is a good number to start with.

Chapter 3: From After Effects to Flash

11. Make sure both checkboxes are checked for **Show Wireframe** and **Show Background**. This makes the drawing much easier to do, as you can see the layers you are working with.

12. Click on **Start Capture** to activate the tool. It doesn't start recording keyframes until you click and drag a layer in the Comp Window.

Figure 3.22: *The Motion Sketch settings control the smoothness of the motion path.*

13. The goal of this animation is to have the ladybug animate over the title and end at the top of the "i" in the word Spring. Click and drag the ladybug in the Comp Window. The Motion Sketch tool records the keyframes as you move the cursor. Release the mouse button when you are done. This stops the tool from recording.

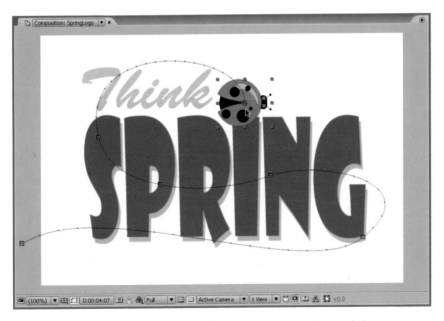

Figure 3.23: *The Motion Sketch records keyframes for the motion path drawn.*

14. Click on the **RAM Preview** button. Save your project.

15. Let's orient the ladybug to follow the path. Select **Layer > Transform > Auto-Orient**. In the Auto-Orientation dialog box, select the option Orient Along Path. Click **OK**.

Figure 3.24: *Orient the ladybug to follow along the path.*

16. You can adjust the recorded motion path in the Comp Window and Timeline panel. Select the layer in the Timeline and press **P** on the keyboard to open the Position property. The recorded keyframes appear in the Timeline section.

Figure 3.25: *Open the Position property in the Timeline to view the recorded keyframes.*

17. Click on the **RAM Preview** button. Save your project.

18. Now that the animation is done, it is time to export the composition. Select **File > Export > Adobe Flash (SWF)**. This opens the Save File As dialog box. Save the SWF file to the 01_SWF folder in Chapter_03.

19. The SWF Settings dialog box appears. In the Images area, set After Effects to **Ignore Unsupported Features**. Since the footage is an Adobe Illustrator file and does not contain any gradients, all the layers will export as vectors.

SpringLogoR

SpringLogo

20. Click **OK**. Locate the exported Flash SWF file. Double-click on it to play the animation in the Flash Player. Notice that After Effects also saves a report HTML file (SpringLogoR.html) within the same folder as the Flash SWF file. This file contains a link to the Flash SWF file and allows you to play the animation in a browser window. This completes the exercise.

To summarize, you can create vector animation directly in After Effects and export it as a Flash SWF file without using Flash at all. This exercise also introduced the Motion Sketch tool, which can save time on animating layers. Flash does not have a tool like this. In order to create a similar motion path, you would need to create a motion guide and attach a layer to it.

Chapter 3: From After Effects to Flash

Exporting PNG Image Sequences

An alternative to exporting a Flash SWF file is to export a PNG image sequence. The raster images can then be imported into Flash as a frame-based animation. Even though the compression is quite good in a PNG file, the image size and the duration of the image sequence needs to be taken into consideration.

This exercise provides a step-by-step tutorial on exporting a PNG sequence from After Effects to Flash. To see an example of what you will build, locate and play **Duel.swf** in the Completed folder inside the 02_PNG folder in Chapter_03. Why use After Effects to create the character animation instead of Flash?

Figure 3.26: *The finished PNG Image Sequence in Flash.*

One awesome new tool that After Effects has over Flash is the Puppet tool. Introduced in After Effects CS3, this tool allows you to easily create natural motion by deforming parts of a layer. We'll take a brief look at how this tool was used for this exercise. Chapter 7 provides more in depth tutorials on character animation using the Puppet tool.

1. Open **Swashbuckler.aep** inside the 02_PNG folder in Chapter_03.

2. The Project panel contains a Flash SWF file and a composition. The character originated in Flash as a one-frame, static vector image. The Puppet tool turns any raster or vector image into a kind of simulated marionette. For this exercise, the "strings" of the marionette were attached using the Puppet Pin Tool . Deform points were added at the shoulders, elbows, wrist, torso, knees, and feet (Figure 3.27). The position of each deform point was animated over time.

   Swashbuckler

   Why export this as a PNG sequence? Even though the artwork is vector-based, with the Puppet effect applied, the layer will only export as a raster image. This would create a large SWF file. PNGs provide a better, much smaller solution.

Figure 3.27: *The Puppet tool simulates a marionette. Deform pins placed at strategic locations allow you to create realistic, natural movement over time.*

3. Before you save the PNG image sequence, crop the Comp Window to help reduce the file size for each exported image. Click on the **Region of Interest** button at the bottom of the Composition panel. The region of interest is the area that is previewed in the Comp Window.

4. Click and drag in the Comp Window to create a smaller region of interest. Scrub through the Timeline to make sure the character remains inside the area as he animates. Use the corner handles to resize the region if necessary.

Figure 3.28: *Reduce the region of interest. Creating a smaller region requires less processing power and helps improve the RAM preview.*

Chapter 3: From After Effects to Flash

5. Select **Composition > Crop Comp to Region of Interest**. The size of the Comp Window is reduced to the dimensions of the region of interest bounding box.

6. Select **Composition > Make Movie**.

7. Click on **Lossless** next to Output Module. Set the Format to **PNG Sequence**. Under the Video Output section, set the channels to **RGB + Alpha**. You need an alpha channel to composite the sequence properly in Flash.

Figure 3.29: *Set the PNG files to render with an alpha channel.*

8. Click on **Output To**. In the dialog box that appears create a new folder in the 02_PNG folder in Chapter_03. Name it **PNG Sequence**. Click **Open**. Click **Save**. It is always a good idea to store image sequences in their own folder.

Figure 3.30: *Create a new folder to save the PNG files into.*

9. Click the **Render** button. Save your project.

10. Locate the PNG Sequence folder. It now contains thirty PNG files each with a sequentially numbered file name. These files will be imported into a movie clip in Flash. Cropping the Comp Window helps reduce the overall file size.

Figure 3.31: *The rendered PNG image sequence contains sequentially numbered file names that Flash can recognize.*

Duel

11. Let's move to Flash. Double-click on **Duel.fla** in the 02_PNG folder to open the file in Flash. It contains two layers: Foreground and Background. The artwork was created in Photoshop and imported as bitmap images.

Figure 3.32: *The Flash file contains the scene for the swashbuckler.*

12. Select **Insert > New Symbol**. Enter **mcSwashbuckler** for the name and make sure that the type is set to Movie Clip. Click **OK**.

13. The Timeline for the new movie clip appears. Highlight the first blank keyframe and select **File > Import > Import to Stage** to open the Import dialog box. Choose the first image in the PNG sequence (Duel_00000). Click **Open**.

14. Flash recognizes the file naming convention as a sequence and prompts you to import the entire sequence. Click **Yes**.

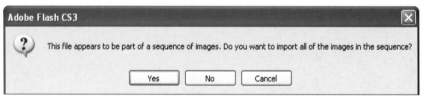

Figure 3.33: *Flash prompts you to import the entire image sequence.*

15. The PNG image sequence appears as a series of keyframes in the movie clip. Scrub through the Timeline to see the animation. Go to the Library. There is a bitmap icon for each image in the sequence.

16. You are going to use multiple instances of this movie clip on the Flash Stage. To maintain a small SWF file size, convert each bitmap image in the Timeline into a graphic symbol. By doing this, Flash will only store the bitmap images once in the final published file.

17. Organize the Library better. Create two new folders; one folder holds the imported PNG sequence and the other holds the graphic symbols.

18. Click on the **New Layer** icon at the bottom of the Timeline panel. Rename the layer to Swashbuckler. Position the new layer in between the Foreground and Background layers.

19. Click and drag the **mcSwashbuckler** symbol from the Library to the Stage. Let's give the character a drop shadow to anchor him in the scene.

20. Click on the swashbuckler and select **Edit > Duplicate**. A copy appears on top of the original movie clip. Click and move the duplicate movie clip off the original so that you will be able to see the drop shadow effect more clearly.

Figure 3.34: *Duplicate the movie clip.*

21. Make sure the duplicate movie clip is still selected. Go to the Properties panel and click on the Filters tab. Click on the "+" to add a new filter to the instance. Select **Drop Shadow** from the popup menu.

22. Click on the checkbox for Hide Object. Adjust the Strength from 100% to 70%. Change the blur factor from 5 to 10 for Blur X and Y. These settings will help make the shadow more convincing in illustrating depth.

23. Skew the drop shadow horizontally to add perspective. The Skew tool is found in the Transform panel. Click on the radio button for Skew and enter **45.0°** in the Skew Horizontally text box.

24. Select **Modify > Transform > Flip Vertical**. This will flip the drop shadow so that it acts more like a cast shadow for the swashbuckler.

25. Select the Free Transform tool. Position the cursor over the top-middle handle. Click and drag down to scale the drop shadow vertically.

26. Position the drop shadow at the base of the swashbuckler. You may need to rotate the shadow to align better with his feet (Figure 3.35).

Figure 3.35: *Position and rotate the drop shadow to align with the swashbuckler.*

27. Select **Modify > Arrange > Send to Back** to adjust the layer stacking order. The drop shadow is now underneath the swashbuckler.

28. Select **Control > Test Movie**. As the movie clip of the swashbuckler animates, the shadow mimics the movements. Save your Flash file. Obviously the raster PNG images do inflate the published file size (575 KB) more that if they were vector shapes. Duplicate the swashbuckler and flip the copy horizontally. Now he has someone to duel against. Adjust the colors of the copy using the Filters tab. Think about animating the position of each character.

Duel
Flash Movie
575 KB

Figure 3.36: *Add another swashbuckler movie clip instance to the Stage.*

Working with Flash Video (FLV)

Flash Video is everywhere on the Web. It provides great image quality and compression. Flash can encode a video from After Effects in the FLV format. When you import a video into Flash, you have a couple of options to choose from. You can either embed the video directly on the Timeline or load it externally as a separate file. Which option is the best to use? That all depends on the video and what you need it for. Table 3.1 offers some suggestions.

Table 3.1: *Embed the Video or Load It Externally?*

Video / Purpose	Embed	External
5 seconds or under with no audio	X	
Used to trace frames for rotoscope animation	X	
Used for interface interactivity (buttons, preloaders)	X	
Longer than 5 seconds with audio		X
Used for instructional training		X
Used in conjunction with cue points		X

Exercise 1: Import Video Wizard

There are also a couple of ways you can import video into Flash. Let's start by using the Import Video Wizard. This tool walks you through a series of screens to create a FLV playback component that contains a link to the FLV video file and controls that allow you to interact with the playback.

1. Open the **03_FLV** folder in the Chapter_03 folder. Open **01_ImportWizard.fla** in Flash. The file contains two layers: Video and Background. Select the blank keyframe on frame 1 of the Video layer (Figure 3.37).

01_ImportWizard

Figure 3.37: *Select the blank keyframe on the Video layer.*

2. Select **File > Import > Import Video**. This opens the Import Video Wizard.

3. The wizard first asks you to locate the video file. Make sure On Your Computer is selected. Click **Browse**. In the Open dialog box, locate the DeepBlueTitle.mov in the Movies folder inside the 03_FLV folder. Select it. Click **Open**.

Figure 3.38: *Locate the video to import on your computer.*

4. The path name to the file appears in the File Path field. Click **Next**.

5. For the deployment options, select **Progressive Download From a Web Server**. This option allows you to stream video using HTTP streaming. Flash will create an external FLV file. That file needs to be uploaded to the server along with the SWF file. Click **Next** to continue.

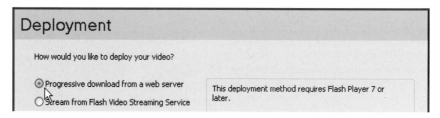

Figure 3.39: *Select Progressive Download as the deployment option.*

6. For the video encoding, select **Flash 8 – High Quality (700 kbps)** from the Encoding Profile popup menu. Flash has several encoding profiles for different Flash Player versions and different download speeds. The higher the quality, the larger the file size. Experiment with different profiles to determine which one provides the best solution for your Flash project.

Figure 3.40: *Select the encoding profile for the video.*

7. The video dimensions are 720 x 480 pixels. This is quite large for a Flash Video file. Common FLV dimensions are 360 x 240, 320 x 240, 240 x 180, and 120 x 90. Click on the **Crop and Resize** tab. Check the Resize checkbox. Enter **360** in the Width field and **240** in the Height field. This will scale the rendered Flash Video (FLV) file and help reduce the overall file size. Click **Next** to continue.

Chapter 3: From After Effects to Flash

Figure 3.41: *Resize the video to 360 x 240 to reduce file size.*

8. The skin provides video controls such as play, stop, and seek. Select **SkinUnder-PlaySeekStop.swf** from the Skin popup menu. Notice that the skin is a SWF file. Flash will save a copy of this file to the same folder it saves the FLV file to.

Figure 3.42: *Select the video controls. Flash refers to this as a Skin.*

9. Click **Next** to continue. Review the settings for the imported video file. Click **Finish** to encode the video. The resulting FLV file will be saved to the same folder as the Flash FLA file.

10. When Flash is done encoding the video, a black box with the selected skin appears on the Flash Stage. The black box is a FLV playback video component. In order to see the video, you need to publish the Flash file.

11. Select **Control > Test Movie**. This completes the exercise on using the Import Video Wizard. The next exercise loads FLV files using ActionScript.

01_ImportWizard

DeepBlueTitle

SkinUnderPlaySeekStop

Figure 3.43:
Flash saves three files to the same folder as the FLA file. These three files need to be uploaded together to a server in order to play on the Web.

Exercise 2: Loading Video Using ActionScript

The Import Video Wizard provides an easy method for creating and importing video files into Flash. ActionScript offers another way to load Flash Video. Unlike the Import Video Wizard, ActionScript does not create the actual FLV file; it can only load FLVs and control their playback.

You must encode the video file in the FLV format using either After Effects, Flash Import Video Wizard, or the Adobe Flash CS3 Video Encoder prior to loading it with ActionScript. The code that imports the FLV file follows a strict procedure that first connects to the FLV file and then streams its content into a Video object added to the Flash Stage (Figure 3.44).

Figure 3.44: *Loading FLV files using ActionScript.*

1. Open **02_VideoActionScript.fla** located in the 03_FLV folder in Chapter_03. The project is already assembled using three layers: buttons, TV, and Screen.

Figure 3.45: *Open 02_VideoActionScript.fla. It contains all the artwork you need.*

Let's deconstruct how the imagery was created in Photoshop. The photo of the vintage television set has a transparent hole where the actual picture tube is. Using the Pen tool, the shape of the picture tube was traced, selected and deleted. The **Screen** layer holds a PNG image of reflective glass. Its opacity was set to 50% in Photoshop. The video will play underneath both layers giving the illusion of a television broadcast.

Figure 3.46: *The television set is made up of two PNG images. The imported video will playback underneath the two layers adding to the illusion of a television broadcast.*

The **buttons** layer holds a movie clip instance. The panel artwork was created in Photoshop and imported as a PNG file. A button symbol was created in Flash and placed over each thumbnail image. Each button has a unique instance name that can be referenced through ActionScript. When the buttons are clicked, Flash will load a specific FLV file into a Video object.

Figure 3.47: *The buttons are invisible button symbols created in Flash. Each has a unique instance name that will load a specific FLV file when clicked on.*

The movie clip also contains an animation of the panel moving up and down. A mask layer is used to hide the panel when not in use. Frame labels are assigned to reference specific frames through code (Figure 3.48). For example, each time a thumbnail image is clicked, ActionScript instructs this movie clip to jump to the frame labeled "close" and play the frames that follow it.

Figure 3.48: *The movie clip contains an animation. Frame labels are used to identify the movement of the video panel.*

FLV

Video1
Flash Video File

Video2
Flash Video File

Video3
Flash Video File

Where are the videos? They are kept external from this Flash file. Locate the FLV folder inside the 03_FLV folder. It contains three FLV files that were rendered out of After Effects through the Render Queue. These files will be loaded externally into Flash using ActionScript. Now that you have an idea of how the Flash file is set up, let's start programming.

2. On the main Timeline add a new layer labeled **actions**. Select the blank keyframe in Frame 1 and open the Actions panel.

3. The first step is to create a **NetConnection** object. This object links, or provides directions, to the FLV file. **Null** is used for the connection name since you are accessing the FLV files locally from your hard drive. Finally, create a **NetStream** object to control the playback of the video. In order to stream the data correctly, the NetConnection is passed into the NetStream. Enter the following code:

```
// create a NetConnection
var vConnection:NetConnection = new NetConnection();
vConnection.connect(null);
// create a NetStream
var vStream:NetStream = new NetStream(vConnection);
```

4. The Flash Player receives descriptive information embedded in the FLV file being played. This information is referred to as metadata. It could contain the title, author, comments, etc. You need to set up an object that will listen for this metadata information. This object will be linked to the NetStream object since that is what is transferring the data into Flash.

Enter the following code in the Actions panel. Add it after the code you entered in Step 3. The code **vStream.client** attaches the metadata object to the NetStream object. The metadata listener calls a function named **onMetaData**. This function will be added later.

```
// create a metaData listener
var metaDataListener:Object = new Object();
metaDataListener.onMetaData = onMetaData;
vStream.client = metaDataListener;
```

5. The next step is to create a **Video Display Object** that will hold the loaded FLV file. The code creates a new object with a size of 320 x 240 pixels. The horizontal and vertical position is set to align the Video object with the television screen.

   The statement, **addChild(myVideo)**, draws the object on the Flash Stage. To affect the layer stacking order, use the **setChildIndex** command. A value of **0** sets the object at the bottom, underneath all other layers. Finally, the NetStream object is attached to the Video object. Enter the following code:

```
// create a video display object
var myVideo:Video = new Video(320, 240);
// set the location of the video
myVideo.x = 116;
myVideo.y = 46;
addChild(myVideo);
// set the depth of the video to be underneath everything
setChildIndex(myVideo, 0);
// attach the NetStream to the video object
myVideo.attachNetStream(vStream);
```

6. Once the NetConnection, NetStream, and Video objects are in place, define all variables and event listeners. The variable named **dropStatus** determines whether the video panel opens or closes on the Stage. The event listeners are attached to the buttons on the thumbnail images. Enter the following code:

```
// define popUp menu variable
var dropStatus:Boolean = true;

// add Event Listeners for buttons
infoPop_mc.popUp_btn.addEventListener(MouseEvent.CLICK, OpenOrClose);
infoPop_mc.info_mc.image1.addEventListener(MouseEvent.CLICK, playVideo1);
infoPop_mc.info_mc.image2.addEventListener(MouseEvent.CLICK, playVideo2);
infoPop_mc.info_mc.image3.addEventListener(MouseEvent.CLICK, playVideo3);
```

7. The last step is to add the Event Handlers. They are functions that execute statements when a specific event is "heard" by the event listeners. For this exercise you will add five handlers, one for each button event listener and a handler for the metaDataListener. The code **vStream.play("FLV file name")** plays the video in the Video object. Enter the code on the following page.

8. Select **Control > Test Movie**. Click on a thumbnail to load a video. ActionScript provides a lot more control over video that will be discussed in the next chapter.

```
// add Event Handlers to respond to the buttons
function OpenOrClose(event:MouseEvent){
     if(!dropStatus)
     {    dropStatus = true;
          infoPop_mc.gotoAndPlay("open");
     }else{
          dropStatus = false;
          infoPop_mc.gotoAndPlay("close");
     }
}
function playVideo1(event:MouseEvent){
   vStream.play("FLV/Video1.flv");
}
function playVideo2(event:MouseEvent){
   vStream.play("FLV/Video2.flv");
}
function playVideo3(event:MouseEvent){
   vStream.play("FLV/Video3.flv");
}
// add Event Handler to respond to the metadata loading
function onMetaData(data:Object){
   dropStatus = false;
   infoPop_mc.gotoAndPlay("close");
}
stop();
```

Summary

This completes the chapter. As you can see, there are several different options available to you when exporting After Effects files to Flash. No matter which option you choose, always optimize the image size and the video encoding to maintain a respectable file size for Web delivery. Exporting vector art from After Effects creates small file sizes but does have its limitations. Rasterized content should be exported as either an image sequence or Flash Video.

When working with Flash Video you can either import the video into an FLV Playback component or stream the video into a Video Display object using ActionScript. Which is better? Using the FLV Playback component can be quite useful and a big time saver in most cases. It provides a lot of functionality with little or no coding effort on your part.

If there is a very strict requirement in terms of file size, creating the Video Display object is better than using components for a number of reasons. First, it creates a lower file size. Components tend to include extra features that you may never actually use. Secondly, if you want to make a video player with more customizable features than what the component includes, you can build them using ActionScript and in the process, learn more about programming.

CHAPTER 4

....

Alpha Channels

Importing video into Flash is nothing new. Now that Flash supports an 8-bit alpha channel, new possibilities emerge for Flash designers. Alpha channels can vastly improve the user experience in your video-based Flash applications.

What Are Alpha Channels?

An RGB image contains three color channels — red, green, and blue. When combined, these channels produce the full color image. The alpha channel is a fourth channel that contains an 8-bit grayscale image. This image determines the transparency of each pixel. Black pixels become transparent, and white pixels are opaque. Any value in between black and white has a certain degree of transparency. A 32-bit color image contains 24-bit color information with an 8-bit alpha channel.

Figure 4.1: *An alpha channel determines the transparency of each pixel.*

When you hear the words alpha channel, most Flash designers think of Adobe Photoshop and PNG files. Those alpha channels are working with still images. Video can also contain an alpha channel and After Effects can create this through keying. **Keying** takes a selected color (the key) in video and removes it from the shot. A prime example is your local weatherman on TV. He is standing in front of a blue or green screen. The colored screen is removed, or keyed out, and a weather map is placed in the resulting transparent area.

Figure 4.2: *Keying takes a selected color (usually blue or green) in video and removes it from the shot.*

Chapter 4: Alpha Channels

In this chapter, you will use the Keylight plug-in in After Effects to key out the background in video. The rendered video with an alpha channel will be layered over different background images in Flash. In addition to keying, you will also learn about setting up cue points in After Effects that can trigger other events in Flash. Let's start by creating an alpha channel video.

Locate the Chapter_04 folder on the DVD. Copy this folder to your hard drive. The folder contains all the files needed to complete the chapter exercises.

Keying in After Effects

Keylight is a keying effect designed for blue or green screen footage. With a couple clicks of the mouse, you can key out a color from a video clip. This high-end keying plug-in is licensed from the Foundry, **www.thefoundry.co.uk**, a visual effects software company.

Before you use the Keylight plug-in, let's talk about what goes into setting up the shot to produce a clean key. It may seem quite simple; stand in front of a green screen and shoot some video. The actual setup is much more involved. The key, forgive the bad pun, starts with good lighting.

Lighting is critical. Typically two or more lights are used to light the green screen. Your background needs to be evenly and brightly illuminated. You want to set up your lights so that they remove as many shadows as possible. A preferred method involves lighting the background and the subject separately. If your subject is framed waist-up have him/her stand at least six feet in front of the background. Make sure that they are not wearing a similar color in their clothing. Figure 4.3 shows the setup used for this chapter. These are general tips to follow. Learning what goes into setting up a green screen shoot is a subject for an entirely different book.

Figure 4.3: *Good lighting is critical in producing a clean chroma key.*

Keying begins with a video clip. Once you have shot your footage in front of the green screen, import the video into After Effects to remove the green color. The word "remove" may not be the best word to use. The keying process actually generates an alpha channel mask around your subject. This mask hides the green background; it doesn't remove it. To see what you will build in this exercise, locate and launch the **Welcome.swf** file in the Completed folder inside the 01_AlphaChannel folder in Chapter_04 (Figure 4.4).

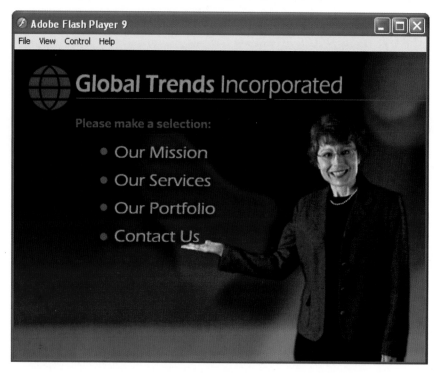

Figure 4.4: *The final SWF file integrates a FLV file with an alpha channel.*

01_Alpha

1. In Adobe After Effects, select **File > Open Project**. Open the 01_AlphaChannel folder inside Chapter_04. Select **01_Alpha.aep** and click **Open**. The Project panel contains the footage needed to complete this exercise.

2. If the **Welcome** composition is not open, double-click on it in the Project panel. The woman was recorded in front of a green screen. Notice that you can see the clamps and sand bags that hold the green screen in place. You need to eliminate them first, before you apply the Keylight plug-in.

3. Select the **Welcome.mov** layer. Select the **Pen** tool from the Tools panel. This creates a mask that will remove unwanted areas in the Comp Window.

4. Go to the Timeline and move the Current Time Indicator (CTI) to three seconds (03:00). The woman is raising her hand. This gives you a better idea of the unwanted areas that you need to mask out.

5. Go to the Comp Window and create a mask shape around the woman using the Pen tool. Click to plot points. When you close the path, the area outside of the mask disappears (Figure 4.5). Scrub through the Timeline to make sure that you do not lose any of the subject in the mask. To adjust the mask, click on the **Selection** (arrow) tool. Click and drag a point to alter the shape of the mask.

Figure 4.5: *Use the Pen tool to create a mask around the woman.*

You just created a **garbage matte**. This is commonly done when dealing with green screen footage. It serves a couple of purposes. First, it removes unwanted areas from the shot. Secondly, it reduces the area that you need to key.

6. Make sure the Welcome.mov layer is still selected in the Timeline. Select **Effect > Keying > Keylight (1.2)**. This applies the plug-in to the layer.

7. In the Effect Controls panel, go to the **Screen Colour** property and select the **eye dropper** icon to activate the tool.

8. With the Eye Dropper tool selected, go to the Comp Window and click on the green area surrounding the woman. As soon as you click, the green screen background disappears or turns black (Figure 4.6). That was easy!

Figure 4.6: *Select the color key using the Eye Dropper tool to remove it.*

9. In the Effect Controls panel, select **Screen Matte** from the **View** popup menu.

10. The Screen Matte displays the alpha channel mask in your keyed footage as a grayscale image. Remember, areas of black are transparent; areas of white are opaque. Notice that there are still shades of gray near the bottom. Although the Keylight plug-in is very effective at keying, you still need to help it out a little. Twirl open the **Screen Matte** properties.

Figure 4.7: *The Screen Matte view displays the alpha channel as a grayscale image.*

11. In the Screen Matte properties, make the following changes to each value:

   ▶ Change the **Screen Pre-blur** property to **1.0**. This smooths the edges.

   ▶ Change the **Clip Black** property to **15**. This increases the black levels.

   ▶ Change the **Clip White** property to **90**. This increases the white levels.

12. In the Effect Controls panel, select **Final Result** from the **View** popup menu. In the Composition panel, click on the **Toggle Transparency Grid** button ▦ to see the image on a transparent background (Figure 4.8). Click on the toggle button again to bring back the black background.

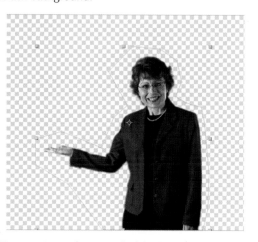

Figure 4.8: *Adjust the Screen Matte properties to fine-tune the keying.*

13. Before you render the composition, crop the Comp Window to help reduce the file size of the FLV file. Click on the **Region of Interest** button 🔲 at the bottom of the Composition panel. The region of interest is the area that is previewed in the Comp Window.

14. Click and drag in the Comp Window to create a smaller region of interest. Scrub through the Timeline to make sure the woman remains inside the area. Use the corner handles to resize the region if necessary.

Figure 4.9: *Reduce the region of interest. Creating a smaller region requires less processing power and helps improve the RAM preview.*

15. Select **Composition > Crop Comp to Region of Interest**. The size of the Comp Window is reduced to the dimensions of the region of interest bounding box.

16. Select **Composition > Make Movie**. This opens the Render Queue.

17. Click on **Best Settings** to open the Render Settings dialog box. In the Frame Rate area, set **use this frame rate** to **15** frames per second.

Figure 4.10: *Change the frame rate of the rendered movie.*

18. Click on **Lossless** next to Output Module. Set the Format to **Adobe Flash Video**. Click on **Format Options** and set the Bitrate setting to **400**. Under **Basic Video Settings**, encode the alpha channel (Figure 4.11).

Figure 4.11: *Render the Flash Video file with an alpha channel.*

19. Click on the Export Audio checkbox. Select the **Audio** tab. Set the Bitrate setting to **96**. This will help reduce the final file size.

Figure 4.12: *Export the audio. Set the Bitrate to 96.*

20. Click on **Output To** and select the 01_AlphaChannel folder in the Chapter_04 folder on your hard drive as the final destination for the rendered movie. Click the **Render** button. Save your project.

01_Welcome

21. Let's move to Flash. Double-click on **01_Welcome.fla** in the 01_AlphaChannel folder to open the file in Flash. It contains two layers: a background image for a fictitious company called Global Trends, and a video layer.

22. Select the blank keyframe on Frame 1 of the video layer. Select **File > Import > Import Video**. The Import Video Wizard appears. To import the FLV file:

   ▸ Locate the **Welcome.flv** file you rendered out of After Effects.
   ▸ Set the deployment for **Progressive Download from a Web Server**.
   ▸ Set the Skin to **None**.
   ▸ Click **Finish** to create the FLVPlayback component on the Flash Stage.

23. With the FLVPlayback component selected, go to the Properties panel and enter an instance name of **display**.

24. Change the position of the FLVPlayback component on the Stage. In the Properties panel, set the **X** value to **220.0** and the **Y** value to **74.0**. The video component moves to the lower right corner of the Stage (Figure 4.13).

25. Select **Control > Test Movie**. The video plays the alpha channel in place.

Figure 4.13: *Position the video component in the lower right corner of the Stage.*

The FLVPlayback component adds about 40K to the published file size. With a "Progressive Download" the file plays from your Web server, currently your hard drive, causing a very slight delay before the video starts. The video just pops up out of nowhere. There are a number of ways to integrate the video in a more seamless fashion. For this exercise, you will use a screen shot of the first frame of the video already layered in the Flash project. The screen shot is provided.

26. Click on the **New Layer** icon at the bottom of the Timeline panel. Rename the layer to **image**. Click and drag the **mcWelcomeFrame1** movie clip from the Library to the Stage. This is a screen shot captured of the first frame. It was saved as a JPEG file and imported into Flash.

27. Go to the Properties panel and enter an instance name of **frame1_mc**. Change the position of the movie clip on the Stage to align with the video. In the Properties panel, set the **X** value to **435.5** and the **Y** value to **238.0** (Figure 4.14).

Figure 4.14: *Position the screen capture on the Flash Stage to align with the video.*

28. Click on the **New Layer** icon at the bottom of the Timeline panel. Rename the layer to **actions**. Click on the blank keyframe in Frame 1 and open the Actions panel. Add the following code:

```
// import Flash Video package
import fl.video.*;

// set variables
var flvScene = display;

// add Event Listeners
flvScene.addEventListener(VideoEvent.READY, videoReady);

// Event handler removes image when video is loaded
function videoReady(event:VideoEvent):void {
    frame1_mc.visible = false;
}
```

The code first imports the Flash video package. A **package** contains a group of classes that provide functionality to Flash. The asterisk causes the Flash compiler to import all classes within the video package, some of which you will not use in this exercise. If file size is a concern, you can import the specific class path you need, such as **fl.videos.FLVPlayback**.

Next, a variable name is assigned to the FLVPlayback component on the Stage. As you saw earlier, the component pauses the progressive video until it is ready to view. An event listener is attached that listens to timing events broadcasted from the FLVPlayback component. Once the video is ready to play, the screen shot is no longer required and is hidden.

Another alternative is to load all the images after the video is loaded into the FLVPlayback component. In addition, it is common practice to display a progress bar while the video is loading. This can be accomplished by using the ProgressBar UI component. That is what you will do in the next exercise.

29. Select **Control > Test Movie**. Having the first frame of the video already on the Flash Stage provides a more seamless video experience versus the video just popping up from nowhere and playing. This completes the exercise.

The goal of this project was to introduce you to the Keylight plug-in in After Effects. It is an effective tool for creating video with alpha channel content. Flash can reference the alpha information contained within the FLV file. This can greatly impact the user experience in your video-based Flash projects. Now that you are aware of how to create alpha channels in video, let's build on your knowledge by adding cue points into the equation.

Adding Cue Points

Watching video in Flash does not have to be a passive experience. You can build standard VCR controls that play — **FLVComponent.play()** — and stop — **FLVComponent.stop()** — video. Let's go beyond that by embedding cue points into the video in After Effects. These assigned navigation or event-based points can be referenced through ActionScript to synchronize the video to the content in the Flash movie. This exercise focuses on adding cue points to your video.

To see what you will build in this exercise, launch the **WantedMan.swf** file in the Completed folder inside the 02_CuePoints folder in Chapter_04 (Figure 4.15). Move the cursor over the outlaw's nose and mouth. Be careful he doesn't eat your cursor. Click on his left eye to give him a good poke in the eye.

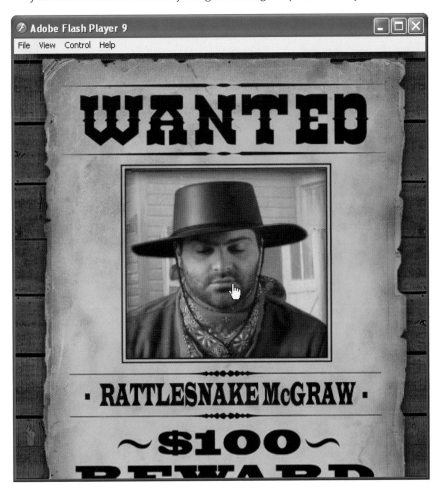

Figure 4.15: *The final SWF file contains a video with embedded cue points.*

02_WantedPoster

1. Open the **02_WantedPoster.aep** inside the 02_CuePoints folder in Chapter_04. The Project panel contains the footage needed to complete this exercise.

2. If the **WantedPoster** composition is not open, double-click on it in the Project panel. The outlaw was recorded in front of a green screen. Scrub through the Timeline. The outlaw has three different facial reactions that dissolve back into the same static image. Select the **WantedPoster.mov** layer in the Timeline.

Figure 4.16: *The QuickTime movie contains three different scenarios for the outlaw.*

3. Select **Effect > Keying > Keylight (1.2)**. This applies the plug-in to the layer.

4. In the Effect Controls panel, go to the **Screen Colour** property and select the **eye dropper** icon to activate the tool. Go to the Comp Window and click on the green area surrounding the outlaw. As soon as you click, the green screen background disappears or turns black (Figure 4.17).

Figure 4.17: *Select the color key using the Eye Dropper tool to remove it.*

5. In the Effect Controls panel, select **Screen Matte** from the **View** popup menu. Twirl open the **Screen Matte** properties. Make the following changes:

   ▸ Change the **Screen Pre-blur** property to **1.0**. This smooths the edges.
   ▸ Change the **Clip Black** property to **15**. This increases the black levels.
   ▸ Change the **Clip White** property to **85**. This increases the white levels.

6. Select **Final Result** from the **View** popup menu. Now that you have keyed out the green background, it is time to add layer-time markers to identify certain frames within the Timeline. These markers can include Flash Video cue points that will be embedded in the rendered FLV file. First, save your project.

Chapter 4: Alpha Channels

7. Make sure the **WantedPoster.mov** layer is still selected. Move the CTI to the one second mark (01:00). Select **Layer > Add Marker**. A triangular marker appears on the selected layer duration bar. Double-click on it.

8. The Layer Marker dialog box opens. Go to the **Flash Video Cue Point and Parameters** section; enter **nose** for the name. Set the cue point to **Navigation** (Figure 4.18). When you render the final composition as a Flash Video file, this marker will be embedded as a cue point. Flash can reference this cue point through ActionScript and navigate to it. Click **OK**.

Figure 4.18: *Add a Flash Video cue point at the one second mark.*

9. Create two more navigation-based cue points. Here is what you need to do:
   ▶ Move the CTI to the four second (04:00) mark. Add a marker and create a Flash Video cue point named **eye**. Set the cue point to **Navigation.**
   ▶ Move the CTI to the seven second (07:00) mark. Add a marker and create a Flash Video cue point named **mouth**. Set the cue point to **Navigation.**

10. Flash will be able to jump to these three navigation-based cue points. You need to set up a couple more cue points to trigger other events internal to the Flash file. Move the CTI to the eight second mark (08:00). Select **Layer > Add Marker**.

11. Double-click on the marker. Go to the **Flash Video Cue Point and Parameters** section; enter **eat** for the name. Set the cue point to **Event** (Figure 4.19). What is the difference between Event and Navigation? Event-based cue points cause some event to happen in Flash. Navigation-based cue points let you shift to a specific frame in the video.

Figure 4.19: *Add a Flash Video cue point at the eight second mark.*

12. Create three more event-based cue points. Here is what you need to do:
   ▶ Move the CTI to the **03:20** mark. Add a marker and create a Flash Video cue point named **noseDone**. Set the cue point to **Event.**
   ▶ Move the CTI to the **06:20** mark. Add a marker and create a Flash Video cue point named **eyeDone**. Set the cue point to **Event.**
   ▶ Press the **End** key to move the CTI to the end of the Timeline. Add a marker and create a Flash Video cue point named **end**. Set the cue point to **Event.**

13. With the cue points in place, add one last effect to the layer. Select **Effect > Color Correction > Hue/Saturation**. You are going to colorize the video to a sepia tone. This will blend in better with the artwork in the Flash file.

14. Go to the Effect Controls panel. Click on the **Colorize** checkbox. Set the **Colorize Hue** to **+30.0** degrees. Set the **Colorize Saturation** to **25**.

Figure 4.20: *Use the Hue/Saturation effect to colorize the video.*

15. The composition is done. Select **Composition > Make Movie**. Click on **Best Settings** to open the Render Settings dialog box. In the Frame Rate area, set **use this frame rate** to **15** frames per second. Uncheck the Audio Export box.

16. Click on **Lossless** next to Output Module. Set the Format to **Adobe Flash Video**. Click on **Format Options** and set the Bitrate setting to **400**. Under **Basic Video Settings**, encode the alpha channel (Figure 4.21).

Figure 4.21: *Render the Flash Video file with an alpha channel.*

17. Click on **Output To** and select the 02_CuePoints folder in the Chapter_04 folder on your hard drive as the final destination for the rendered movie. Click the **Render** button.

18. Let's move to Flash. Double-click on **02_WantedMan.fla** in the 02_CuePoints folder to open the file in Flash.

WantedMan

19. The Flash file is already set up with five layers. The **poster** layer contains a PNG file with a transparent hole where the actual video will appear. The video will play underneath this layer on top of a **background** image. This image was imported into Flash as a JPEG image. Both images were converted into movie clip symbols with instance names of **poster_mc** and **scene_mc**. Both movie clip instances will be hidden initially before the video loads.

Figure 4.22: *The imported FLV file is layered between two Photoshop images.*

The **progressBar** layer holds a Flash ProgressBar UI component. This bar will provide user feedback as the video progressively downloads from the Web. Its instance name is **pBar**.

The **buttons** layer holds three invisible button symbols. When the cursor rolls over or clicks on a button, the FLVPlayback component will navigate to embedded cue points. Let's add the video.

20. Select the blank keyframe on Frame 1 of the video layer. Select **File > Import > Import Video**. The Import Video Wizard appears. To import the FLV file:

   ▸ Locate the **WantedPoster.flv** file you rendered out of After Effects.
   ▸ Set the deployment for **Progressive Download from a Web Server**.
   ▸ Set the Skin to **None**.
   ▸ Click **Finish** to create the FLVPlayback component on the Flash Stage.
   ▸ Go to the Properties panel and enter an instance name of **display**.

21. Click on the **New Layer** icon at the bottom of the Timeline panel. Rename the layer to **actions**.

22. Select the keyframe in Frame 1 of the **actions** layer. Open the Actions panel. Enter the code to import the Flash packages needed for this project. Also define the variables that will be used later.

```
// import Flash packages
import fl.video.*;
import fl.controls.ProgressBarMode;

// set variables
var flvScene = display;
var flvRespond:Boolean = false;
```

23. Set up the progress bar to manually update the number of bytes loaded using the **setProgress()** method later in the code. The code **pBar.indeterminate** tells Flash that the file you are importing has a determinate (known) file size. Also, hide the poster and background image movie clips by setting their visible properties to false.

```
// Set progress bar state
pBar.mode = ProgressBarMode.MANUAL;
pBar.indeterminate = false;

// hide movie clips
poster_mc.visible = false;
scene_mc.visible = false;
```

24. Define the Event Listeners for the FLVPlayback component and the buttons.

```
// add Event Listeners and load the video
flvScene.addEventListener(VideoProgressEvent.PROGRESS, onLoading);
flvScene.addEventListener(VideoEvent.READY, videoReady);
flvScene.addEventListener(MetadataEvent.CUE_POINT, onCue);

// add Event Listeners for the buttons
nose_btn.addEventListener(MouseEvent.ROLL_OVER, cueNose);
mouth_btn.addEventListener(MouseEvent.ROLL_OVER, eatCursor);
eye_btn.addEventListener(MouseEvent.CLICK, pokeEye);
```

25. Define the Event Handlers that respond to the listeners. The first event handler manually updates the ProgressBar UI component. It monitors the bytesLoaded versus the bytesTotal values in the setProgress function.

```
// Event handler controls the progressbar
function onLoading(event:VideoProgressEvent):void {
    var bLoaded = Math.round(event.bytesLoaded/1000);
    var bTotal = Math.round(event.bytesTotal/1000);
  // Update progress...
    pBar.setProgress(bLoaded, bTotal);
}
```

26. The next event handler removes the progress bar from the Stage and turns the visibility of the image layers back on. This occurs when the video is loaded.

```
// Event handler removes progress bar when video is loaded
function videoReady(event:VideoEvent):void {
    flvScene.stop();
    removeChild(pBar);
    scene_mc.visible = true;
    poster_mc.visible = true;
}
```

27. Enter the code that controls the embedded navigation-based cue points. The code **seekToNavCuePoint(cueName)** accurately jumps to the embedded navigation cue point by using the cue point's name. The video plays from there.

```
// create Event Handlers for navigation-based cue points
function cueNose(event:MouseEvent):void {
    if(!flvRespond){
        playCue("nose");
    }
}
function pokeEye(event:MouseEvent):void {
    if(!flvRespond){
        playCue("eye");
    }
}
function eatCursor(event:MouseEvent):void {
    if(!flvRespond){
        playCue("mouth");
    }
}
function playCue(cueName){
    flvRespond = true;
    flvScene.seekToNavCuePoint(cueName);
    flvScene.play();
}
```

28. The last function handles the event-based cue points embedded in the Flash Video file. These cue points tell the FLVPlayback component to stop the video playback when a certain cue point is reached. It also hides the cursor when the outlaw eats it. The cursor reappears when the video reaches the end.

```
// Event Handler for event-based cue points
function onCue(event:MetadataEvent):void{
    if(event.info.name == "noseDone"){
        flvRespond = false;
        flvScene.stop();
    }
```

...code continues on next page

```
    if(event.info.name == "eyeDone"){
       flvRespond = false;
       flvScene.stop();
    }
    if(event.info.name == "eat"){
       Mouse.hide();
    }
    if(event.info.name == "end"){
       flvRespond = false;
       flvScene.stop();
       Mouse.show();
    }
}
```

29. Select **Control > Test Movie**. This completes the exercise. In addition to keying out the green screen in a video, you can now add cue points to your After Effects skills. Cue points allow you to turn linear video into a nonlinear, interactive experience for the user. The last exercise continues with the western theme. You will build a simple shootout game using cue points and ActionScript.

Figure 4.23: *Cue points add interactivity to video.*

Creating an Interactive Video Game

The previous two exercises used the FLVPlayback component to display the video and access the embedded cue points. How do you control streamed video with cue points using just code without a video component? This exercise answers this question as you build a basic interactive video game (Figure 4.24).

To see an example of what you will build in this exercise, locate and launch the **HighNoon.swf** file located in the 03_VideoGame folder inside Chapter_04. The video is loaded using the NetConnection and NetStream objects. As mentioned earlier, this exercise continues with the western theme. You will now become the outlaw, Rattlesnake McGraw. The sheriff in town has you cornered. Click on the bull's-eye when the sheriff draws his gun. Who will survive?

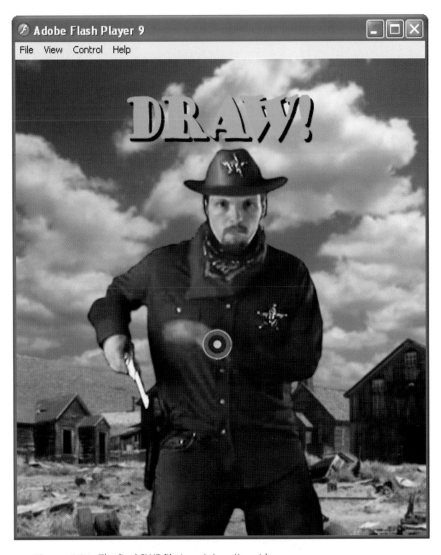

Figure 4.24: *The final SWF file is an interactive video game.*

03_Sheriff

1. Open the **03_Sheriff.aep** inside the 03_VideoGame folder in Chapter_04. The Project panel contains the footage needed to complete this exercise.

2. If the **Sheriff** composition is not open, double-click on it in the Project panel. The sheriff was recorded in front of a green screen. Scrub through the Timeline. The video has four basic sections: ready to shoot, drawing the gun, getting shot, and winning the gunfight. Select the **Sheriff.mov** layer in the Timeline.

Figure 4.25: *The QuickTime movie contains four different scenarios for the sheriff.*

3. Select the **Pen** tool 🖊 from the Tools panel. This creates a mask that will remove unwanted areas in the Comp Window.

4. Use the Pen tool to create a garbage matte around the sheriff (Figure 4.26). Scrub through the Timeline to make sure that you do not lose any of the sheriff in the mask.

Figure 4.26: *Use the Pen tool to create a mask around the sheriff.*

Chapter 4: Alpha Channels

5. Select **Effect > Keying > Keylight (1.2)**. This applies the plug-in to the layer.

6. In the Effect Controls panel, go to the **Screen Colour** property and select the **eye dropper** icon to activate the tool. Go to the Comp Window and click on the green area surrounding the outlaw. As soon as you click, the green screen background disappears or turns black (Figure 4.27).

Figure 4.27: *Select the color key using the Eye Dropper tool to remove it.*

7. In the Effect Controls panel, select **Screen Matte** from the **View** popup menu. Twirl open the **Screen Matte** properties. Make the following changes:

   ▸ Change the **Screen Pre-blur** property to **1.0**. This smooths the edges.
   ▸ Change the **Clip Black** property to **25**. This increases the black levels.
   ▸ Change the **Clip White** property to **65**. This increases the white levels.
   ▸ Change the **Screen Shrink** property to **–1**. This clips the sheriff's outline.

8. Select **Final Result** from the **View** popup menu. Now that you have keyed out the green background, it is time to add layer-time markers and the Flash Video cue points that will be embedded in the rendered FLV file.

9. Make sure the **Sheriff.mov** layer is still selected. For this exercise, you will create all event-based cue points. Here is what you need to do:

   ▸ Move the CTI to the **02:00** mark. Add a marker and create a Flash Video cue point named **loop**. Set the cue point to **Event.**
   ▸ Move the CTI to the **02:06** mark. Add a marker and create a Flash Video cue point named **draw**. Set the cue point to **Event.**
   ▸ Move the CTI to the **03:00** mark. Add a marker and create a Flash Video cue point named **bang**. Set the cue point to **Event.**
   ▸ Move the CTI to the **05:09** mark. Add a marker and create a Flash Video cue point named **dead**. Set the cue point to **Event.**
   ▸ Press the **End** key to move the CTI to the end of the Timeline. Add a marker and create a Flash Video cue point named **end**. Set the cue point to **Event.**

10. Click on the **Region of Interest** button in the Composition panel. Click and drag in the Comp Window to create a smaller region of interest. Scrub through the Timeline to make sure the sheriff remains inside the area.

Figure 4.28: *Reduce the region of interest. Creating a smaller region requires less processing power and helps improve the RAM preview.*

11. Select **Composition > Crop Comp to Region of Interest**. The size of the Comp Window is reduced to the dimensions of the region of interest bounding box.

12. The composition is done. Select **Composition > Make Movie**. Click on **Lossless** next to Output Module. Set the Format to **Adobe Flash Video**. Click on **Format Options** and set the Bitrate setting to **400**. Under **Basic Video Settings**, encode the alpha channel.

13. Click on the Export Audio checkbox. Select the **Audio** tab. Set the Bitrate setting to **96**. This will help reduce the final file size.

Figure 4.29: *Export the audio. Set the Bitrate to 96.*

14. Click on **Output To** and select the 03_VideoGame folder in the Chapter_04 folder on your hard drive as the final destination for the rendered movie. Click the **Render** button.

03_HighNoon

15. Let's move to Flash. Double-click on **03_HighNoon.fla** in the 03_VideoGame folder to open the file in Flash.

16. The Flash file is already set up with three frames. Frames 1 and 3 play and restart the game on Frame 2. The actions layer contains code for each button on the screen. Click on **Frame 2**.

Figure 4.30: *The artwork is in place on Frame 2. You will add the video through code.*

17. The second frame in the Flash file contains a background JPEG image, a movie clip instance that contains the word "draw," and a bull's-eye movie clip instance. Select the keyframe in Frame 1 of the **actions** layer. Open the Actions panel. You will add the video to this frame using the NetConnection and NetStream objects. Enter the following code:

```
// create video netconnection and netstream
var vConnection:NetConnection = new NetConnection();
vConnection.connect(null);
var vStream:NetStream = new NetStream(vConnection);
```

The **NetConnection** object links to the FLV file. **Null** is used for the connection name since you are accessing the FLV files locally from your hard drive. The **NetStream** object controls the playback of the video. In order to stream the data correctly, the NetConnection is passed into the NetStream.

18. The Flash Player receives the cue point information embedded in the FLV file being played. You need to set up an object that will listen for this information. Enter the following code in the Actions panel. Add it after the code you entered in Step 17. The code **vStream.client** attaches the metadata object to the NetStream object. The listener calls a function named **onCuePoint**. This function will be added later.

```
// create a cuePoint listener
var client:Object = new Object();
client.onCuePoint = onCuePoint;
vStream.client = client;
```

19. The next step is to create a **Video Display Object** that will hold the loaded FLV file. The code creates a new object with a size of 418 x 480 pixels, the size of the video file. You may need to adjust this to match your video size if it is different. The vertical position is set to align the video object at the bottom of the screen. The statement, **addChild(myVideo)**, draws the object on the Flash Stage. The NetStream object is attached to the Video object.

```
// create a video display object
var myVideo:Video = new Video(418, 480);
myVideo.y = 60;
addChild(myVideo);
myVideo.attachNetStream(vStream);
vStream.play("Sheriff.flv");
```

20. Next, create a new Sound object that will play a rifle sound effect when the user clicks on the target. The audio file is stored externally from the Flash movie in a folder labeled **Audio**. Enter the following code:

```
// create sound Object
var rifle:Sound
// create new Sound Objects and link audio files
rifle = new Sound(new URLRequest("audio/rifle.mp3"));
```

21. Once the NetConnection, NetStream, and Video objects are in place, define the variables needed for the game. The variable **loopTime** will store the position in time for the cue point labeled loop. This will be used to cycle a small portion of the video before the sheriff draws his gun. The boolean variable **hitHim** will be set to true if the user clicks on the target on the Stage. Enter the code:

```
// define variables
var loopTime
var hitHim:Boolean = false;
```

22. Define the Event Listeners for the target movie clip. Set its visible property to false, hiding it on the Stage.

```
// create Event Listeners and hide objects on Stage
target_mc.addEventListener(MouseEvent.CLICK, shoot);
target_mc.buttonMode = true;
target_mc.visible = false;
draw_mc.visible = false;
```

23. Define the Event Handler that responds to the **onCuePoint** listener. To reference the cue point name use the code **cuePoint.name**. To reference the specific time of the cue point, use **cuePoint.time**. To jump to a certain point in time, use the code **videoStream.seek (time in seconds)**.

```
// add Event Handler to respond to the metadata loading
function onCuePoint(cuePoint:Object):void {

    if(cuePoint.name == "loop"){
        loopTime = cuePoint.time;
    }

    if(cuePoint.name == "draw"){
        var randomLoop:Number = Math.random()*10; // random number 0 to 9
        // if random number is greater than 2
        if(randomLoop > 2){
            vStream.seek(loopTime);                    // cycle the video loop
        }else{
            setChildIndex(target_mc, numChildren - 1); // set target on top
            target_mc.visible = true;
            draw_mc.visible = true;
        }
    }

    if(cuePoint.name == "bang"){
        draw_mc.visible = false;
        target_mc.visible = false;
        if(!hitHim){
            vStream.seek(6);
        }
    }
    if(cuePoint.name == "dead"){
        vStream.close();
        myVideo.clear();
        gotoAndStop(3);
    }
    if(cuePoint.name == "end"){
        gotoAndStop(3);
    }
}
```

24. The last function you need to create sets the boolean variable **hitHim** to true if the user clicks on the target movie clip while it is visible. It also plays the sound effect of the rifle. Enter the code:

```
function shoot(event:MouseEvent){
    rifle.play();
    hitHim = true;
}

stop();
```

25. Select **Control > Test Movie**. This completes the exercise. The code used to reference cue points using the NetStream object is not that much different than the ActionScript used for the FLVPlayback component. Save your project.

Figure 4.31: The final SWF file uses the cue points to determine user feedback.

Summary

This completes the chapter on creating alpha channels and embedding cue points. Some key concepts to remember include:

- ▸ Keying takes a selected color (the key) in video and removes it from the shot.
- ▸ In After Effects, the keying process actually generates an alpha channel mask around your subject.
- ▸ A garbage matte removes unwanted areas from the shot and reduces the area that you need to key.
- ▸ Event-based cue points cause some event to happen in Flash.
- ▸ Navigation-based cue points let you shift to a specific frame in the video.

The next chapter continues your journey into the world of motion graphics where After Effects is the industry standard. You will learn more about the Type tool, using prebuilt text animation presets and custom animators.

CHAPTER 5

....

Type in Motion

Motion Graphics has become synonymous with text, specifically animated text. This chapter shows you how to apply typography and movement to create a variety of motion graphics solutions in After Effects that can be integrated into Flash.

Creating and Animating Type

The text engine in After Effects is an incredible tool. It is one of the best out there. You have at your disposal an arsenal of text animators and properties to control and animate over time. With all this power comes a certain amount of complexity. Figure 5.1 shows a typical text layer in the Timeline. It may look a little intimidating with all those properties, but by the time you complete this chapter, you'll discover that creating text in After Effects is as easy as A-B-C.

Figure 5.1: *Text layers include animator groups that provide many properties.*

Adding text to a composition is a simple process. Select the **Type** tool in the Tools panel, click anywhere in the Comp Window, and start typing. When you finish, press the Enter key on the numeric keypad to exit typing mode. If you press the Return/Enter key on the main keyboard, the type cursor drops down to the next line, just like in a word processor. You can also click anywhere outside the Comp Window or select another tool such as the Selection (arrow) tool when you are done typing.

Figure 5.2: *There are two Type tools: the Horizontal and the Vertical Type tool.*

When you click in the Comp Window an insertion point for the text appears at the cursor's location. If you want to center the text in the Comp Window select **Layer > New > Text**. After Effects places the insertion point in the center of the Comp Window. The text is set to center alignment as well. A text layer is automatically created in the composition and appears in the Timeline. It does not appear in the Project panel.

Text in After Effects falls into two categories, **Point Text** and **Paragraph Text**. When you click and start typing in the Comp Window you are creating Point Text. Each line of type is a continuous block of text (Figure 5.3). New lines will only be created when you press the Return/Enter key.

Figure 5.3: *Point Text is one block of text. Paragraph Text automatically wraps the text to fit inside its bounding box.*

Click and drag the Type tool in the Comp Window to create Paragraph Text. Paragraph Text automatically wraps text around to the next line to fit within the bounding box (Figure 5.3). The text's bounding box is defined by how far you dragged the cursor when you created the Paragraph Text layer.

If needed, you can resize the bounding box for Paragraph Text by first selecting the text using the Type tool. Then click and drag on one of the handles around the perimeter of the bounding box. Hold down the Shift key to constrain the proportions of the bounding box.

Double-clicking a text layer in the Comp Window will highlight all of the text and switch you to the Type tool. Once the text is selected, you can adjust Text properties such as font size and alignment using the Character and Paragraph panel. Both panels, by default, open when a text layer is created.

You can select all of the text or individual characters. Based on your selection, the adjustments you make only affect the highlighted characters. You can control the font, its size, leading (space between lines), kerning (space between individual characters), and tracking (space between all characters).

1. Launch **Adobe After Effects**. Select **Composition > New Composition**. You will set up the project for a typical Flash movie. Make the following settings:

    ▸ Composition Name: **SupernovaText**
    ▸ Width: **550**
    ▸ Height: **400**
    ▸ Pixel Aspect Ratio: **Square Pixels**
    ▸ Frame Rate: **15**
    ▸ Duration: **0:00:05:00**

    Click **OK**. The new composition opens with a black screen in the Composition panel. The Timeline opens a tab.

2. Select **Layer > New > Text**. After Effects places the insertion point in the center of the Comp Window. Type "SUPERNOVA." A text layer is automatically created in the composition and appears in the Timeline.

    The type layer in the Timeline is automatically named after the text you type. You can change its name the same way you'd change any layer name — select the layer name and press the Return/Enter key to rename the layer.

3. Double-click on the text to select all. Change the font and font size to whatever you want using the Character panel. Arial Black was used for this exercise. The font size was set to 60 pixels (Figure 5.4).

Figure 5.4: *Double-click on the text to highlight all the characters. Change the Character properties to whatever you want.*

4. In the Timeline twirl open the **SUPERNOVA** text layer to reveal its properties. There are two: Text and Transform. Twirl open the transform properties. These are the same layer properties that you have been working with in the previous chapters: Anchor Point, Position, Scale, Rotation, and Opacity.

5. The position of a layer's anchor point affects how it scales and rotates. It is the point at which all the transform properties are calculated from. Set the **Anchor Point** value to **0.0, –20.0**. This changes the vertical position of the layer's anchor point from the baseline of the text to the center of the text.

Chapter 5: Type in Motion

6. Let's animate some of the transform properties. Move the Current Time Indicator (CTI) to the two second mark (02:00). Click on the **stopwatch** icon ⏱ for Position, Scale, and Rotation. This sets keyframes for each property at that point in time.

7. Press the **Home** key to move the CTI to the beginning of the composition (00:00). Make the following changes to the transform properties:

   ▸ Set the **Scale** value to **600%**.

   ▸ Set the **Rotation** value to **–30.0**.

8. Reposition the text in the Comp Window. Click and drag the text layer down, off the bottom right corner of the window (Figure 5.5).

Figure 5.5: *Reposition the text layer in the Comp Window.*

9. Click on the **RAM Preview** button. The text layer flies in from the right side of the Comp Window. The transform properties affect the entire layer of text, similar to other footage layers in a composition. Save your project.

10. Let's apply a blur effect to add more dynamic movement to the composition. Make sure the text layer is still selected in the Timeline. Move the Current Time Indicator (CTI) to the two second mark (02:00) so that you can see the effect. Select **Effect > Blur & Sharpen > CC Radial Fast Blur**.

Figure 5.6: *Apply the CC Radial Fast Blur to the text layer.*

11. Go to the Effect Controls panel and change the **Amount** value to **100**. This increases the amount of blur, producing what looks like rays of light coming from the text. Click on the **stopwatch** icon ⏱ to set a keyframe.

12. Move the CTI to the three second mark (03:00).

13. Go to the Effect Controls panel and change the CC Radial Fast Blur **Amount** value to **30**. Click on the **stopwatch** icon ⏱ next to the **Center** property. This property controls the position of the radial blur.

14. Move the CTI to the four second mark (04:00). Change the **Center** value to **0.0, 200.0**. This moves the radial blur to the left edge of the Comp Window.

15. Move the CTI to the five second mark (05:00). Change the **Center** value to **550.0, 200.0**. This moves the radial blur to the right edge of the Comp Window.

16. Select **Effect > Hue/Saturation**. Go to the Effect Controls panel and click on the **Colorize** checkbox. Make the following changes:

    ▸ Set the **Colorize Hue** to **–140** degrees.
    ▸ Set the **Colorize Saturation** to **100**.
    ▸ Set the **Colorize Lightness** value to **–30**.

17. Click on the **RAM Preview** button. The animation resembles the opening credits to the "Superman" movies (Figure 5.7). Save your project. This completes this exercise on creating and animating a text layer. If you want to export the file to Flash, render the composition as a Flash Video (FLV) file with an encoded alpha channel. Import the video into Flash using "progressive download."

Figure 5.7: *The final text animation using the CC Radial Fast Blur.*

The goal of this exercise was to introduce you to the Type tool and demonstrate how to animate a text layer in After Effects. As you can see, you can animate text layers as you would any other layer in a composition. But there is so much more you can do, such as animating the individual characters or words.

You can attach text to a curved path. In the next exercise, you will place your text on a mask path and animate it sliding along that path. Masks can also be animated by keyframing the Mask Shape property so your attached text can follow a morphing, undulating path. It is so cool and easy to do!

Animating Text Along a Path

In this exercise you will attach a text layer to a mask path to create a simple text animation for a fictional perfume called "Captivate." The path is created using the Pen tool in the Tools panel. Let's get started.

 Locate the Chapter_05 folder on the DVD. Copy this folder to your hard drive. The folder contains all the files needed to complete the chapter exercises.

1. Open the **TextonPath.aep** inside the 01_AnimatingType folder in Chapter_05. The Project panel contains the footage needed to complete this exercise.

TextonPath

2. If the **Captivate** composition is not open, double-click on it in the Project panel. It contains one layer, a photo of a woman (courtesy of **www.istockphoto.com**).

3. Select **Layer > New > Text**. After Effects places the insertion point in the center of the Comp Window. Type "CAPTIVATE." A text layer is automatically created in the composition and appears in the Timeline.

4. Double-click on the text to select all. Change the font and font size to whatever you want using the Character panel. Felix Titling was used for this exercise. The font size was set to 72 pixels (Figure 5.8)

Figure 5.8: *Create a text layer in the Comp Window.*

5. Select the **Captivate** text layer in the Timeline. Select the **Pen** tool from the Tools panel. This creates the path for the text. The path can be open or closed. If you close the mask path, set its mode to None and attach the text.

6. Go to the Comp Window and create a mask path that follows the contour of the woman's shoulder using the Pen tool (Figure 5.9). Start the path on the left side of the Comp Window. To adjust the mask, click on the **Selection** (arrow) tool. Click and drag a point to alter the shape of the mask.

Figure 5.9: *Create a mask path using the Pen tool on the text layer.*

7. In the Timeline, twirl open the **Captivate** layer to reveal its properties. Twirl open the **Text** properties. Twirl open the **Path Options** property group.

8. Select **Mask 1** from the Path property's popup menu (Figure 5.10). After Effects will instantly attach the text to the path in the Comp Window.

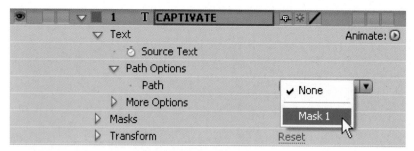

Figure 5.10: *Attach the text layer to the mask path.*

9. Several new properties appear under the Path Options. Scrub through the **First Margin** value to move the text off the right side of the screen. To animate the text moving along the path, keyframe the First Margin property by clicking on its **stopwatch** icon.

10. Press the **End** key on the keyboard to move the CTI to the end of the composition. Go to the Timeline and scrub through the First Margin property to move the text off the left side of the Comp Window.

11. Click on the **RAM Preview** button. The text animates in from the right side of the Comp Window and follows the woman's shoulder across the screen. Save your project.

12. Experiment with the other Path Options. Turn the **Perpendicular to Path** option **OFF** and your text remains vertically aligned as it animates across the woman's shoulder (Figure 5.11).

Chapter 5: Type in Motion

Figure 5.11: *Turn off the Perpendicular to Path option (right image).*

As you learned in Chapter 3, text is vector-based in After Effects. Static text layers and basic text animation export as vector objects. The best way to save this animation to Flash is to export the text as an Adobe Flash SWF file.

13. Turn off the visibility of the **Woman.jpg** layer by clicking on its Video switch 👁 . You do not need this layer exported because it will be included in the Flash file.

14. Select **File > Export > Adobe Flash (SWF)**. This opens the Save File As dialog box. Save the SWF file to the 01_AnimatingType folder in Chapter_05.

15. The SWF Settings dialog box appears. In the Images area, set After Effects to **Ignore Unsupported Features**. There is no audio so leave that unchecked. Leave the rest of the settings as the default (unchecked). Click **OK**. That's it.

16. To see the final results, double-click on **Captivate.fla** in the Completed folder. The Flash file is already built. The SWF file was imported into a movie clip and layered underneath a PNG image of the woman. The final file size is 145 KB.

Captivate

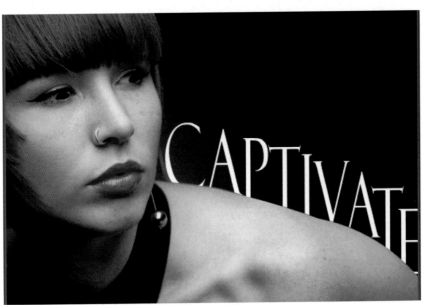

Figure 5.12: *Export the text animation as an Adobe Flash SWF file.*

Applying Text Animation Presets

After Effects ships with a ton of text animation presets. These are prebuilt animation effects sorted by category in the Effects & Presets panel. They can be easily applied to a text layer by a simple drag and drop interaction.

For this exercise, you will build a Flash ad using the Web Banner composition preset. The motion graphics banner ad will be created using the text animation presets. You will build a movie teaser trailer for a direct-to-DVD fictional horror movie called "Contagion." Let's start by creating the new composition.

1. Create a new project in **After Effects**. Select **Composition > New Composition**. Enter **DVDAd** as the Composition Name. Select **Web Banner, 468 x 60** from the Preset popup menu. Set the duration to **0:00:20:00**. Click **OK**.

2. Select **Layer > New > Text**. After Effects places the insertion point in the center of the Comp Window. Type "Deep inside..." Go to the Character panel and change the font to whatever you want. Arial Black was used for this exercise. The font size was set to 30 pixels (Figure 5.13).

3. Type **A** on the keyboard to display the layer's Anchor Point property. Change its second value to **–9.0**. This vertically centers the text in the Comp Window.

Figure 5.13: *Change the Anchor Point value to center the text in the Comp Window.*

4. Select **Layer > New > Text**. Type "a new terror awaits." The font and font size is set automatically to match the previous text layer. Vertically center the text in the Comp Window using the Anchor Point transform property (Figure 5.14).

Figure 5.14: *Create a new Point Text layer.*

5. Select **Layer > New > Text**. Type "Coming soon to DVD." Vertically center the text in the Comp Window using the Anchor Point transform property.

Figure 5.15: *Create a new Point Text layer.*

6. One last text layer is needed — the title of the movie. Select **Layer > New > Text**. Type "CONTAGION." Go to the Character panel and change the font to whatever you want. The Stencil font was used for this exercise. The font size was set to 60 pixels and the color changed to a light green. Vertically center the text in the Comp Window using the Anchor Point transform property.

Figure 5.16: *Create the title text layer. Vertically center it in the Comp Window.*

7. All the text is created. Notice that each layer's duration bar spans the entire Timeline. You need to reposition some of the duration bars so that the text layers appear at different times in the Comp Window. To do this:

   ▸ Move the CTI to the three second mark (03:00). Click and drag the **"a new terror awaits"** duration bar so that its starting point (left edge) aligns with the Current Time Indicator (Figure 5.17).

Figure 5.17: *Reposition the layer's duration bar in the Timeline to align with the CTI.*

   ▸ Move the CTI to the fifteen second mark (15:00). Click and drag the **"Coming soon to DVD"** duration bar so that its starting point (left edge) aligns with the Current Time Indicator.

   ▸ Move the CTI back to the eight second mark (08:00). Click and drag the **"CONTAGION"** duration bar so that its starting point (left edge) aligns with the Current Time Indicator (Figure 5.18).

0:00:08:00 (15.00 fps)
Source Name
1 T CONTAGION
2 T Coming soon to DVD.
3 T a new terror awaits.
4 T Deep inside...

Figure 5.18: *Reposition the layer's duration bar in the Timeline to align with the CTI.*

8. Press the **Home** key to move the CTI back to the beginning of the composition (00:00). Select the **"Deep inside"** layer in the Timeline.

   ▸ Type **T** on the keyboard to display the layer's Opacity property. Set its value to **0**. Click on the Opacity **stopwatch** icon 🕐 to add a keyframe.

   ▸ Move the CTI to the one second mark (01:00). Set the layer's Opacity value back to **100**. The text now fades in.

9. Move the CTI to the three second mark (03:00). Select the **"a new terror awaits"** layer in the Timeline.

   ▸ Type **T** on the keyboard to display the layer's Opacity property. Set its value to **0**. Click on the Opacity **stopwatch** icon 🕐 to add a keyframe.

   ▸ Move the CTI to the four second mark (04:00). Set the layer's Opacity value back to **100** to fade the text layer in.

10. Let's apply some text animation presets to the text layers. Go to the **Effects & Presets** panel. Twirl open the **Animation Presets** folder. Twirl open the **Text** folder. This contains all the different preset folders of text animation. Here is what you need to do:

   ▸ Move the CTI to the three second mark (03:00). Open the **Miscellaneous** preset folder. Click and drag the **Explosion** effect from the Effects & Presets panel to the **"Deep inside"** layer in the Timeline. This effect scatters each letter randomly as if the text exploded.

   ▸ Move the CTI to the six second mark (06:00). Twirl open the **Animate Out** preset folder. Click and drag the **Fade Out Slow** effect from the Effects & Presets panel to the **"a new terror awaits"** layer in the Timeline. This effect fades each letter from left to right.

   ▸ Move the CTI to the eight second mark (08:00). Open the **Miscellaneous** preset folder. Click and drag the **Wiggly Lines** effect from the Effects & Presets panel to the **"CONTAGION"** layer in the Timeline.

   ▸ Move the CTI to the fourteen second mark (14:00). Make sure you still have the **Miscellaneous** preset folder twirled open. Click and drag the **Explosion 2** effect from the Effects & Presets panel to the **"CONTAGION"** layer in the Timeline. This is a variation of the first explosion effect.

   ▸ Move the CTI to the fifteen second mark (15:00). Twirl open the **Organic** preset folder. Click and drag the **Insects** effect from the Effects & Presets panel to the **"Coming soon to DVD"** layer in the Timeline.

11. Click on the **RAM Preview** button to preview your motion graphics project. With just a simple drag and drop interaction, you can easily create effective text animation quickly. With the basic animation in place, let's tweak it a bit. Before you do that, save your project.

12. The title animation could be more dynamic. Turn on the **Motion Blur** switch 🔘 for the **"CONTAGION"** layer in the Timeline. This switch simulates the motion blur captured by a camera. In order to see the motion blur in the Comp Window, click on the **Enable Motion Blur** button 🔘 at the top of the Timeline. Whenever this button is activated, any layer with the Motion Blur switch enabled will display the blur in the Comp Window (Figure 5.19).

Figure 5.19: *Enable the Motion Blur switch and button to enhance the animation.*

13. Turn on the **Motion Blur** switch for the **"Coming soon to DVD"** text layer in the Timeline. That one switch can greatly enhance the motion in the text animation. It is also important to note that these two layers will no longer export as vectors.

Figure 5.20: *Enable the Motion Blur switch for the second text layer.*

14. Click on the **RAM Preview** button. This completes the text animation. What's missing is a good, creepy background. In addition to text animation presets, After Effects also ships with several animated background presets.

15. Deselect all text layers in the Timeline. Make sure nothing is highlighted. Go to the **Effects & Presets** panel. Twirl open the **Backgrounds** folder. Double-click on **Germs**. A new solid layer is added to the Timeline and Project panel. In the Comp Window you see the background effect — instant undulating germs.

Figure 5.21: *Add a background preset to the composition.*

16. In the Timeline, move the **Solid 1** layer to the bottom of the stack. Type the **U** key to reveal all its keyframed properties. The **Evolution** property for Fractal Noise appears twice. This property controls the undulating movement. Click and drag both keyframes at the five second mark to the end of the composition.

Figure 5.22: *Move the second Evolution keyframes to the end of the composition.*

17. Now that the background preset animates for the entire duration of the composition, the last step is to adjust the preset colors to provide better contrast between the text and the floating germs.

18. Go to the Effect Controls panel. It contains all the effects used to create the background preset animation. Go to the **Colorama** effect and twirl open the **Output Cycle**. Select **Solarize Green** from the **Use Preset Palette** popup menu.

19. Double-click on the bright green ◬ triangle at the bottom of the color wheel. The Color dialog box appears. Select a darker green color. Click **OK**.

Figure 5.23: *Adjust the Colorama effect to darken the green color. This creates better contrast between the text and background animation.*

20. Click on the **RAM Preview** button. This completes this exercise on applying text animation presets. If you want to export the file to Flash, render the composition as a Flash Video (FLV) file. Click on **Format Options** and select **Web Banner, 468 x 60** from the Preset popup menu. This preset is optimized for Web delivery. Import the video into Flash using "progressive download."

Think about what you just built. This entire composition was created in After Effects without any imported footage. Twirl open the text layers and look at the properties used by the presets (Figure 5.24). A good way to start learning about text animation in After Effects is to dissect a text animation preset. In the next exercise you will use some of these properties and animator groups to create your own custom text animation.

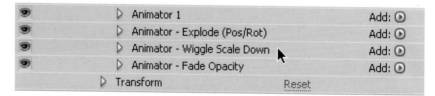

Figure 5.24: *Examine the animated properties of a text animation preset to start learning about the different animators and properties available.*

Chapter 5: Type in Motion

Using Text Animators

Let's create a text animation from scratch. For this technique you will not use any of the text animation presets. First you need to create a composition the same size as your Flash movie.

1. Create a new project in After Effects. Select **Composition > New Composition**. Make the following settings:

   ▸ Composition Name: **DownloadText**
   ▸ Width: **550**
   ▸ Height: **400**
   ▸ Pixel Aspect Ratio: **Square Pixels**
   ▸ Frame Rate: **15**
   ▸ Duration: **0:00:05:00**
   ▸ Click **OK**.

2. Select **Layer > New > Text**. After Effects places the insertion point in the center of the Comp Window. Type "DOWNLOAD."

3. Double-click on the text to select all. Change the font and font size to whatever you want using the Character panel. Avant Garde was used for this exercise. The font size was set to 60 pixels (Figure 5.25).

Figure 5.25: *Double-click on the text to highlight all the characters. Change the Character properties to whatever you want.*

4. Duplicate the layer in the Timeline. Turn off the visibility of the original text layer by clicking on its Video switch 👁 .

Figure 5.26: *Duplicate the text layer. Hide the original text layer by clicking on its video toggle switch.*

5. Select the duplicate text layer (**DOWNLOAD 2**) and twirl open the text layer to display the Text and Transform options. On the **Text** layer click on the arrow ⏵ next to the word **Animate**. The popup menu contains all the Text properties you can animate on a per character basis. Select **Scale** (Figure 5.27).

Figure 5.27: *Select the Scale animation property.*

6. The Timeline instantly has more layers added that may be a little confusing at first. Let's deconstruct the layers you need to work with. **Animator 1** is an animator group that holds the property that you chose to animate and a **Range Selector**. Let's focus on the Range Selector and the Scale property. Scrub through the Scale value and set it to **500%**. All the letters scale up at once.

Figure 5.28: *Increase the scale of each character to 500%.*

7. What happens if you want the letters to scale separately? To do this, twirl open the **Range Selector**. Scrub through the **Offset** value to scale each letter separately. The Offset value ranges from 0 to –100 or +100. Set the Offset value to **0**. Click on its **stopwatch** icon to set a keyframe at the current time.

Figure 5.29: *Scrub through the Offset value in the Range Selector.*

Chapter 5: Type in Motion

8. Move the Current Time Marker (CTI) to the two second mark (02:00). Set the **Offset** value to **100**. A new keyframe is automatically generated.

9. Click on the **RAM Preview** button to see the results. Each letter starts out at 500% and scales down to its original size at 100%. It's a good start, but let's add more properties to create a more interesting animation. Save your project.

10. Now that you have set up the keyframes for the Range Selector, this will be applied to any additional property added to the text layer. On the **Animator 1** layer, select the popup menu next to the word **Add**. Select **Property > Opacity**.

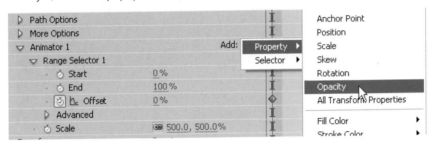

Figure 5.30: *Add the Opacity animation property to the animator group.*

11. The Opacity property is added underneath Scale. Just like with the Scale property, the Opacity's value indicates the starting property for the text. Scrub through the value and set it to **0**. Now each letter will fade in one-by-one as they scale down to 100% (Figure 5.31).

Figure 5.31: *The text nows fades in as it scales to 100%.*

12. The animation is getting better, but the scaling occurs at the baseline of the text. What if you want to scale from the center of the text? On the **Animator 1** layer, select the popup menu next to the word **Add**. Select **Property > Anchor Point**.

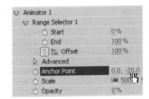

13. The Anchor Point property is added to the Animator 1 group. Scrub through the second value and set it to **-20**. This lowers the text vertically. Each letter will fade in and scale from the center of the text. Click on the **RAM Preview** button to see the results. Now that you have added a couple of text animation properties and set up the keyframes for the Range Selector, let's experiment with some of the advanced settings.

14. In the **Range Selector 1**, twirl open the **Advanced** section. Turn on **Randomize Order**. Click on the **RAM Preview** button to see the results. Each letter animates in random order (Figure 5.32).

Figure 5.32: Turn on Randomize Order in the Advanced settings.

15. In the Advanced section, go to the **Based On** layer; click on the popup menu and select **Words** instead of Characters. Click on the **RAM Preview** button. Now the whole word animates. Change the property back to **Characters.**

Figure 5.33: You can animate the entire word or the individual characters.

DownloadText
Flash Movie
2 KB

Let's take a quick break from After Effects. Currently, this text animation could be used in Flash as a preloader animation. It will export as vector art. The exported SWF file size is 2 KB. This is still small enough that it will not impact the actual preloading of the file. To see an example of a preloader in Flash, locate and open the **Loader.fla** file in the **Preloader** folder inside Chapter_05.

Loader

The file contains two layers: preloader and actions. The SWF file was imported into a movie clip symbol with an instance name of **text_mc**. The text animation appeared as a series of keyframes in the Timeline. A graphic symbol for each letter appeared in the Library. The animation was set up to loop back and forth by copying and pasting the keyframes and then reversing the frames. Click on the keyframe in Frame 1 of the **actions** layer. Open the Actions panel to see the ActionScript. The Loader class is used to import an external JPEG image.

```
// import Flash package
import flash.display.LoaderInfo;
import flash.net.URLRequest;

// define new loader object and URL request
var myLoader:Loader = new Loader();
var myFile:URLRequest = new URLRequest("JPEG/image1.jpg");
myLoader.load(myFile);

// create event listener
myLoader.contentLoaderInfo.addEventListener(Event.COMPLETE, loadImage);

// create event handler
function loadImage(event:Event){
   text_mc.visible = false;
   addChild(myLoader);
}
```

To simulate the file download, select **Control > Test Movie**. In the new SWF window that opens, select **View > Download Settings**. Make a selection from the different bandwidth profiles in the popup menu. Select **View > Simulate Download** to preview how fast the image will load under the chosen bandwidth. The text animation loops until the image is completely loaded.

Figure 5.34: *In Flash you can simulate file download for different bandwidths.*

The break is over. Let's get back into After Effects and explore another advanced technique using text selectors. In this next part of the exercise, you are going to focus on animating the original text layer that is currently hidden.

16. Turn off the visibility of the duplicate text layer by clicking on its video switch. Turn on the visibility of the original text layer (**DOWNLOAD**).

17. Double-click on the text to select all. Change the text color to a bright green. Increase the font size so that the text fills the width of the Comp Window (Figure 5.35). For this exercise, the font size was set to 104 pixels.

Figure 5.35: *Change the text color and increase the font size.*

18. In the Timeline, twirl open the text layer to display the Text and Transform options. Click on the arrow next to the word **Animate** and select **Position**.

19. In the **Range Selector 1** section, scrub through the Position value and set it to **0.0, 500.0**. This changes the vertical position of the text in the Comp Window.

20. On the **Animator 1** layer, select the popup menu next to the word **Add**. Select **Selector > Wiggly**. A new Wiggly Selector appears underneath the Range Selector 1 in the Timeline. The letters appear at different vertical locations in the Comp Window (Figure 5.36). A Wiggly Selector adds randomness to the overall text animation. You can control its affect through the Wiggly properties.

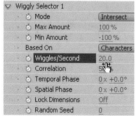

Figure 5.36: *Apply the Wiggler Selector to the text layer.*

21. Twirl open the **Wiggly Selector 1**. Change the **Wiggles/Second** value to **20.0**. The text now "wiggles" much faster in the Comp Window. To enhance the motion, let's activate the motion blur for this layer.

22. Turn on the **Motion Blur** switch for both text layers in the Timeline. Click on the **Enable Motion Blur** button at the top of the Timeline. Whenever this button is activated, any layer with the Motion Blur switch enabled will display the blur in the Comp Window (Figure 5.37).

23. Turn on the visibility of the duplicate text layer (**DOWNLOAD 2**) by clicking on its Video switch.

24. Click on the **RAM Preview** button. Your motion graphics project is starting to look like it belongs in the opening credits to "The Matrix." Save your project.

Figure 5.37: *Enable the Motion Blur switch and button to enhance the animation.*

25. Press the **Home** key to move the CTI to the beginning of the composition.

26. Deselect all text layers in the Timeline. Make sure nothing is highlighted. Go to the **Effects & Presets** panel. Twirl open the **Backgrounds** folder. Double-click on **Circuit**. A new solid layer is added to the Timeline and Project panel.

27. In the Timeline, move the **Solid 1** layer to the bottom of the stack. Type the **U** key to reveal all its keyframed properties. The **Scale** and **Evolution** properties appear. Click and drag both keyframes to the beginning of the composition.

28. Type **T** on the keyboard to display the layer's Opacity property. Set its value to **40%**. This provides better contrast between the text and the background. Click on the **RAM Preview** button to see the final results.

Figure 5.38: *The final composition includes an animated background preset.*

29. The composition is done. The project has evolved from a Flash preloading animation to a title sequence. Since you added motion blur to the text layers, exporting to a SWF file is now not the best solution. Render the composition as a Flash Video (FLV) file.

30. Select **Composition > Make Movie**. Click on **Lossless** next to Output Module. Set the Format to **Adobe Flash Video**. Click on **Format Options** and set the Bitrate setting to **400**.

31. Click on **Output To** and select the Chapter_05 folder on your hard drive as the final destination for the rendered movie. Click the **Render** button. The final file size for the FLV file is 270 KB. Import the video into Flash using "progressive download."

Summary

This completes the chapter on type in motion. You covered a lot of ground with text and all its properties. This chapter only scratches the surface of what you can do with the text engine in After Effects. The possibilities are endless. The best way to keep learning is to apply the text animation presets and examine their structure. From there, you can start creating your own custom presets. In the next chapter you cross over into the third dimension.

CHAPTER 6

....

The Third Dimension

Step into the third dimension. After Effects allows you to position and animate layers in 3D space. This chapter continues your journey into a new frontier of creativity for Flash Web and broadcast design using the Z-axis as your guide.

Entering 3D Space

The third dimension unleashes a lot of creative possibilities. Up to this point in the book, you have worked exclusively in two dimensions — X and Y. After Effects travels beyond 2D by allowing you to move layers along the Z-axis (depth). In addition, you can rotate the layers, add cameras, and even lights that illuminate 3D layers, creating realistic cast shadows. It is so much fun and all it takes is one simple click and you are in 3D space.

This chapter explores how to create, adjust, and animate 3D layers. Each exercise builds on your 3D skills. The chapter projects are geared either towards integrated Flash and After Effects for Web output or broadcast video. Let's cross over into the third dimension.

 Locate the Chapter_06 folder on the DVD. Copy this folder to your hard drive. The folder contains all the files needed to complete the chapter exercises.

The first exercise starts with the basics, converting layers into 3D layers. Any layer, other than an adjustment layer, can be positioned in 3D space as long as it contains content. You will create a 3D animation using a text animation preset and render the composition as a Flash Video file optimized for the Web.

Once imported into Flash, the FLV file will be used as a navigational button. To see what you will build, locate and launch the **3DSpaceConsole.swf** file in the Completed folder inside the 01_3DSpace folder in Chapter_06 (Figure 6.1). Click on the video. The Flash playback head jumps to another frame and plays an animation that zooms out of the scene.

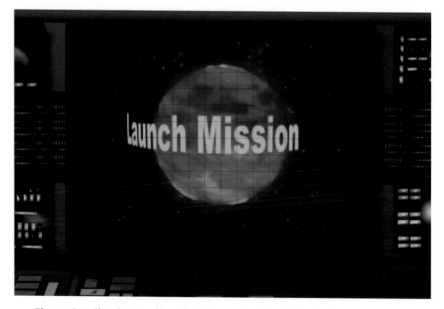

Figure 6.1: *The planet and text are 3D layers in After Effects.*

1. In Adobe After Effects, select **File > Open Project**. Navigate to the 01_3DSpace folder inside Chapter_06. Select **01_3DSpace.aep**, and click **Open**.

01_3DSpace

2. The project contains one composition named 3DSpace. It holds two layers: a QuickTime movie of a planet rotation and a Photoshop still image of a star field.

Figure 6.2: *The composition holds two layers: a QuickTime movie and a still image.*

3. Select the **Planet30.mov** layer. Type **P** on the keyboard to display the layer's Position property. Hold down the **Shift** key and type **R** to open the Rotation property as well. Notice that these properties work in two-dimensional space (Figure 6.3). The layer's position can only move along the X-axis (left and right) and the Y-axis (up and down).

Figure 6.3: *By default, all layers in After Effects are displayed in two-dimensional space.*

4. In the Timeline panel, locate the **3D Layer** switch in the switches column. Its icon is a cube ⬚. Select the 3D Layer switch for the Planet30.mov layer. You just crossed over into the third dimension. Exciting... huh? Well, nothing much happened in the Comp Window, but take a look at the transform properties you opened in the previous step (Figure 6.4).

Figure 6.4: *3D layers acquire additional transform properties.*

When a layer is converted into a 3D layer, it acquires the Z-axis. There are now six Rotate properties to choose from. A new transform property called **Orientation** represents the layer's absolute rotational XYZ angles. It is best to use the other XYZ Rotation properties for any type of 3D animation. Only use Orientation to set a 3D layer's rotation angle that does not animate.

5. Let's rotate the planet in 3D space. Select the **X Rotation** value. Scrub through the second value by moving your cursor left and right. The layer rotates around the X-axis (Figure 6.5). The Rotation value is measured in degrees.

Figure 6.5: *X Rotation rotates the layer around the X-axis.*

6. When you are done, set the **X Rotation** property back to **0** degrees.

7. Select the **Y Rotation** value. Scrub through the second value by moving your cursor left and right. The layer rotates around the Y-axis (Figure 6.6).

Figure 6.6: *Y Rotation rotates the layer around the Y-axis.*

8. When you are done, set the **Y Rotation** property back to **0** degrees.

9. Select the **Z Rotation** value. Scrub through the second value by moving your cursor left and right. The layer rotates around the Z-axis (Figure 6.7).

Figure 6.7: *Z Rotation rotates the layer around the Z-axis.*

10. Set the **Z Rotation** property back to **0** degrees. Deselect the layer.

You may have noticed that the 3D layer does not contain any thickness to it. After Effects allows you to position flat 2D layers in three-dimensional space. Think of it as holding a sheet of paper up in front of you and turning it from side to side. You cannot model spherical-shaped objects in After Effects. For that, you would need an actual 3D program such as Autodesk Maya or Maxon's Cinema 4D.

11. Let's continue with your project by adding another 3D layer. For this, you will add a 3D text animation preset. Make sure that none of the layers are selected in the Timeline. Go to the **Effects & Presets** panel. Twirl open the **Animation Presets** folder. Twirl open the **Text** folder.

12. Twirl open the **3D Text** folder and double-click on **3D Rotate around Circle**. This creates a new text layer in the Timeline. It is already set as a 3D layer.

Figure 6.8: *Double-click on the 3D animation preset to add it to the composition.*

13. A yellow circle appears around the layers in the Comp Window. You need to adjust its rotation on the X-axis to see the letters. Go to the Timeline and select the 3D text layer. Type **R** on the keyboard to open its Rotation property.

14. Scrub through the **X Rotation** value and set it to **–85** degrees.

15. Go to the Comp Window. Double-click on the yellow line to select the path. The best place to double-click is in the gray area. Click and drag the bottom left handle in closer to the planet. Do the same with the right handle.

Figure 6.9: *Scale the 3D text path to be closer to the planet.*

16. Type the **U** key on the keyboard to reveal all the keyframed properties for the layer. The **First Margin** property appears with two keyframes in the Timeline. This controls the text animation around the circular path.

17. Press the **Home** key on the keyboard. This moves the Current Time Indicator to the beginning of the composition (00:00).

18. Scrub through the **First Margin** value to position the text behind the planet.

19. Press the **End** key to move the CTI to the end of the Timeline.

20. Click and drag the second keyframe to the end of the composition. Hold the Shift key while dragging and the keyframe will snap to the CTI.

    ► Scrub through the **First Margin** value to position the text behind the planet.

Figure 6.10: *Click and drag the second keyframe to the end of the composition.*

21. Scrub through the Timeline until the text is in front of the planet in the Comp Window. Select the Text tool and highlight all the text.

    ► Change the default text from Adobe After Effects to **Launch Mission**.

    ► Go to the Character panel and change the text to whatever font and size you want. Arial Black was used for this exercise.

    ► The text color is set to yellow.

Figure 6.11: *Click and drag the second keyframe to the end of the composition.*

22. Click on the **RAM Preview** button. Notice that the text goes behind the planet even though in the Timeline the text layer is stacked on top of the planet layer. Why is this happening? 3D layers ignore the stacking order. The layer's distance from the active camera determines which layer is in front (Figure 6.12).

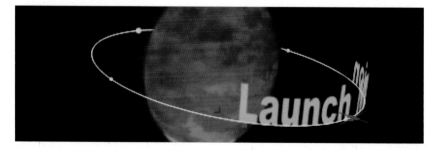

Figure 6.12: *3D Layers ignore the stacking order in the Timeline panel.*

Chapter 6: The Third Dimension

23. Leave the **starfield.psd** layer as a 2D layer. You can mix 2D and 3D layers within the same composition. Save your project. Select **Composition > Make Movie**.

24. Click on **Lossless** next to Output Module. Set the Format to **Adobe Flash Video**. Click on **Format Options** and set the Bitrate setting to **400**. The correct dimensions (320 x 240) and frame rate (15 fps) were set when the composition was initially created using the Web Video (320 x 240) preset.

25. Click on **Output To** and select the Chapter_06 folder on your hard drive as the final destination for the rendered movie. Click the **Render** button.

26. Let's move to Flash. Double-click on **3DSpaceConsole.fla** in the 01_3DSpace folder to open the file in Flash. It contains four layers: actions, grid, video, and console. Everything is in place except for the video.

3DSpaceConsole

Figure 6.13: *The Flash file is assembled and ready for the FLV file.*

27. Select the blank keyframe on Frame 1 of the video layer. Select **File > Import > Import Video**. The Import Wizard dialog box appears. To import the FLV file:

   ▸ Locate the **3DSpace.flv** file you rendered out of After Effects.
   ▸ Set the deployment for **Progressive Download from a Web Server**.
   ▸ Set the Skin to **None**.
   ▸ Click **Finish** to create the FLVPlayback component on the Flash Stage.

28. Center the FLVPlayback component within the grid artwork on the Stage. Go to the Properties panel and give the component an instance name of **myVideo**. You will next add ActionScript to loop the video and turn it into a navigational button. To do this, the code must reference the instance name.

29. Select the keyframe in Frame 1 of the **actions** layer. Open the Actions panel. Enter the following code before the "stop" action in the Actions panel.

The code imports the Flash Video package. This allows Flash to access video events such as when it is done playing (COMPLETE). An event listener "listens" for the video to complete. When it "hears" the event, the linked event handler (loopVideo) instructs the FLVPlayback component to rewind the video back to the first frame (0) and starts playing it again.

Another event listener detects a mouse click on the video component itself. When that event occurs, the Flash movie jumps to the second frame in the Timeline and plays the animation. To provide user feedback, the buttonMode for the FLVPlayback component is set to true. This will change the appearance of the cursor when it rolls over the video indicating that the video is clickable.

```
// import Flash Video package
import fl.video.*;

// add Event Listeners
myVideo.addEventListener(VideoEvent.COMPLETE, loopVideo);
myVideo.addEventListener(MouseEvent.CLICK, startMission);

// enable the cursor change for a button
myVideo.buttonMode = true;

// add Event Handlers
function loopVideo(event:VideoEvent){
    // go back to the beginning and start playing
    event.target.seek(0);
    event.target.play();
}

function startMission(event:MouseEvent){
    gotoAndPlay(2);
}

stop();
```

30. Select **Control > Test Movie**. Click on the video.

This completes the exercise. In this exercise you converted a 2D layer into a 3D layer. When a layer becomes three-dimensional, it acquires additional Z-axis transform properties. You experimented with the layer's XYZ Rotation properties in 3D space. You also added a 3D text animation preset. 3D layers ignore the layer stacking order in the Timeline. Let's switch our focus from rotation to position. The next exercise continues your 3D trek using the Z-axis Position property.

Animating in 3D Space

The goal of this exercise is to animate a layer's position in three-dimensional space. Position in 3D space is defined by X-, Y-, and Z-coordinates. Changing the X-position of a layer moves it left or right. Changing the Y-position moves a layer up or down. The Z-axis moves a layer towards or away from the active camera. Table 6.1 describes how 3D space works in After Effects.

Table 6.1: *Understanding X-Y-Z in After Effects*

Axis	Position	+ Value	- Value
X	Left and Right	Moves Right	Moves Left
Y	Up and Down	Moves Up	Moves Down
Z	Toward and Away	Moves Away	Moves Toward

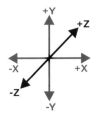

To see an example of what you will build in this exercise, locate and play the **RomanMarch.mov** in the Completed folder inside the 02_3DAnimation folder in Chapter_06. You will build a 3D animation using an imported Flash SWF file. The final composition will be prepared for NTSC video.

Figure 6.14: *The final movie contains a Flash SWF file animated along the Z-axis.*

1. In Adobe After Effects, select **File > Open Project**.

2. Navigate to the 02_3DAnimation folder inside Chapter_06. Select **02_3DAnimation.aep** and click **Open**.

02_3DAnimation

3. The Project panel contains all of the footage you need to complete the exercise. Deselect any highlighted footage in the Project panel by clicking on the gray area under the footage. Click on the **New Folder** icon at the bottom of the Project panel. Rename the new folder to **Comps**.

Figure 6.15: *Create a new folder and name it Comps.*

4. Select **Composition > New Composition**. Enter **RomanMarch** as the Composition Name. Select **NTSC D1** from the Preset popup menu. Set the duration to **0:00:15:00**. Click **OK**.

Figure 6.16: *Create a new composition.*

5. Click and drag the **RomanGROUP.swf** footage from the Project panel to the Timeline. Release the mouse. A group of Roman soldiers appear in the Composition panel. This animation was created in Flash and published as a SWF file. Let's quickly deconstruct the walk cycle.

Motion tweens are applied to nested graphic symbols that only change in position over time. These include the head, shield, spear and arm. The torso and skirt are vector shapes that morph. Shape hints were used to achieve the desired effect. The leg movement is a frame-by-frame animation.

The entire animation is encapsulated within a graphic symbol. This symbol was placed on the Flash Stage and duplicated three times. The symbols occupy 32 frames in the main Timeline, the number of frames contained in the walk cycle.

Chapter 6: The Third Dimension

Figure 6.17: *The marching soldier animation is made up of several layers in Flash.*

6. The Flash Stage is set to 720 x 540 to compensate for non-square pixels. In After Effects, select the layer and then **Layer > Transform > Fit to Comp**.

7. Conform the frame rate of the footage file to 29.97 fps. To do this, select the footage item in the Project panel. Select **File > Interpret Footage > Main**.

   ▸ In the Frame Rate section, select **Conform to frame rate** and enter **29.97**.
   ▸ In the Other Options section, enter **15** for the number of loops.
   ▸ Click **OK**.

8. After you have looped the SWF animation, a ghosted bar now extends to the end of the composition in the Timeline. Re-trim its Out Point by clicking and dragging it to the end of the composition.

Figure 6.18: *Re-trim the Out Point to extend to the end of the composition.*

9. Duplicate the layer four times. Select the layer and press **Command + D** (Mac) or **Control + D** (Windows). You should have five layers in the Timeline.

Figure 6.19: *Duplicate the RomanGROUP.swf layer four times.*

10. Select all the layers in the Timeline. Select the 3D Layer switch 🔲 for any one of the selected layers. This will turn all of the selected layers into 3D layers.

11. Type **P** on the keyboard to display each layer's Position property (Figure 6.20).

Figure 6.20: *Turn on the 3D Layer switch and open the Position property for each layer.*

12. Now it is time to position each duplicate row of Roman soldiers in 3D space. To do this you are going to change the Z-position for each layer (Figure 6.21). First, deselect all the layers by clicking in the gray area underneath Layer 5.

   ▸ Select **Layer 2** and change the Z-position value from 0 to **300**.
   ▸ Select **Layer 3** and change the Z-position value from 0 to **600**.
   ▸ Select **Layer 4** and change the Z-position value from 0 to **900**.
   ▸ Select **Layer 5** and change the Z-position value from 0 to **1200**.

Figure 6.21: *Change the Z-position for each layer.*

The Comp Window currently displays a limited view of the new 3D positioning. Luckily, the Composition panel provides you with multiple views to choose from when working in three dimensions. The ability to view the composition from various angles helps you fine-tune 3D layer placement and alignment.

Chapter 6: The Third Dimension

13. Go to the Composition panel. From the **3D View** popup menu, select **Custom View 1**. The Comp Window now displays a better angle to see the 3D positioning. There are several views to choose from (Figure 6.22).

Front View

Custom View 2

Custom View 3

Figure 6.22: *3D views allow you to see 3D layers from different angles.*

> *The Active Camera view is the default and the view that will be rendered when you export your final movie. Use the other views to position and align 3D layers. Before you render, return to the Active Camera view to evaluate the final composition.*

14. You can also easily change any of the custom camera views using the Orbit Camera Tool, Track XY Camera Tool, and Track Z Camera Tool in the Tools panel. Go to the Tools panel and select the **Orbit Camera Tool** (Figure 6.23).

Figure 6.23: *3D Camera tools allow you to change any custom view.*

15. Go to the Comp Window and click and drag the cursor across the image to rotate around your composition in 3D space. Experiment with the other Camera tools. Select them from the Tools panel and click and drag in the Comp Window.

> ▸ The **Orbit Camera Tool** rotates around the composition.
> ▸ The **Track XY Camera Tool** pans left, right, up and down.
> ▸ The **Track Z Camera Tool** controls how close the layers are to the view.
> ▸ None of these tools affect the position of your layers, only the view.

16. Return the 3D view to the **Active Camera** view. Now that you are aware of how to maneuver around the composition using the views, it is time to animate. Instead of animating each layer separately, you will use parenting to link four of the layers to one "parent" layer. All you need to do is animate the parent layer.

17. Go to the Timeline panel. Click on the menu popup arrow in the upper right corner of the panel. Select **Columns > Parent**. The Parent column appears next to the switches. Parenting allows you to attach one layer or layers to another layer. This is similar to grouping. Chapter 7 covers parenting in detail. For now:

   ▸ Select Layers 2 through 5.

   ▸ From the Parent popup menu, select layer **1.RomanGROUP.swf**.

   ▸ Layers 2 through 5 are now attached to Layer 1. Any changes made to this layer, the parent, will affect all the attached layers, the children.

Figure 6.24: *Parenting allows you to attach one or multiple layers to another.*

18. Press the **Home** key on the keyboard to move the CTI to 00:00.

19. Select **Layer 1**. Click on the **stopwatch** icon next to the Position property. This records the layer's position at the start of the composition.

20. Move the CTI to the **eleven second** mark (11:00). `0;00;11;00`

21. Set the Z-position of Layer 1 to **–2800**. A negative value on the Z-axis moves the layer towards the active camera. A new keyframe is also generated.

22. Click on the **RAM Preview** button. The Roman soldiers march into the camera. Notice that all the soldiers animate even though Layer 1 contains the only keyframed animation. This is a result of parenting. Save your project.

23. Click and drag the **Rome.psd** file from the Project panel to the Timeline. Position it at the bottom of the layers. The background image appears in the Comp Window. For this exercise, leave this layer as a 2D layer.

Figure 6.25: *Add the background image to the composition.*

Chapter 6: The Third Dimension

24. Let's add a camera to the composition. Select **Layer > New > Camera**. The Camera Settings dialog box appears. Enter **myCamera** for the name. Set the preset to **50mm** and check the checkbox to enable depth of field. Click **OK**.

Figure 6.26: *Add a 3D camera to the composition. They appear on their own layer.*

25. By default, cameras are 3D layers. Twirl open the camera transform properties.

   ▶ Change the **Point of Interest's** second value (Y-position) to **220**.

   ▶ Change the **Position's** second value (Y-position) to **160**.

   ▶ This camera adjustment changes the viewed perspective of the 3D layers slightly to align better with the linear perspective in the background image.

Figure 6.27: *Adjust the vertical position of the camera.*

26. Click and drag the **RomansLogo.ai** file from the Project panel to the Timeline. Position it under the **myCamera** layer.

   ▶ Turn on the **3D Layer** switch for the layer.

   ▶ Turn on the **Continuously Rasterize** switch to maintain the smooth detail in the vector artwork as it scales larger than its original size.

Figure 6.28: *Turn on the 3D Layer and the Continuously Rasterize switch.*

27. Let's animate the logo along the Z-axis. It will animate in the opposite direction of the marching Roman soldiers. Type **P** on the keyboard to display the layer's Position property. Set the third value (Z-axis) to **−1000**. The position of the logo is now set behind the camera. This will be its starting position.

28. Move the CTI to the **eight second** mark (08:00). Click on the **stopwatch** icon next to the Position property. This records the starting position of the logo.

29. Move the CTI to the **eleven second** mark (11:00). Set the third Position value (Z-axis) to **200**. The logo is now centered in front of the camera. This is the ending position for the logo animation. A keyframe is automatically created.

30. Click on the **RAM Preview** button. After the Roman soldiers march off the screen, the logo animates in. You have just animated several layers along the Z-axis. Changing the Z-value from positive to negative moves a layer (Roman soldiers) towards the active camera. Changing the Z-value from negative to positive moves a layer (ROMANS logo) away from the camera. This 3D effect would be extremely difficult to replicate in Flash. Save your project.

Figure 6.29: *The Roman soldiers and logo animate along the Z-axis.*

31. Let's add some finishing touches to the project before you render it. Select the **Rome.psd** layer in the Timeline. Type **T** on the keyboard to open the layer's Opacity property. You are going to fade the background image out when the logo animates in.

32. Move the CTI to the **eight second** mark (08:00). Click on the **stopwatch** icon next to the Opacity property. This records a starting opacity of 100%.

33. Move the CTI to the **eleven second** mark (11:00). Set the Opacity value to **0**.

Figure 6.30: *Fade out the background image as the logo animates in.*

34. Select the **RomansLogo.ai** layer in the Timeline. Let's add an effect to this layer.

35. Select **Effect > Generate > CC Light Sweep**. This simulates a beam of light.

36. Move the CTI to the **eleven second** mark (11:00).

37. Go to the Effect Controls panel. Click on the **stopwatch** icon next to the **Center** property. Change the first value to **–100**. This positions the beam of light off the left edge of the layer.

38. Move the CTI to the **thirteen second** mark (13:00). Set the Center property's first value to **730**. This places the beam of light off the right edge of the layer.

39. Click on the **RAM Preview** button. After the logo animates in, a beam of light moves across the letterforms adding a small highlight to the logo artwork.

Figure 6.31: *Add the CC Light Sweep effect to highlight the logo.*

40. Click and drag both audio footage files from the Project panel to the Timeline. Position them above the **myCamera** layer. This completes the composition.

Figure 6.32: *Add the audio files to the Timeline.*

41. Select **Composition > Make Movie**. This opens the Render Queue.

42. Click on **Lossless** next to Output Module. Set the Format to **QuickTime** movie.

43. Click on **Format Options** and set the compression setting to **MPEG-4 Video**. Enable the Audio export for the music and marching sound effect.

44. Click on **Output To** and select the Chapter_06 folder on your hard drive as the final destination for the rendered movie. Click the **Render** button.

This exercise focused on animating a layer's position along the Z-axis. As you create 3D layers, use the different 3D views in the Composition panel to see the layers from multiple angles. These views help with positioning and alignment. After Effects also lets you create your own 3D cameras to view the composition. The next exercise focuses more in depth on adding and animating cameras.

Creating 3D Environments

In the previous exercise you explored the 3D views available in the Composition panel. The default view is the Active Camera. The first two projects dealt with animating layers in 3D space. What if you want to animate the Active Camera? Well, you can't. Instead, After Effects allows you to add your own camera as a 3D layer in a composition and animate it in 3D space.

This exercise provides a step-by-step tutorial on adding a camera, positioning it in your 3D world, and finally setting keyframes to animate the camera through a 3D environment. The environment you will build out of 3D layers. The composition will be rendered as a Flash Video file for Web delivery.

You will then use ActionScript to add interactivity to the 3D world. To see what you will build, locate and launch the **HauntedHallway.swf** file in the Completed folder inside the 03_3DEnvironment folder in Chapter_06. Position the cursor over the arrow on the floor (Figure 6.33). As you proceed down the hallway, other animations are triggered to play based on cue points set in the FLV file.

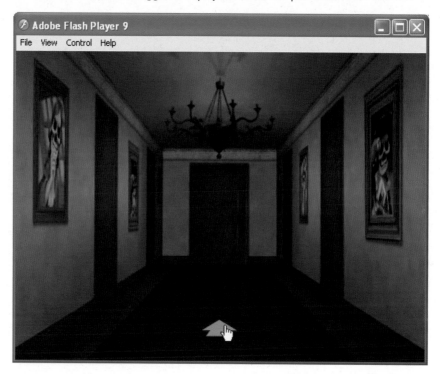

Figure 6.33: *The final SWf file is an interactive 3D environment.*

Let's deconstruct how the artwork was created for this project. Open the layered Photoshop file in the 03_Footage folder. The Photoshop file contains six layers. These layers will be imported and converted into 3D layers in After Effects. Each layer will be oriented in 3D space to create the final hallway scene.

HallwayScene

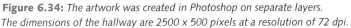

Figure 6.34: *The artwork was created in Photoshop on separate layers. The dimensions of the hallway are 2500 x 500 pixels at a resolution of 72 dpi.*

1. In Adobe After Effects, select **File > Open Project**. Open the 03_3DEnvironment folder inside Chapter_06. Select **03_HauntedHallway.aep** and click **Open**. The Project panel contains footage of each layer in the Photoshop file.

03_HauntedHallway

2. Select **Composition > New Composition**. You need to make the composition the same size as the Flash Stage you will be importing the 3D animation into. Make the following settings:

   ▸ Composition Name: **HauntedHallway**
   ▸ Width: **550**
   ▸ Height: **400**
   ▸ Pixel Aspect Ratio: **Square Pixels**
   ▸ Frame Rate: **30**
   ▸ Duration: **0:00:10:00**

   Click **OK**. The new composition opens in the Composition panel.

3. Click and drag the **floor/HallwayScene.psd** footage file from the Project panel to the Timeline. Turn on the **3D Layer** switch for the layer. Type **P** on the keyboard to display the layer's Position property. Hold down the **Shift** key and type **R** to open the Rotation property as well.

4. Set the **X Rotation** and **Z Rotation** to **90**.

5. Set the **Position** property to **275.0**, **450.0**, and **0.0**.

1	floor/HallwayScene.psd		
	Position	275.0, 450.0, 0.0	
	Orientation	0.0°, 0.0°, 0.0°	
	X Rotation	0x +90.0°	
	Y Rotation	0x +0.0°	
	Z Rotation	0x +90.0°	

Figure 6.35: *Rotate and position the floor layer in 3D space.*

6. Click and drag the **wall/HallwayScene.psd** footage file from the Project panel to the Timeline. Position it on top of the previous layer. Turn on the **3D Layer** switch for the layer. Open the Position and Rotation transform properties.

   ▸ Set the **Y Rotation** to **90**.

   ▸ Set the **Position** property to **525.0**, **200.0**, and **0.0**.

1	wall/HallwayScene.psd		
	Position	525.0, 200.0, 0.0	
	Orientation	0.0°, 0.0°, 0.0°	
	X Rotation	0x +0.0°	
	Y Rotation	0x +90.0°	
	Z Rotation	0x +0.0°	

Figure 6.36: *Rotate and position the wall layer in 3D space.*

7. Duplicate the **wall/HallwayScene.psd** layer. Select the layer and press **Command + D** (Mac) or **Control + D** (Windows).

   ▸ Set the **Y Rotation** to **270**.

   ▸ Set the **Position** property to **25.0**, **200.0**, and **0.0**.

1	wall/HallwayScene.psd		
	Position	25.0, 200.0, 0.0	
	Orientation	0.0°, 0.0°, 0.0°	
	X Rotation	0x +0.0°	
	Y Rotation	0x +270.0°	
	Z Rotation	0x +0.0°	

Figure 6.37: *Rotate and position the duplicate wall layer in 3D space.*

8. Click and drag the **ceiling/HallwayScene.psd** footage file from the Project panel to the Timeline. Position it on top of the previous layer. Turn on the **3D Layer** switch for the layer. Open the Position and Rotation transform properties.

   ▸ Set the **X Rotation** and **Z Rotation** to **90**.

   ▸ Set the **Position** property to **275.0**, **–50.0**, and **0.0**.

This sets up the basic structure of the hallway. Next you will add the doorframe, door, and chandelier to the 3D scene.

Chapter 6: The Third Dimension

9. Click and drag the **doorframe/HallwayScene.psd** footage file to the Timeline. Position it at the top of the layers. Turn on the **3D Layer** switch.

   ▶ Set the **Position** property to **275.0, 200.0,** and **1245.0**.

#	Source Name				
1	🗋 doorframe/HallwayScene	🔲	╱		📦
	🕑 Position		275.0, 200.0, 1245.0		
2	🗋 ceiling/HallwayScene.ps	🔲	╱		📦
3	🗋 wall/HallwayScene.psd	🔲	╱		📦
4	🗋 wall/HallwayScene.psd	🔲	╱		📦
5	🗋 floor/HallwayScene.psd	🔲	╱		📦

Figure 6.38: *Position the doorframe layer in 3D space.*

10. Click and drag the **door/HallwayScene.psd** footage file to the Timeline. Position it at the top of the layers. Turn on the **3D Layer** switch. Type **A** on the keyboard to display the layer's Anchor Point property. Hold down the **Shift** key and type **P** to open the Position property as well.

    ▶ Set the **Anchor Point** to **0.0, 211.5,** and **0.0**.

    ▶ Set the **Position** property to **155.0, 238.0,** and **1245.0**.

#	Source Name				
1	🗋 door/HallwayScene.psd	🔲	╱		📦
	🕑 Anchor Point		0.0, 211.5, 0.0		
	🕑 Position		155.0, 238.0, 1245.0		
2	🗋 doorframe/HallwayScene	🔲	╱		📦
	🕑 Position		275.0, 200.0, 1245.0		
3	🗋 ceiling/HallwayScene.ps	🔲	╱		📦

Figure 6.39: *Position the door layer in 3D space.*

11. Click and drag the **chandelier/HallwayScene.psd** footage file to the Timeline. Position it at the top of the layers. Turn on the **3D Layer** switch.

    ▶ Set the **Position** property to **275.0, 20.0,** and **0.0**.

    ▶ Twirl open the **Materials Options**. Turn on the **Casts Shadows** property. This layer will now cast realistic shadows when a 3D light is added to the scene.

#	Source Name				
1	🗋 chandelier/HallwayScene	🔲	╱		📦
	Transform		Reset		
	Material Options				
	Casts Shadows		On		
	🕑 Light Transmission		🔲		
	Accepts Shadows		On		

Figure 6.40: *Position the chandelier layer in 3D space.*

This completes the 3D environment. Next, you will add a 3D camera.

12. Select **Layer > New > Camera**. The Camera Settings dialog box appears. Enter **myCamera** for the name. Set the preset to **50mm** and check the checkbox to enable depth of field. Click **OK**.

13. Go to the Composition panel. From the **3D View** popup menu, select **Custom View 1**. The Comp Window now displays a better angle to see the camera and the 3D hallway.

14. Use the Orbit Camera Tool, Track XY Camera Tool, and Track Z Camera Tool in the Tools panel to rotate and zoom out to see the entire composition.

Figure 6.41: *Rotate and zoom out using the 3D Camera tools.*

15. The camera has handles and an axis similar to other 3D layers. The triangular shape attached to it defines the field of view from the camera lens. The straight line with a cross hair target at the end is the point of interest. This indicates which way the camera is pointing. Twirl open the camera transform properties.

   ▸ Change the **Point of Interest** property to **275.0**, **200.0**, and **1250.0**.
   ▸ Change the **Position property** to **275.0**, **260.0**, and **–1939.0**.

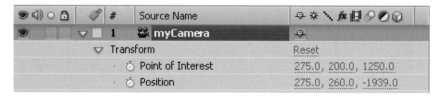

Figure 6.42: *Change the Point of Interest and the Position properties.*

The point of interest moves to the door at the end of the hallway. This guarantees that the camera will always be facing that door as it animates down the hall. The camera position is moved to the opposite end of the hallway. This will be the starting point for the animation. The vertical position was lowered to enhance the linear perspective in the scene.

Figure 6.43: *The custom view (left) and the Active Camera view (right) show the results of changing the camera's position and point of interest.*

16. Return the 3D view to the **Active Camera** view. This view is now the same as **myCamera** view. If you add more cameras to the composition, the Active Camera view will display the view for the selected camera in the Timeline.

17. Let's add some lights to the composition. Select **Layer > New > Light**. The Light Settings dialog box appears. Set the Light Type to **Point** and click **OK**.

> ℹ️ *A point light is an omnidirectional light source. Think of it as a bare light bulb. When a light is added to a composition, the default lighting turns off. Lights only affect 3D layers.*

18. Twirl open the Light transform properties in the Timeline. Set the **Position** property to **275.0**, **150.0**, and **450.0**.

19. Twirl open the Light Options. Set the Intensity to **90%**. Turn on the **Casts Shadows** option. Click on the color swatch. The Parameter Colors dialog box appears. Change the RGB values to **180**, **208**, and **240**. This will cast an eerie blue light over the 3D scene. Notice the cast shadow projected from the chandelier. Lighting can greatly enhance your 3D layers.

Figure 6.44: *Add a point light to the composition.*

20. Duplicate the **Light 1** layer. Set the duplicate light's **Position** property to **275.0**, **400.0**, and **−1000.0**. Set the Intensity to **95%**. This completes the lighting.

21. It is time to animate the camera. Press the **Home** key on the keyboard to move the CTI to 00:00.

22. Select the **myCamera** layer in the Timeline. Click on the **stopwatch** icon next to the Position property. This records the camera's current position.

23. Move the CTI to the **nine second** mark (09:00). Change the camera's **Position property** to **275.0**, **260.0**, and **625.0**. The camera moves in close to the door at the end of the hallway. A new keyframe is created.

Figure 6.45: *Animate the camera along the Z-axis.*

24. Click on the **RAM Preview** button. The camera slowly moves down the hallway. Save your project.

0:00:09:10

25. The door is a separate 3D layer. Let's create an animation that opens the door. Move the CTI slightly past the **nine second** mark (09:10).

26. Select the **door/HallwayScene.psd** layer in the Timeline. Click on the **stopwatch** icon next to the **Y Rotation** property. This records the starting keyframe.

27. Press the **End** key on the keyboard to move the CTI to the end of the composition. Change the **Y Rotation** property to **–102.0** degrees. This rotates the door around the Y-axis. Since you moved the layer's Anchor Point to the left edge of the door in step 10, the door rotates at that point.

Figure 6.46: *Rotate the door layer around the Y-axis to open the door.*

0:00:09:19

28. Move the CTI in between the two keyframes you just created (09:19).

Chapter 6: The Third Dimension

29. Select the **myCamera** layer in the Timeline. Click on the gray diamond to the left of the word Position. This adds a keyframe at the current time.

Figure 6.47: *Add a keyframe at the current time.*

30. Press the **End** key on the keyboard to move the CTI to the end of the composition. Change the camera's **Position property** to **275.0**, **260.0**, and **1025.0**. The camera now animates through the open door.

31. Just a couple of more steps needed before you render the Flash Video file. First, select the **doorframe/HallwayScene.psd** layer. Select **Effect > Color Correction > Hue/Saturation**. Go to the Effect Controls panel and adjust the **Master Lightness** to **−70**. This darkens the doorframe to match the lighting.

32. Select the **door/HallwayScene.psd** layer. Select **Effect > Color Correction > Hue/Saturation**. Go to the Effect Controls panel and adjust the **Master Lightness** to **−70**. This darkens the door to match the lighting.

33. Select the **myCamera** layer in the Timeline. Move the CTI to the **four second** mark (04:00). Select **Layer > Add Marker**. Layer-time markers allow you to label specific points in time within the Timeline area. These markers are included in the rendered movie. A triangular marker appears on the selected layer duration bar. Double-click on it.

34. The Layer Marker dialog box opens. Go to the **Flash Video Cue Point and Parameters** section; enter **bat** for the name. Set the cue point to an **Event**. When you render the final composition as a Flash Video file, this marker will be included as a cue point. Flash can reference this cue point through ActionScript. Click **OK**.

Figure 6.48: *Add a Flash Video cue point at the four second mark.*

35. Move the CTI to the **nine second** mark (09:00). Select **Layer > Add Marker**. Double-click on the new marker in the Timeline. In the **Flash Video Cue Point and Parameters** section, enter **ghost** for the name. Click **OK**.

Figure 6.49: *Add a Flash Video cue point at the nine second mark.*

36. Click on the **RAM Preview** button to view the final composition.

37. Select **Composition > Make Movie**. This opens the Render Queue.

38. Click on **Lossless** next to Output Module. Set the Format to **Adobe Flash Video**. Click on **Format Options** and set the Bitrate setting to **700**.

39. Click on **Output To** and select the Chapter_06 folder on your hard drive as the final destination for the rendered movie. Click the **Render** button.

40. Let's move to Flash. Double-click on **03_HauntedHallway.fla** in the 03_3DAnimation folder to open the file in Flash. It contains six layers: actions, buttons, bat, ghost, progressBar, and video. Let's deconstruct a few layers.

03_HauntedHallway

The bat layer contains a movie clip of a bat flying across the Stage. It has an instance name of **bat_mc**. The ghost layer contains a frame-by-frame animation of a floating ghost. Its instance name is **ghost_mc**. These movie clips will play when the corresponding cue point in the FLV file is reached during playback.

Figure 6.50: *The Flash file contains two movie clips that will play based on the embedded Flash Video cue points.*

The **progressBar** layer holds a Flash ProgressBar UI component. The FLV file was encoded at high quality in After Effects. This bar will provide user feedback as the video progressively downloads from the Web. Its instance name is **pBar**.

The **buttons** layer holds a button symbol. When the cursor rolls over the button the FLVPlayback component will play the video file. When the cursor rolls off, the video stops. It has an instance name of **forward_btn**. Let's add the video.

41. Select the blank keyframe on Frame 1 of the video layer. Select **File > Import > Import Video**. The Import Wizard dialog box appears. To import the FLV file:

   ▶ Locate the **HauntedHallway.flv** file you rendered out of After Effects.
   ▶ Set the deployment for **Progressive Download from a Web Server**.
   ▶ Set the Skin to **None**.
   ▶ Click **Finish** to create the FLVPlayback component on the Flash Stage.
   ▶ Go to the Properties panel and enter an instance name of **display**.

42. Select the keyframe in Frame 1 of the **actions** layer. Open the Actions panel. Enter the following code to import the Flash packages needed for this project. Also define the variables that will be used later.

```
// import Flash packages
import fl.video.*;
import fl.controls.ProgressBarMode;

// define Variables
var flvScene = display;
var flvSource = "HauntedHallway.flv";
```

43. Next, create four new sound objects that will play the sound effects and the background sound. The audio files are stored externally from the Flash movie in a folder labeled **Audio**.

Audio

```
// define sounds
var windSound:Sound
var batSound:Sound
var ghostSound:Sound
var laughSound:Sound
// create new Sound Objects and link audio files
windSound = new Sound(new URLRequest("Audio/wind.mp3"));
batSound = new Sound(new URLRequest("Audio/bat.mp3"));
ghostSound = new Sound(new URLRequest("Audio/ghost.mp3"));
laughSound = new Sound(new URLRequest("Audio/laugh.mp3"));
```

 bat

 ghost

 laugh

44. Set up the progress bar to manually update the number of bytes loaded using the **setProgress()** method later in the code. The code **pBar.indeterminate** tells Flash that the file you are importing has a determinate (known) file size.

 wind

```
// set progress bar state
pBar.mode = ProgressBarMode.MANUAL;
pBar.indeterminate = false;
```

45. Define the Event Listeners for the FLVPlayback component and the buttons.

```
// add Event Listeners and load the video
flvScene.addEventListener(VideoProgressEvent.PROGRESS, onLoading);
flvScene.addEventListener(VideoEvent.READY, videoReady);
flvScene.addEventListener(MetadataEvent.CUE_POINT, onCue);
flvScene.source = flvSource;

// add Event Listeners for the buttons
forward_btn.addEventListener(MouseEvent.ROLL_OVER, moveForward);
forward_btn.addEventListener(MouseEvent.ROLL_OUT, stopMoving);
forward_btn.visible = false;
ghost_mc.addEventListener(MouseEvent.CLICK, enterDoor);
ghost_mc.visible = false;
```

46. Define the Event Handlers that respond to the listeners.

```
// Event Handler controls the progressbar
function onLoading(event:VideoProgressEvent):void {
    var bLoaded = Math.round(event.bytesLoaded/1000);
    var bTotal = Math.round(event.bytesTotal/1000);
    // Update progress...
    pBar.setProgress(bLoaded, bTotal);
}
// Event Handler removes progress bar when video is loaded
function videoReady(event:VideoEvent):void {
    removeChild(pBar);
    forward_btn.visible = true;
    flvScene.stop();
    windSound.play(0, int.MAX_VALUE);  // loop audio indefinitely
}
// Event Handler controls the video playback
function moveForward(event:MouseEvent):void {
    flvScene.play();
}
function stopMoving(event:MouseEvent):void {
    flvScene.stop();
}
// Event Handler for video cue points
function onCue(event:MetadataEvent):void{
    if(event.info.name == "bat"){
        bat_mc.play();
        batSound.play();
    }
    if(event.info.name == "ghost"){
        forward_btn.visible = false;
        ghost_mc.visible = true;
        ghost_mc.play();
        ghostSound.play();
        ghost_mc.buttonMode = true;
    }
}
// Event Handler for ghost button
function enterDoor(event:MouseEvent):void {
    ghost_mc.visible = false;
    flvScene.play();
    laughSound.play();
}
```

47. Select **Control > Test Movie**. This completes the exercise.

Summary

In this exercise you created a 3D environment using 3D layers, a camera and 3D lights. Cue points were also added for Flash interactivity. Through the use of ActionScript you controlled the playback of the video simulating a first-person style game. The cue points triggered other movie clips to play (Figure 6.51).

Figure 6.51: *The published SWF file allows the user to walk down the hallway. Cue points embedded within the FLV file trigger other movie clips to play.*

Before you leave this chapter, let's take a closer look at the camera settings. For this exercise and the previous one you added a camera with a 50mm lens. Why that lens? When dealing with 35mm film, a 50mm focal length creates an image that most closely approximates human sight. Changes in the focal length can drastically impact the depth perceived in your 3D environment. Wide angle lenses have much shorter focal lengths and tend to exaggerate depth. Figure 6.52 shows the same 3D environment seen through a 20mm focal length. It now looks like those never-ending hallways that occur in nightmares.

Figure 6.52: *A camera focal length of 20mm produces exaggerated depth.*

A telephoto lens uses a longer focal length. It does not capture a wide area of the 3D scene. The perceived depth is reduced considerably. Figure 6.53 shows the same 3D environment seen through a 135mm focal length. The hallway now looks like a very small, compressed space.

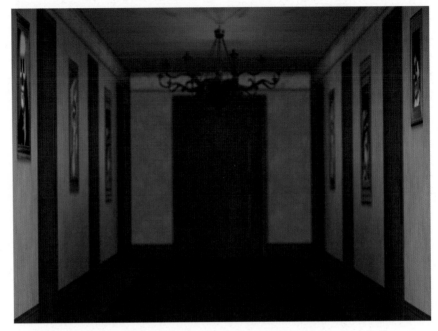

Figure 6.53: *A camera focal length of 135mm compresses the perceived depth.*

This completes the chapter. After Effects allows you to move layers in three dimensions with the click of a button. Although you cannot model realistic shapes, you can orient the flat layers to create unique 3D environments. In addition, you can rotate the layers, and add cameras and lights that add dramatic impact to your rendered movie. You also explored using video cue points to turn linear video into interactive 3D spaces in Flash.

Some key concepts to remember from this chapter include:

▸ When a layer is converted into a 3D layer, it acquires the Z-axis.
▸ A 3D layer does not contain any thickness to it.
▸ It is best to use the XYZ Rotation properties for any type of 3D animation.
▸ Use the 3D views in the Composition panel to position and align 3D layers.
▸ The Active Camera view is the default 3D view and the view that will be rendered when you export your final movie.
▸ When a 3D light is added to a composition, the default lighting turns off. Lights only affect 3D layers.
▸ Changes in a camera's focal length can drastically impact the depth perceived in your 3D scene.

CHAPTER 7

Character Animation

Bringing characters to life in Flash can be quite time consuming. After Effects offers a couple of creative tools that can help reduce production time when animating 2D characters. This chapter explores parenting and the Puppet tools.

Flash Character Animation

The art of character animation requires a lot of patience and practice. Flash provides many great tools for designing 2D characters. Using keyframes or ActionScript, these characters become virtual puppets that can walk, run, and jump. It is the act of linking each individual limb, such as a hand to an arm or a foot to a leg, where Flash could use some assistance.

In practice, a character is divided up into several layers in the Flash Timeline. Each limb is typically a nested graphic or movie clip symbol (Figure 7.1). To rotate a limb correctly, the symbol's registration point must be repositioned to where the joint would be if it were an actual puppet. The character comes to life through the use of a lot of keyframes. Where Flash is lacking is in providing a tool to hinge these character joints (layers) together.

 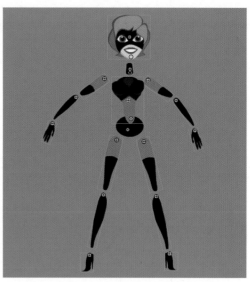

Figure 7.1: *The anatomy of a Flash character is divided up into separate layers. Each limb is a nested symbol. The registration point for each symbol is positioned at the joints in the character.*

Parenting

After Effects offers a technique called **parenting** that can assist in speeding up character animation for Flash. This method attaches one or more layers to a parent layer. If a parent layer moves across the Comp Window, the child layers follow. With the exception of opacity, any changes made to the parent layer's transform properties are inherited by the child layers. Child layers can have their own animation, but these do not affect the parent.

 Locate the Chapter_07 folder on the DVD. Copy this folder to your hard drive. The folder contains all the files needed to complete the chapter exercises.

In this first exercise, you will learn how to assign parenting to several layers. Once the layers are linked together, you will then animate the character and export the final composition as a Flash SWF file. The SWF file will be imported into Flash. To see an example of what you will build, locate and launch the **SuperHero.swf** file in the Completed folder inside the 01_Parenting folder in Chapter_07 (Figure 7.2). Welcome to parenthood!

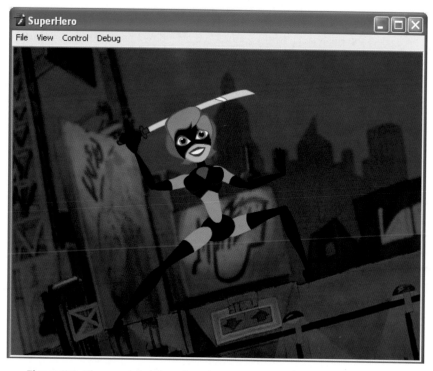

Figure 7.2: *The completed character animation uses parenting in After Effects.*

1. Create a new project in **Adobe After Effects**.

2. Import the footage file. Double-click inside the Project panel. This opens the Import File dialog box. Locate the **Superhero.ai** file inside the 01_Footage folder in 01_Parenting/Chapter_07. Select the file. Choose **Composition – Cropped Layers** as the Import type. Click **OK**.

Figure 7.3: *Import the Adobe Illustrator file into the Project panel as a composition with cropped layers.*

3. Double-click on the Superhero composition in the Project panel to open it in the Timeline and Composition panels. Why import an Illustrator file instead of a Flash file? Each Illustrator layer imports with their original dimensions. Flash SWF files are imported as flattened rasterized files.

4. Before you "parent" the layers, you need to move each layer's anchor point. This allows the character's limbs to rotate correctly at the joints rather than at the center which is an anchor point's default location. To do this:

   ▶ Select the **Head** layer. Notice in the Comp Window the small cross hair target that appears between the superhero's eyes. That is the anchor point.
   ▶ Go to the **Tools** panel and select the **Pan Behind Tool** .
   ▶ Go back to the Comp Window and click and drag the anchor point down to the superhero's chin. This is similar to using the Free Transform tool in Flash to reposition a symbol's registration point.

Figure 7.4: *Change the anchor point's position using the Pan Behind Tool.*

5. With the Pan Behind Tool still selected, click on the **torso** layer. Reposition the anchor point at the bottom of the torso (Figure 7.5).

6. Move the remaining anchor points. With the Pan Behind Tool still selected:

   ▶ Click on a layer in the Comp Window.
   ▶ Click and drag the anchor point to the proper location for the wrist, elbow, knee, and ankle joints.
   ▶ The anchor point position for the upper arms should be close to the shoulder.
   ▶ The anchor point position for the thighs should be at the hips.
   ▶ The only layer that you will keep the anchor point at its default location in the center is the **hips** layer.

7. To set up the parenting structure, you need to open the Parent column in the Timeline panel. If it is not already visible, you can right-click on the **Layer Name** column header and select **Columns > Parent**. Now it is time to figure out which layers are going to be the parents and which are the children.

8. Let's start by connecting the **Head** layer (child) to the **neck** layer (parent). There are a couple of ways to attach a child to a parent. You can use the Parent popup menu to select the appropriate parent. You can also use the Pick Whip tool located to the left of the popup menu. Click on the **spiral icon** (pick whip) for the **Head** layer and drag it to the name column of the **neck** layer (Figure 7.6). Release the mouse. You just linked the head and neck layers.

Figure 7.5: *Change the anchor point's position using the Pan Behind Tool.*

Chapter 7: Character Animation

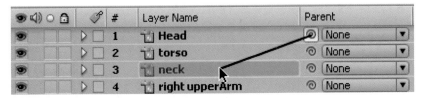

Figure 7.6: *Use the Parent pick whip to link layers in After Effects.*

9. Link the other layers using the same technique. Click on the Parent pick whip for each child layer and use it to point to its parent layer. Figure 7.7 shows you how to set up the parenting structure. If you study the parenting scheme, you will notice that the **hips** layer is the main parent layer for all the other layers. When it moves or rotates, all the layers will follow. Save your project.

Figure 7.7: *Parent the remaining layers as shown.*

10. Now the fun begins. Select the **right UpperArm** layer in the Timeline. Type **R** on the keyboard to display the layer's Rotation property. Scrub through the Rotation value. In the Comp Window the right upper and lower arm rotates along with the right hand. The child layers inherit the transform properties of the parent layer. The upper arm's parent layer (torso) does not rotate.

Figure 7.8: *Rotate the upper arm. Its child layers rotate but the parent layer does not.*

11. Select the **right lowerArm** layer in the Timeline. Open the layer's Rotation property. Scrub through the Rotation value. In the Comp Window the right lower arm and right hand rotate. The upper arm does not (Figure 7.9).

▷	□	3	🛈 neck	🔁 ✷ /
▽	□	4	🛈 right upperArm	🔁 ✷ /
			⊙ Rotation	0 x +45.0°
▽	□	5	🛈 right lowerArm	🔁 ✷ /
			⊙ Rotation	0 x +90.0°
▷	□	6	🛈 right thigh	🔁 ✷
▷	□	7	🛈 right lowerLeg	🔁 ✷ /
▷	□	8	🛈 right foot	🔁 ✷ /

Figure 7.9: *Rotate the lower arm. Its child layers rotate but the parent layer does not.*

Let's do a quick review. A child layer inherits transform properties from its parent layer. These include position, rotation, and scale. Opacity is not passed from parent to child. Also, any effect that is applied to the parent layer does not affect its children. A child layer can also animate on its own without affecting its parent. A child layer can only have one parent. So now that you have "parented" the layers, it is time to create the character animation.

12. For this exercise, rather than stifle your creativity with step-by-step instructions, just play and have fun animating the superhero character. To animate, set keyframes for the layers you want to move or rotate, drag the Current Time Indicator (CTI) to a new time in the Timeline and change the transform properties. Remember to save often.

01_Parenting_DONE

13. If you would like to see one possible solution, open the **01_Parenting_DONE** project in the Completed folder. The superhero composition is set to 30 frames per second and has a duration of two seconds. You can set the duration of your character animation to whatever you want.

Select all the layers in the Timeline and type **U** on the keyboard. This opens all transform properties that contain keyframes (Figure 7.10). Let's deconstruct how the character animation was done.

▸ First, the vertical position of the **hips** layer was animated moving down in the Comp Window. All child layers moved with it.

▸ Next, the left and right thighs were rotated to spread the legs apart.

▸ The lower legs and feet were then rotated to maintain an invisible ground plane that the superhero was standing on.

▸ Finally, the left and right arms were animated in the Comp Window.

When creating character animation using the parenting technique, focus on one particular region at a time. Then go back and animate another section. By making multiple passes through the composition, you will create a much more effective animation and not become overwhelmed by all the layers and keyframes.

Chapter 7: Character Animation

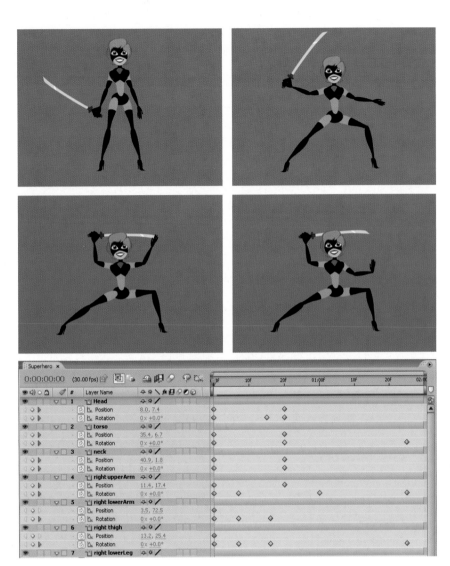

Figure 7.10: *Create a character animation using keyframed properties in the Timeline.*

14. Once you have finished the character animation, it is time to export it. Before you do that, delete the **background color** layer. You want to export the SWF file with an alpha channel.

15. Select **File > Export > Adobe Flash (SWF)**. This opens the Save File As dialog box. Save the SWF file to the 01_Parenting folder in Chapter_07.

16. The SWF Settings dialog box appears. In the Images area, set After Effects to **Ignore Unsupported Features**. Since the footage is an Adobe Illustrator file and does not contain any gradients, all the layers will export as vectors.

17. Click **OK**. Save your After Effects project. Locate the exported Flash SWF file. Double-click on it to play the animation in the Flash Player.

SuperHero

18. Let's move to Flash. Double-click on **SuperHero.fla** in the 01_Parenting folder to open the file in Flash. It contains two layers: foreground and background.

19. Select **Insert > New Symbol**. Enter **mcSuperhero** for the name and make sure that the type is set to Movie Clip. Click **OK**.

20. The Timeline for the new movie clip appears. Highlight the first blank keyframe and select **File > Import > Import to Stage** to open the Import dialog box. Choose the SWF file you created in After Effects. Click **Open**.

21. When the SWF file is imported into the movie clip, it appears as a series of keyframes. Scrub through the Timeline to see the animation.

Figure 7.11: *The imported SWF file appears as a series of keyframes in the Timeline.*

22. The character animation was rather complex and there are a lot of symbols now in the Library. For each keyframe in After Effects, a new graphic symbol was created for the layer. Organize the Library better. Create a new folder labeled **SWF Import** to hold the imported SWF sequence.

23. Click on the **New Layer** icon at the bottom of the Timeline panel. Rename the layer to superhero. Position the new layer in between the foreground and background layers.

24. Click and drag the **mcSuperhero** symbol from the Library to the Stage. Rotate and scale the movie clip into position. Save and test your movie. This completes the exercise. The next exercise focuses on linking 3D layers to a null object. It also introduces expressions and explains how to use them in After Effects.

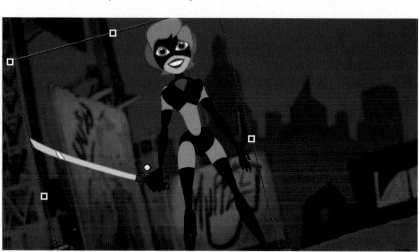

Figure 7.12: *Position the imported character animation on the Flash Stage.*

Chapter 7: Character Animation

Parenting Plus Expressions

Parenting in After Effects can save a lot of time and headaches when trying to animate a character. The previous exercise introduced the concept of parenting using two-dimensional layers. What about 3D? Parenting works for both 2D and 3D layers as you will soon see. In fact, you can assign a 3D layer to a 2D layer. This exercise also introduces expressions, which are JavaScript-based instructions that can streamline complex animation in After Effects.

1. Open **02_Parent_Expression.aep** inside the 02_Expression folder in Chapter_07.

2. The Project panel contains all the footage you need to complete this exercise. There are two compositions already set up for you in a Comps folder. Double-click on the **Wings** composition to open its Timeline and Composition panels.

Figure 7.13: *Open the Wings composition. It contains two Illustrator layers.*

3. You are going to animate the wings fluttering in 3D space. The anchor points for each layer have been repositioned to the center of the image so that they will rotate properly. Turn on each layer's **3D Layer** switch 🔲.

4. Select the **rightWing** layer in the Timeline. Type **R** on the keyboard to open the Rotation properties. Instead of scrubbing through a rotation value, you are going to use an expression to rotate the wings. Hold down the **Option** key (Mac) or the **Alt** key (Windows) and click on the **stopwatch** icon ⏱ next to **Y Rotation**. This enables expressions to control the property (Figure 7.14).

Figure 7.14: *Enable expressions for the Y Rotation property.*

5. The code **transform.yRotation** appears in the Timeline area. When expressions are enabled, they take over for keyframes. The Y Rotation numerical values turn red, indicating that they will not accept manual changes. In the Expression layer, click on the **Expression Language Menu** arrow ⏵. Select **Random Numbers > Random(minValOrArray, maxValOrArray)** from the popup menu.

Figure 7.15: *Add a random number expression to the layer.*

6. The code appears in the Timeline. Change the code to **random(0, 60)**. Press the Enter key on the numeric keypad to accept the expression. Scrub through the Timeline. The right wing now rotates along the Y-axis randomly from 0 degrees to a maximum of 60 degrees. Imagine trying to keyframe that animation.

7. Select the **leftWing** layer in the Timeline. Type **R** on the keyboard to open the Rotation properties. Hold down the **Option** key (Mac) or the **Alt** key (Windows) and click on the **stopwatch** icon ⏱ next to **Y Rotation**.

8. Click on the **spiral icon** next to Expression: Y Rotation — this is a Pick Whip tool. Drag it up to the Y Rotation property in the right wing (Figure 7.16). This Pick Whip tool links the two properties together. Scrub through the Timeline.

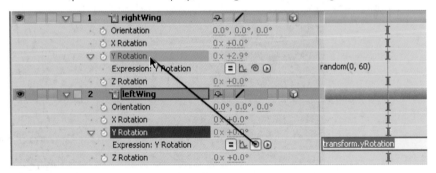

Figure 7.16: *Use the Pick Whip tool to link the two properties together.*

9. The wings are now fluttering in 3D space, however the left wing is rotating in the wrong direction. Go to the left wing expression and click on the code. Change the expression to **thisComp.layer("rightWing").transform.yRotation * –1**. Press Enter on the numeric keypad to accept the new expression.

Figure 7.17: *Multiply the expression by –1 to get the opposite effect.*

Chapter 7: Character Animation

10. Turn on the **Continuously Rasterize** switch ✻ for both layers to maintain the smooth vector quality. Now that the wings are fluttering correctly in 3D space, it is time to create a new composition.

11. Select **Composition > New Composition**. You need to make the composition the same size as the Flash Stage you will be importing the animation into. Make the following settings:

   ▸ Composition Name: **FairyFlight**
   ▸ Width: **550**
   ▸ Height: **400**
   ▸ Pixel Aspect Ratio: **Square Pixels**
   ▸ Frame Rate: **30**
   ▸ Duration: **0:00:05:00**

   Click **OK**. The new composition opens in the Composition panel.

12. Click and drag the **Fairy.swf** footage file from the Project panel to the Timeline. Turn on the **3D Layer** switch. Type **S** on the keyboard to display the layer's Scale property. Scrub through the Scale property to set its value to **40%** (Figure 7.18).

Figure 7.18: *Add the SWF footage file to the Timeline. Scale it to 40%.*

13. Click and drag the **Wings** composition from the Project panel to the Timeline. Position it underneath the **Fairy.swf** layer. Turn on the **Continuously Rasterize** and **3D Layer** switch.

14. Type **R** on the keyboard to open the Rotation properties. Hold down the **Shift** key and type **S** and **T** to open the Scale and Opacity properties as well.

   ▸ Set the **Scale** value to **40%**.
   ▸ Set the **Orientation** value to **75.0, 340.0**, and **65.0**.
   ▸ Go to the Comp Window and click and drag the wings into position on the fairy's back (Figure 7.19).
   ▸ Set the **Opacity** value to **70%**.

Figure 7.19: *Position the wings.*

15. To set up the parenting structure, you need to open the Parent column in the Timeline panel. If it is not already visible, right-click on the **Layer Name** column header and select **Columns > Parent**. You are going to assign the wings (child) to the fairy (parent).

16. Click on the **spiral icon** (pick whip) for the **Wings** layer and drag it to the name column of the **Fairy.swf** layer. Release the mouse. This links the two 3D layers.

Figure 7.20: *Link the two 3D layers using parenting.*

17. Go to the Composition panel and click and drag the Fairy artwork to the upper left edge of the Comp Window (Figure 7.21). Keep the fairy's hand visible. Notice that the **Wings** layer follows along as a result of parenting. This will be the starting position for the fairy's animated flight.

Figure 7.21: *Move the fairy in the Comp Window. Keep some of it visible.*

18. You are going to use Motion Sketch to animate the fairy's position over time. There is one small problem — Motion Sketch does not work with 3D layers. So what do you do? You need to create a **Null Object** and assign the fairy to it. What is a null object? It is a layer that contains nothing, yet has all the transform properties of a normal layer. Select **Layer > New > Null Object**.

19. A Null layer appears in the Timeline. Click and drag the null object in the Comp Window. Align the top left corner of the null object with the fairy's hand.

Figure 7.22: *Position the null object in the Comp Window.*

20. Click on the **spiral icon** (pick whip) for the **Fairy.swf** layer and drag it to the name column of the **Null 1** layer. Release the mouse.

21. Select **Window > Motion Sketch**. This opens the Motion Sketch panel in the bottom right corner of the Workspace.

Chapter 7: Character Animation

22. Set the Smoothing to **10**. This reduces the number of keyframes recorded and produces a much smoother motion path.

23. Select the **Null 1** layer in the Timeline. Click on **Start Capture** to activate the tool. It doesn't start recording keyframes until you click and drag a layer in the Comp Window. Click and drag the null object across the Comp Window. Release the mouse when you are done. A motion path is created.

Figure 7.23: *The Motion Sketch records keyframes for the motion path drawn.*

24. Now that the flight of the fairy is done, let's add some pixie dust to the composition. Make sure the Timeline panel is highlighted. Press the **Home** key to move the CTI to the beginning of the composition (00:00).

25. Select **Layer > New > Solid**. The Solid Settings dialog box appears.

   ▶ Enter **PixieDust** for the solid name.
   ▶ Click on the **Make Comp Size** button.
   ▶ Click **OK**. The color of the solid layer doesn't matter.

26. A solid layer of color appears at the top of the Timeline and in the Composition panel. Go to the Effects & Presets panel. Enter **Foam** into the Contains field. The item in the effects list that matches is displayed.

27. To apply the Foam effect to the solid layer, click and drag the effect to either the layer in the Comp Window or the Timeline panel. A red box with an X highlights the layer that will receive the effect. Release the mouse.

28. Go to the Effect Controls panel. Click on the twirler to the left of **Producer**. This controls where the bubbles originate from.

   ▶ Click on the cross hair target button ⊕ .
   ▶ In the Comp Window click on the fairy's hand. This repositions the point.

29. Select the **Null 1** layer in the Timeline. Type **P** on the keyboard to open the Position property. Click on the word Position to select all of the keyframes recorded using the Motion Sketch tool. Select **Edit > Copy**. You will paste a copy of these keyframes in the Producer Point property.

30. Select the **PixieDust** solid layer. Go to the Effect Controls panel and click on the **stopwatch** icon ⏱ for the **Producer Point** property.

31. Go to the Timeline. While the PixieDust layer is still selected, type **U** on the keyboard to open all keyframed properties. Select the Producer Point keyframe and then **Edit > Paste**. Now, the Producer Point's position matches the null object's position. Scrub through the Timeline and the bubbles follow along with the fairy. Now the only problem is that you don't want bubbles; you want pixie dust coming out of the fairy's hand.

Figure 7.24: *The Producer Point animates to follow the null object.*

32. The Foam effect allows you to replace the default bubbles with other artwork contained within a composition in the Timeline. Click and drag the **Starburst** comp from the Project panel to the Timeline. Its stacking order doesn't matter. This composition contains a Photoshop still image of a starburst. Hide the layer by turning off the Video switch 👁. Foam only needs to have the composition in the Timeline for reference. It doesn't have to be visible.

33. Select the **PixieDust** solid layer. Go to the Effect Controls panel and click on the twirler to the left of **Rendering**. This controls the visual look of the bubbles. Make the following changes:

   ▸ Bubble Texture: Change from **Default Bubble** to **User Defined**.
   ▸ Bubble Layer Texture: **Starburst.**

34. To see the finished results, select **Rendered** from the View popup menu at the top of the Effect Controls panel. You now have pixie dust.

Figure 7.25: *Change the view from Draft to Rendered to see a better representation of the bubbles in the Comp Window.*

Figure 7.26: *The Foam effect can use another composition's artwork for a texture.*

35. Click on the **RAM Preview** button to view the final composition.

36. Select **Composition > Make Movie**. This opens the Render Queue.

37. Click on **Lossless** next to Output Module. Set the Format to **Adobe Flash Video**. Click on **Format Options** and set the Bitrate setting to **400**. Under **Basic Video Settings**, encode the alpha channel (Figure 7.27).

Figure 7.27: *Render the Flash Video file with an alpha channel.*

38. Click on **Output To** and select the Chapter_07 folder on your hard drive as the final destination for the rendered movie. Click the **Render** button.

39. Let's move to Flash. Double-click on **02_FairyFlight.fla** in the 02_Expressions folder to open the file in Flash. It contains one layer, a background image.

02_FairyFlight

40. Click on the **New Layer** icon at the bottom of the Timeline panel. Rename the layer to **Fairy**. For this exercise, let's embed the FLV file created in After Effects into a movie clip symbol on the Flash Timeline. Since the duration of the video is 5 seconds with no audio, the embedded FLV file will not drastically increase the final published SWF file size (500 KB).

41. Select the blank keyframe on Frame 1 of the **Fairy** layer.

42. Select **File > Import > Import Video**. The Import Video Wizard dialog box appears. To import the FLV file:

   ▸ Locate the **FairyFlight.flv** file you rendered out of After Effects.

   ▸ Set the deployment to **Embedded Video in SWF and Play in Timeline.**

   ▸ Set the Embedding type to a **Movie Clip**.

   ▸ Click **Finish** to embed the video. The first frame of the video appears on the Stage and a video symbol is added to the Library.

Figure 7.28: The embedded FLV file plays back the animation inside a movie clip.

43. Save and test your movie. This completes the exercise. You covered a lot of ground in both of the parenting exercises. Hopefully you can see a benefit in using parenting to assist with your character animation.

   Let's review some of the key concepts from this exercise. Parenting is assigning one layer or layers to another parent layer. The assigned child layers can contain their own animation but also inherit the transform properties of the parent layer.

   Expressions in After Effects are JavaScript-based commands that streamline complex animation. When an expression is applied to a transform property, all manual input is deactivated in favor of the expression instruction. The next section of this chapter focuses on the Puppet tools in After Effects.

The Puppet Tools

An amazing new set of tools introduced in After Effects CS3 are the Puppet tools. They allow you to quickly add joints (deform pins) to raster images and vector graphics, including still images, shapes, and text characters. These joints can then be animated over time, bringing the static image to life.

The Puppet tools work within an effect (the Puppet effect). The effect works by deforming parts of a layer according to the positions of pins that you place and move. These pins define what parts of the image should move, what parts should remain rigid, and what parts should overlap. In addition, the Puppet tools allow you to record real-time animation using the Motion Sketch tool.

Let's create a puppet. This exercise provides a step-by-step tutorial on using the three Puppet tools to animate characters. You will use the Puppet tools in the Tools panel to directly apply and work with the effect in the Comp Window.

1. In Adobe After Effects, select **File > Open Project**. Open the 03_Puppet folder inside Chapter_07. Select **03_PuppetTool.aep** and click **Open**. The Project panel contains a composition and the footage needed to complete this exercise.

Figure 7.29: *The project contains a composition with a raster image of a court jester.*

2. Select the **Puppet Pin Tool** [🖈] from the Tools panel. It is the last tool on the right. This tool places and moves **Deform pins**.

3. Go to the Composition panel and click in the center of the jester's belt buckle to add a new Deform pin. Click on his left shoulder and left hand to create two additional pins (Figure 7.30). As soon as you create the first Deform pin, the Puppet effect is added to the Timeline and Effect Controls panel.

4. Drag the pin on the left hand of the court jester up and down. Notice the realistic movement. This is a result of a mesh applied to the layer's outline.

Figure 7.30: *Add Deform pins to the waist, left shoulder, and left hand (left image). Click and drag the left hand Deform pin to see the Puppet tool in action (right image).*

5. Select the **Show Mesh** box in the Tools panel. When you place the first Deform pin, the layer's outline is automatically divided into a mesh of triangles (Figure 7.31). Each triangle in the mesh is associated with the pixels of the image, so the image's pixels move with the mesh, creating natural movement.

Figure 7.31: *A mesh is created and applied to the layer's outline. Each triangle controls how the image's pixels move.*

The Expansion field in the Tools panel lets you increase the mesh size to catch any stray pixels not included in the mesh. You can also increase the number of triangles within the mesh. The higher the number, the more processing time required, as well as an increase in the rendering time.

6. Turn off the mesh. As you moved the Deform pin you may have noticed that the court jester's feet did a little dance as well. To keep the jester's feet firmly planted on the ground, add two more pins to the character's ankles. Also pin the jester's right shoulder and hand.

7. Drag the Deform pin on the left hand up and down again. Notice that the jester's feet stayed pinned in their position. When you move a Deform pin, the mesh changes shape to match the movement. It also tries to keep the other parts of the mesh as rigid as possible. The result is a more natural, lifelike movement in your character. The movement of the arm is greater than the motion in the waist and feet, just as a body moves in the real world.

8. Let's animate the Deform pins. Make sure the **Jester.psd** layer is still selected in the Timeline and type the **U** key on the keyboard. This opens the Mesh property along with the seven created Deform pins and their position values.

> *Keyframes are automatically enabled for Deform pins. After Effects assumes that you will use these pins to create an animation. This is different from other transform properties where you have to manually click the stopwatch to enable keyframes.*

Figure 7.32: *Puppet pins automatically enable position keyframes.*

9. Drag the Current Time Indicator (CTI) to the one second mark (01:00). Click and drag the Deform pin on the right hand of the character down. A motion path appears and a keyframe is automatically added to the Timeline.

Figure 7.33: *Change the position of a Deform pin to record the keyframe.*

10. Have some fun animating the character's arms and legs. Move the CTI to a new point in time and change the positions of the Deform pins. If you want to move multiple pins at once, select a pin and then hold down the Shift key and click on another. Click the **RAM Preview** button to preview the character animation.

11. Move the CTI to the beginning of the Timeline. The Puppet tool can also record pin movements using Motion Sketch. To record a pin movement, move the cursor over the Deform pin in the center belt buckle and hold down the **Command** (Mac) or **Control** (Windows) key. The stopwatch cursor appears over the Deform pin indicating the Motion Sketch tool.

12. Click and drag the pin back and forth. When you are done, release the mouse. After Effects records the animation and the court jester is now belly dancing. After you release the mouse, the motion path appears in the Comp Window along with the accompanying keyframes in the Timeline.

13. Move the CTI to the beginning of the Timeline. Select the Deform pin over the right hand and move it to the right. Notice that the character's right hand moves behind his head. You can control whether the image moves in front of or behind another using the **Puppet Overlap Tool**.

The Puppet Tools

14. Select the **Puppet Overlap Tool** from the Puppet Pin Tool popup menu. This tool places Overlap pins, which control which parts of an image should appear in front of others when the animation creates overlapping images.

Figure 7.34: *Select the Puppet Overlap Tool from the Puppet Pin Tool popup menu.*

15. Click to add an Overlap pin on the right hand, directly over the Deform pin. Change the **In Front** value to **50%** in the Tools panel. Change the **Extent** value to 100 to extend the Overlap mesh up the right arm. Now you can control how the arm overlaps the head by increasing (moves in front) or decreasing (moves behind) the In Front property.

Figure 7.35: *Add an Overlap pin and change its In Front value to move the image in front of or behind another image.*

16. The Overlap pin also appears in the Timeline below all of the Deform pins. Its properties can be keyframed over time.

Figure 7.36: *The Overlap pin also appears in the Timeline under the Deform pins.*

Chapter 7: Character Animation

What happens when you stretch a Deform pin too far and start seeing unwanted artifacts or tearing in the mesh? Use the **Puppet Starch Tool** which stiffens parts of the image so that they are distorted less.

17. In Figure 7.37 the court jester is doing an extreme split. That must explain his facial expression. His left leg has been stretched too far, causing a distortion in his right thigh. Select the **Puppet Starch Tool** from the Puppet Pin Tool popup menu. An outline view of the character appears in the Comp Window.

Figure 7.37: *Select the Puppet Starch Tool from the Puppet Pin Tool popup menu.*

18. Click and add a Starch pin on the right hip in the outline. Increase the **Extent** value to **80** and the **Amount** value to **30%** in the Tools panel. Notice that the right thigh of the character moves back closer to its original shape (Figure 7.38).

Figure 7.38: *Add a Starch pin to decrease the amount of distortion in the mesh.*

19. Before you render the final composition, turn on the Motion Blur switch for the **Jester.psd** layer (Figure 7.39). Enable the Motion Blur button above the Timeline to activate motion blur for the composition.

Figure 7.39: *Turn on motion blur for the layer to improve your character animation.*

20. You may want to increase the triangles of the mesh to make the deformation more smooth and accurate. Select the **Show Mesh** box in the Tools panel and scrub the Triangles value. Increasing the triangles increases the render time.

Figure 7.40: *Increase the triangles in the mesh for smoother deformations.*

This completes this exercise. Keep playing with the Puppet tools to create your own unique character animation using the court jester. Add your own image or 2D character to the project. Remember to save often.

This exercise introduced you to the Puppet tools in After Effects. The Puppet deformation effect produces natural, lifelike movement in a static image. There are three Puppet tools. The Puppet Pin Tool creates and moves the Deform pins. The Puppet Overlap Tool allows you to control which image moves in front of or behind another image. The Puppet Starch Tool stiffens parts of the image so that they are distorted less.

These Puppet tools are a lot of fun to play around with. There are many creative possibilities open to you using these tools. The last exercise in this chapter integrates the Puppet tools in After Effects with ActionScript in Flash. You will create an interactive dancing puppet for the Web.

Interactive Puppets

In this exercise you will create an interactive Flash project that incorporates character animation created using the Puppet tools. It is a simple version of those funny Internet toys that entertain us for hours online. These time killer websites are a waste of time, but they are a good waste of time.

To see what you will build, locate and play the **04_VideoCreator.swf** file located in the Completed folder in 04_Interactive/Chapter_07. Click and drag the different thumbnail images of dance moves to the disco track. When you are done, click on the dance button that appears. The character dances in the order of your placed disco moves. Click on the clear track button to reset the dancer and start again.

Figure 7.41: *The final interactive Flash project incorporates character animation created with the Puppet tools in After Effects.*

The mechanics behind this project are fairly basic in Flash. It involves a drag and drop interaction, an array that stores the different dance moves and plays them back in the correct sequence, and the NetConnection and NetStream class objects that connect and stream the videos. Think of it as a starting point for your own creative designs. The exercise is meant to get you thinking about how you can control linear animation created in After Effects using the power of ActionScript in Flash.

The character was designed in a 3D application and rendered out as a still image. That image was imported into After Effects as a footage file. It was added to a composition and animated using the Puppet tools. The only trick that you need to be aware of is how to make all the dance moves work seamlessly together.

Figure 7.42 shows an image sequence for each character animation used in the completed project. It should become quite obvious that the first and last frames for all three dance moves are the same starting image. This creates the seamless playback in Flash as one video is replaced by another.

Figure 7.42: *The first and last frame for each animation are identical.*

04_DiscoMan

1. In Adobe After Effects, select **File > Open Project**. Open the 04_Interactive folder inside Chapter_07. Select **04_DiscoMan.aep** and click **Open**. The Project panel contains three folders. The **Footage** folder holds the rendered 3D character image. The **Completed** folder holds the three final compositions used. The **Create Your Own** folder has a composition ready for you.

2. Double-click on the **CreateYourOwn** composition to open its Timeline and Composition panels. The composition has a duration of two seconds.

3. Before you start using the Puppet Pin Tool, double-click on the layer-time marker ⌂ at the end of the Timeline. It contains a Flash Video cue point labeled "end." The cue point has been set to an event. This event tells Flash that the current video is done and to load in the next video in the sequence. Click **OK** to close the dialog box.

Chapter 7: Character Animation

4. Select the **Puppet Pin** Tool [icon] from the Tools panel.

5. Go to the Composition panel and click in the center of the disco character to add a new Deform pin. Add additional pins at all the joints (Figure 7.43).

Figure 7.43: *Add the Puppet pins to the character.*

6. Select the **DiscoMan.png** layer in the Timeline. Type the **U** key on the keyboard. Get into the habit of renaming your Deform pins so that you know what they are deforming. To do this, select the name and press the Return/Enter key on the keyboard. This highlights the name and allows you to rename it.

7. Now it is time to animate the Puppet pins. Move the Current Time Indicator (CTI) to new points in the Timeline. Click and drag the Deform pins to create your own unique disco moves. If needed, use the Puppet Overlap Tool and Puppet Starch Tool to achieve the desired results you want. Have fun!

8. Once you have created your character animation, press the **End** key to move the CTI to the end of the Timeline. Click on the **Reset** button to the right of the word Puppet. This restores the Puppet pins to their original location. Now the first and last frames are identical, which is what you want. Save your project.

Figure 7.44: *Click Reset to reposition the Deform pins back to their original placed location.*

9. Click on the **RAM Preview** button to view the final composition.

10. Select **Composition > Make Movie**. This opens the Render Queue.

11. Click on **Best Settings** to open the Render Settings dialog box. Change the Resolution from Full to **Half** (Figure 7.45). The dimensions of the rendered Flash Video (FLV) file will now be 320 x 240.

Figure 7.45: *Render the Flash Video file at half resolution (320 x 240).*

12. Click on **Lossless** next to Output Module. Set the Format to **Adobe Flash Video**. Click on **Format Options** and set the Bitrate setting to **400**. Under **Basic Video Settings**, encode the alpha channel (Figure 7.46).

Figure 7.46: *Render the Flash Video file with an alpha channel.*

13. Click on **Output To** and select the **videos** folder inside the 04_Interactive folder in the Chapter_07 folder on your hard drive as the final destination for the rendered movie. Click the **Render** button.

04_VideoCreator

14. Let's move to Flash. Double-click on **04_VideoCreator.fla** in the 04_Interactive folder to open the file in Flash. It contains all the files you need to complete this exercise. Let's deconstruct the file.

   ▶ The three thumbnail images are movie clips with instance names of **clip1**, **clip2**, and **clip3**. The registration point has been set to the left center.

   ▶ The disco track is a movie clip with an instance name of **holder**. Its registration point has been set to the left center as well.

   ▶ The two button symbols have instance names of **reset_btn** and **play_btn**.

15. Select the keyframe in Frame 1 of the **actions** layer. Open the Actions panel. The ActionScript is already set up. Let's deconstruct sections of the code and show you where you can add your character animation.

The code defines some variables to store information. The variable **numClips** stores the number of clips used. The variable **openSlot** refers to the open slot available in the disco track. It holds three slots, one for each thumbnail image. The thumbnail images are 80 x 80 pixels. The variable **clipOffset** stores that information. This is used to properly place each image when dragged to the disco track movie clip.

```
// define the number of clips, open slots, space between each clip
var numClips:uint = 3;
var openSlot:uint = 0;
var clipOffset:uint = 80;
```

Next, the starting horizontal and vertical positions for each thumbnail image need to be stored into a variable. These six variables hold that information.

```
// variables to store original clip location
var startX1:Number
var startY1:Number
var startX2:Number
var startY2:Number
var startX3:Number
var startY3:Number
```

A new Array Object is created to hold the playback sequence for the video clips. Another variable named **videoIndex** is defined to store the array index number of the current video clip.

```
// array to store the video playback sequence
var videoSequence:Array = new Array();
var videoIndex:uint = 0;
```

A new Sound Object is created to play the disco music. The audio file is stored externally from the Flash file in a folder labeled **audio**. A SoundChannel Object is created to stop the audio from playing when the reset button is clicked.

```
// create a new Sound object and SoundChannel
var disco:Sound
disco = new Sound(new URLRequest("audio/disco.mp3"));
var discoControl:SoundChannel = new SoundChannel();
```

audio

disco

Flash Video

Net Connection

links to FLV

Net Stream

transfers data

Video Object

Each video clip is loaded into a Video Object created in ActionScript. The code creates the NetConnection and NetStream Objects. The embedded cue point is listened for using the code **vStream.client**. This metadata listener (**client. onCuePoint**) calls a function named **onCuePoint** that will be added later. The last part of the code creates the Video Display Object and positions it on the Flash Stage. The NetStream object is attached to the video object.

```
// create video netconnection and netstream
var vConnection:NetConnection = new NetConnection();
vConnection.connect(null);
var vStream:NetStream = new NetStream(vConnection);

// create a cuePoint listner
var client:Object = new Object();
client.onCuePoint = onCuePoint;
vStream.client = client;

// create a video display object
var myVideo:Video = new Video(320, 240);
myVideo.x = 344;
myVideo.y = 120;
addChild(myVideo);
setChildIndex(myVideo, 0);
myVideo.attachNetStream(vStream);
```

Next, the event listeners are defined. A "for loop" generates an event listener for each thumbnail image. It also records each movie clip's position on the Flash Stage and stores that information into the **startX** and **startY** variables.

```
// loop through the movie clips to assign event listeners
for(var i:uint = 1; i <= numClips; i++){
  // create temp variable
  var currentClip:MovieClip = this["clip" + i];
  // record original Stage location
  this["startX" + i] = currentClip.x;
  this["startY" + i] = currentClip.y;
  // add button mode and event listeners
  currentClip.buttonMode = true;
  currentClip.addEventListener(MouseEvent.MOUSE_DOWN, dragIt);
  currentClip.addEventListener(MouseEvent.MOUSE_UP, stopdragIt);
}

// create event listeners for play and reset buttons
play_btn.addEventListener(MouseEvent.CLICK, onPlay);
play_btn.visible = false;
reset_btn.addEventListener(MouseEvent.CLICK, onReset);
```

With the event listeners, objects, and variables defined, the next part of the code creates the event handlers and methods.

Chapter 7: Character Animation

The first two event handlers set up the drag and drop interaction. The draggable area is confined to a **new Rectangle** over the thumbnail images and disco track.

```
// define the event handlers
function dragIt(event:MouseEvent):void{
    // set the depth to be on top
    setChildIndex(MovieClip(event.currentTarget), numChildren - 1);
    event.target.startDrag(false, new Rectangle(10, 100, 210, 200));
    stage.addEventListener(MouseEvent.MOUSE_UP, stopdragIt);
}

function stopdragIt(event:MouseEvent):void{
    event.target.stopDrag();
    stage.removeEventListener(MouseEvent.MOUSE_UP, stopdragIt);
    placeClip(event.target);
}
```

When a clip is released, the function **placeClip** is called. This function contains a conditional that places the clip either in the disco track or back to its starting position based on where the clip is on the Stage when you let go of the mouse.

```
function placeClip(draggedClip){
    if(draggedClip.hitTestObject(holder)){
        draggedClip.x = holder.x + openSlot;
        draggedClip.y = holder.y;
        openSlot += clipOffset;
        // remove button properties
        draggedClip.buttonMode = false;
        draggedClip.removeEventListener(MouseEvent.MOUSE_DOWN, dragIt);
        draggedClip.removeEventListener(MouseEvent.MOUSE_UP, stopdragIt);
        // call function to add the corresponding video clip to the array
        addVideo(draggedClip.name);
        // show the PLAY button when all three slots are filled
        if(openSlot == 240){ play_btn.visible = true; }
    }else{
        // reset the clip back to its original Stage location
        var clipNumber:uint =  draggedClip.name.substr(4);
        draggedClip.x = this["startX" + clipNumber];
        draggedClip.y = this["startY" + clipNumber];
    }
}
```

videos

DiscoDance01

DiscoDance02

DiscoDance03

The video sequence array is populated if the movie clip is successfully dragged to the disco track. The function **addVideo** checks to see which clip was dragged to the disco track and loads the corresponding external video file. If you would like to swap the existing videos with your own, this is the part of the code you would change. Select the file name and change it to the name of your Flash Video (FLV) file (see code on next page).

```
function addVideo(whichClip){
    // add the correspoding video to the array
    if(whichClip == "clip1"){ videoSequence.push("videos/DiscoDance01.flv") };
    if(whichClip == "clip2"){ videoSequence.push("videos/DiscoDance02.flv") };
    if(whichClip == "clip3"){ videoSequence.push("videos/DiscoDance03.flv") };
}
```

The function **onCuePoint** listens for the embedded cue point at the end of each video clip. When that frame is played, the next video in the array sequence is streamed into the video object. Since the first and last frames are identical for all video clips, the video swap is unnoticeable.

```
// add Event Handler to respond to the metadata loading
function onCuePoint(cuePoint:Object):void {
    if(cuePoint.name == "end"){
        videoIndex++;
        if(videoIndex == videoSequence.length){
            videoIndex = 0;
        }
        vStream.play(videoSequence[videoIndex]);
    }
}
```

16. Select **Control > Test Movie**. This completes the exercise.

Summary

This completes the chapter on character animation using the parenting and Puppet tools in After Effects. Both tools can save a lot of time and headaches when trying to animate a character. Parenting assigns one or more layers to another parent layer. The Puppet effect deforms parts of a layer according to the positions of pins that you place and move. The next chapter focuses on creating visual effects in After Effects and then integrating them into your Flash projects.

CHAPTER 8

···

Visual Effects

Stunning visual effects can add dramatic punch to any Flash project. This chapter focuses on creating different kinds of visual effects, from very subtle to explosive, using the tools in After Effects.

Controlling the Weather

Visual effects are an art form all to themselves. After Effects provides a myriad of effects that you can apply to your moving and still images. With a plethora of plug-ins available, this chapter focuses on some of the more popular ones that can enhance your Flash projects. Let's start by creating your own dramatic weather full of blizzards and torrential downpours. After Effects offers you hundreds of effects to make it all happen.

 Locate the Chapter_08 folder on the DVD. Copy this folder to your hard drive. The folder contains all the files needed to complete the chapter exercises.

Exercise 1: Let It Snow

In this first exercise, you will learn how to create snow in After Effects and apply that effect to a Flash animation. You were exposed to the CC Snow effect briefly in Chapter 2, but that project was intended for broadcast. To see an example of what you will build, locate and launch the **01_WinterScene.swf** file in the Completed folder inside the 01_Weather folder in Chapter_08.

Figure 8.1: *The completed animation integrates the CC Snow effect in After Effects.*

1. Launch **Adobe After Effects**. Select **Composition > New Composition**. The Composition Settings dialog box appears. You will set up the composition to match the Flash file you are integrating the effect into.

2. Make the following settings and then click **OK** to create the new composition.

   ▸ Composition Name: **Snow**
   ▸ Width: **550**
   ▸ Height: **400**
   ▸ Pixel Aspect Ratio: **Square Pixels**
   ▸ Frame Rate: **30**
   ▸ Duration: **0:00:01:00**

3. Make sure the Timeline panel is highlighted. Select **Layer > New > Solid**. The Solid Settings dialog box appears. Make the following settings:

   ▸ Enter **Snow** for the solid name.
   ▸ Click on the **Make Comp Size** button.
   ▸ Set the color of the solid layer to **Black**. It needs to be black in order for the effect to composite correctly in Flash.
   ▸ Click **OK**.

4. A solid layer of color appears in the Timeline and in the Composition panel. Select **Effect > Simulation > CC Snow**. This is a third-party plug-in from Cycore that ships with After Effects. If you do not see this effect in your Effects menu, you may need to install this plug-in from the After Effects installation CD.

5. The CC Snow effect gives you just that, falling snowflakes (Figure 8.2). It is a fairly simple effect. Go to the Effect Controls panel. Increase the **Amount** to **400** and the **Speed** to **1.5**. Since you are going to composite this effect in Flash, increase the **Opacity** to **70%**.

Figure 8.2: *Apply the CC Snow effect to a black solid layer. Use the Effect Controls panel to adjust the effect's properties.*

6. Click on the **RAM Preview** button. The duration of the composition is set to one second. Although the snow effect does not create a continuous loop, you will not notice with all those snowflakes falling. Save your project.

7. Select **Composition > Make Movie**. This opens the Render Queue.

8. Click on **Lossless** next to Output Module. Set the Format to **Adobe Flash Video**. Click on **Format Options** and set the Bitrate setting to **400**. Click on **Output To** and select the Chapter_08 folder on your hard drive as the final destination for the rendered movie. Click the **Render** button.

01_WinterScene

9. Let's move to Flash. Double-click on **01_WinterScene.fla** in the 01_Weather folder to open the file in Flash. It contains three layers: a background image, a movie clip instance of a skater, and a snow layer (Figure 8.3).

Figure 8.3: *The Flash file contains all the artwork you need to complete this exercise.*

10. Select the blank keyframe on Frame 1 of the **snow** layer.

11. Select **File > Import > Import Video**. The Import Video Wizard dialog box appears. To import the FLV file:
    - ► Locate the **Snow.flv** file you rendered out of After Effects.
    - ► Set the deployment to **Embedded Video in SWF and Play in Timeline**.
    - ► Set the Embedding type to a **Movie Clip**.
    - ► Click **Finish** to embed the video. The first frame of the video appears on the Stage and a video symbol is added to the Library.

12. Now that the video is imported, it is time to composite it with the other layers. Select the snow movie clip instance. Go to the Properties panel and change **Blend** mode to **Add** (Figure 8.4). This blend mode causes the black background to disappear and you are left with only the white snowflakes.

Figure 8.4: *Change the Blend mode from Normal to Add.*

13. Save and test your movie. This completes the exercise. Snow is quite simple to create in After Effects and integrate in Flash. With a minimal amount of time and effort, you can create realistic snow. Imagine the time it would take to animate or program the snow falling using ActionScript.

Figure 8.5: *The final snow effect in Flash.*

Why embed a FLV file? Out of all the possible outputs for this exercise, this file format produces the smallest size file that doesn't drastically increase the Flash movie. The final published SWF file with the embedded video is 63 KB. If you rendered out a PNG sequence and imported the files into Flash, its final published size would have been around 375 KB.

You could have also rendered out the FLV file with an encoded alpha channel. You would then have to link the video externally for Flash to utilize the transparency. For this scenario, it is much simpler to embed the video. As you watch the final animation, notice that while the snow enhances the scene, it doesn't interact with the other elements. In the next exercise you will create raindrops that react to the artwork in Flash.

Exercise 2: Raindrops Keep Falling on His Head

In this exercise, you will go from winter to summer and create a rainstorm. Instead of using the CC Rain plug-in, also from Cycore, you will use **Particle Playground** which provides you with much more control over each particle. To see an example of what you will build, play the **02_RainyDays.swf** file in the Completed folder inside the 01_Weather folder in Chapter_08. Notice that the raindrops bounce off the boy (Figure 8.6).

Figure 8.6: *The completed animation integrates the Particle Playground effect.*

02_Rain

1. Open **02_Rain.aep** inside the 01_Weather folder in Chapter_08.

2. The Project panel contains all the footage you need to complete this exercise. A composition is already set up for you in a Comps folder. Double-click on the **Raining** composition to open its Timeline and Composition panels. It contains two layers: a Flash animation of a boy tossing a baseball and a nested composition that contains a PNG raster image of a raindrop. Both layers will be used to create the final effect.

3. Make sure the Timeline panel is highlighted. Select **Layer > New > Solid**.

   ▸ Enter **Rain** for the solid name.
   ▸ Click on the **Make Comp Size** button.
   ▸ Set the color of the solid layer to **Black**.
   ▸ Click **OK**.

4. A solid layer of color appears in the Timeline and in the Composition panel. Select **Effect > Simulation > Particle Playground**. The Particle Playground effect lets you animate a large number of similar objects independently, such as raindrops in a rainstorm.

5. The black solid color disappears. Scrub through the Timeline. A small red fountain of squares appears in the center of the Comp Window. The red circle is the particle cannon that streams the particles (Figure 8.7).

Figure 8.7: *Apply the Particle Playground effect to the black solid layer.*

6. Go to the Effect Controls panel. It contains a lot of properties. Let's examine each set of properties that you will need to change. Twirl open the **Cannon** properties. The Cannon creates the stream of particles from a specific point on the layer. It also controls the number of particles and their movement. Make the following changes:

   ▸ Change the **Position** to **275.0, –10.0**. This moves the cannon to the top of the Comp Window.

   ▸ Set the **Barrel Radius** to **275.0**. This enlarges the cannon opening from which all the particles fall from.

   ▸ Change the **Particles Per Second** value to **1200.0**.

   ▸ Change the **Direction** value to **+180** degrees. All the particles will instantly drop down from the cannon's position.

   ▸ Change the **Velocity** value to **300.0**.

7. Scrub through the Timeline to see the changes you made. Now there are a lot more particles that span the entire width of the Comp Window (Figure 8.8).

Figure 8.8: *Change the Cannon properties to increase the number of particles.*

8. Twirl open the **Layer Map** properties. By default, the Cannon creates dot particles. To replace the dots with a layer in the composition, select the raindrop composition from the **Use Layer** popup menu. After Effects replaces all dots with an instance of the raindrop (Figure 8.9). A particle source layer can be a still image, a solid, or a nested After Effects composition.

Figure 8.9: *Change the layer map to replace the red dots with raindrops.*

9. Twirl open the **Gravity** properties. Gravity controls the pull on existing particles in a direction you specify. Change the **Force** value to **600.0**. Positive values increase the force, pulling particles more strongly.

10. Twirl open the **Repel** properties. Repel controls how nearby particles repel or attract each other. Twirl open the **Repeller** controls. Set the **Selection Map** to the **Rain_Kid.swf** layer. After Effects imports SWF files with their alpha channel preserved so the raindrops will repel only on top of the boy or ball. Change the **Force** value to **10.0** and the **Force Radius** to **40.0**.

Figure 8.10: *Change the Repel properties to control how the raindrops interact with the boy.*

11. Click on the **RAM Preview** button. Save your project.

12. Before you render the composition, turn off the visibility of the **Rain_Kid. swf** layer and the **raindrop** layer by clicking on their Video switches ![eye icon]. The animation of the boy is already in the Flash file. You only need to render the particles as a Flash Video file.

Figure 8.11: *Hide the Flash animation and the nested raindrop composition.*

13. Select **Composition > Make Movie**. This opens the Render Queue.

14. Click on **Lossless** next to Output Module. Set the Format to **Adobe Flash Video**. Click on **Format Options** and set the Bitrate setting to **400**. Click on **Output To** and select the Chapter_08 folder on your hard drive as the final destination for the rendered movie. Click the **Render** button.

02_RainyDays

15. Let's move to Flash. Double-click on **02_RainyDays.fla** in the 01_Weather folder to open the file in Flash. It contains three layers: a background image, an animated graphic symbol of the boy tossing a baseball, and a rain layer.

Figure 8.12: *The Flash file contains all the artwork you need to complete this exercise.*

16. Select the blank keyframe on Frame 1 of the **rain** layer.

17. Select **File > Import > Import Video**. The Import Video Wizard dialog box appears. To import the FLV file:

   ▸ Locate the **Raining.flv** file you rendered out of After Effects.
   ▸ Set the deployment to **Embedded Video in SWF and Play in Timeline**.
   ▸ Set the Embedding type to a **Movie Clip**.
   ▸ Click **Finish** to embed the video.

18. Select the rain movie clip instance. Go to the Properties panel and change **Blend** mode to **Add**.

19. Save and test your movie. This completes the exercise.

   As you can see, the Particle Playground effect provides a lot of control over the individual particles. In addition to repelling particles, you can also attract them to stick to other layers in After Effects. Use the layer map to specify what happens to any particle that passes over a specific pixel in the layer. The next part of the chapter also deals with particles — the exploding kind.

Blowing Stuff Up

In this section of the chapter, you can take out your frustrations by blowing stuff up. Let's start with another popular particle generator, **Shatter**. The name says it all. The Shatter effect explodes graphic images. The effect's controls allow you to set explosion points and adjust the strength and radius of the blast.

Exercise 1: The Shatter Zone

For this exercise, you will create a title sequence for a Flash project called "The Shatter Zone." The project incorporates Shatter and the CC Star Burst effects. To see an example of what you will build, launch the **01_Shatter.swf** file in the Completed folder inside the 02_Mayhem folder in Chapter_08.

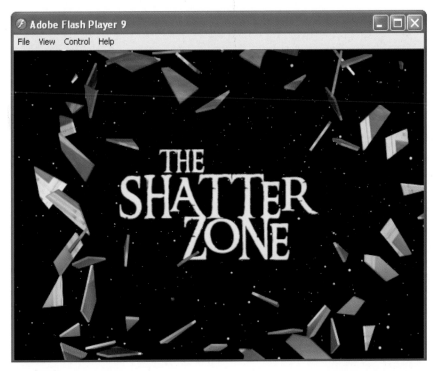

Figure 8.13: *The title sequence integrates the Shatter effect in After Effects.*

1. Open **01_ShatterZone.aep** inside the 02_Mayhem folder in Chapter_08.

2. The Project panel contains all the footage you need to complete this exercise. A composition is already set up for you in a Comps folder. Double-click on the **ShatterZone** composition to open its Timeline and Composition panels.

01_ShatterZone

   It contains two layers: a nested window composition and a vector logo created in Adobe Illustrator. Both layers have been converted into 3D layers and animate over time. The first thing you need to create is the starfield background. To do this you need a new solid layer.

3. Make sure the Timeline panel is highlighted. Select **Layer > New > Solid**.

   ▶ Enter **Starfield** for the solid name.

   ▶ Click on the **Make Comp Size** button.

   ▶ Set the color of the solid layer to **White**.

   ▶ Click **OK**.

4. A solid layer of color appears in the Timeline and in the Composition panel. Click and drag the solid layer to the bottom of the stack underneath the window and logo layers (Figure 8.14).

Figure 8.14: *Create a new white solid layer and position it at the bottom of the layer stack in the Timeline.*

5. Select **Effect > Simulation > CC Star Burst**. This is another third-party plug-in from Cycore that ships with After Effects. The white solid layer is replaced with white stars that zoom toward the active camera. Go to the Effect Controls panel and change the **Size** value to **30.0**. This creates a more realistic starfield.

Figure 8.15: *Apply the CC Star Burst effect to create the animated starfield background.*

Chapter 8: Visual Effects

6. Select the **WindowComp** layer in the Timeline. Select **Effect > Simulation > Shatter**. The image of the window turns into a wire frame view of the Shatter effect. Scrub through the Timeline and you will see that the effect starts immediately by exploding wire frame bricks across the Comp Window.

Figure 8.16: *Apply the Shatter effect to the window. The layer turns into a wire frame view of the effect.*

7. Move the Current Time Indicator (CTI) to the five second mark (05:00). This is the point in time where the window has completed its animation.

8. In the Effect Controls panel, select **Rendered** in the **View** popup menu. The grid will disappear and you will see the layer's content, or what's left of it.

9. Twirl open the **Shape** properties and make the following changes:

   ▶ Set the Pattern from **Bricks** to **Glass**.

   ▶ Change the **Repetitions** value to **15.0**. This value specifies the scale of the shards of glass. Increasing this value increases the number of pieces by scaling down the size of the shatter map. Consequently, the layer breaks into more and smaller pieces of glass.

   ▶ Change the **Extrusion** value to **0.10**. This will reduce the thickness for each shattered particle.

10. Force 1 and Force 2 controls define the blast areas. Twirl open the **Force 1** properties and change the **Radius** value to **0.0**. The window reassembles itself in the Comp Window. Click on the **stopwatch** icon 🕐 for **Radius** to record its value at the current time.

11. Move the CTI to the seven second mark (07:00). Change the **Radius** value to **2**.

12. Physics control how the pieces move and fall through space. Twirl open the **Physics** properties and change the **Gravity** value to **0.0**.

13. Click on the **RAM Preview** button. The window now shatters into several shards of glass particles after it finishes animating in. Save your project.

Figure 8.17: *The final effect shatters the window layer.*

14. Select **Composition > Make Movie**. This opens the Render Queue.

15. Click on **Lossless** next to Output Module. Set the Format to **Adobe Flash Video**. Click on **Format Options** and set the Bitrate setting to **400**.

16. Click on **Output To** and select the Chapter_08 folder on your hard drive as the final destination for the rendered movie. Click the **Render** button.

17. The final size for the FLV file is around 510 KB. Create a new Flash file at 30 frames per second. Import the video using "progressive download."

18. Save and test your Flash movie. This completes this exercise. Experiment with the other properties within the Shatter effect. The effect even contains a 3D camera built into it. You can set the camera to fly around the exploded particles. It is truly an amazing and powerful effect.

So far in this chapter you have been building visual effects using only the tools available in After Effects. Some visual effects are extremely hard to replicate and require actual footage. Realistic fire and explosions are a couple of these types of effects that do not have a plug-in readily available in After Effects.

There are several good companies that provide royalty free stock footage that can help you out. One such company is Artbeats (**www.artbeats.com**). In the next exercise you will use one of their stock footage files from the Reel Explosion series to enhance a Flash game.

Chapter 8: Visual Effects

Exercise 2: Meteor Blast

Flash games are incorporating more video and visual effects to enhance the online experience. In this exercise, you will take existing footage of an explosion and create an alpha channel for it. The rendered PNG sequence will be imported into a Flash game. To see an example of the finished Flash game, launch the **02_MeteorBlast.swf** file in the Completed folder inside the 02_Mayhem folder in Chapter_08. Blast the falling meteors out of the sky (Figure 8.18).

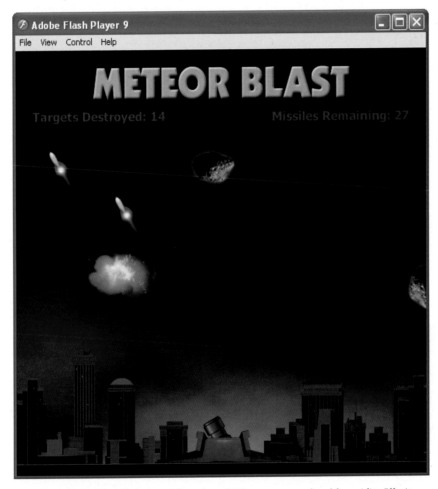

Figure 8.18: *The Flash game integrates a PNG sequence rendered from After Effects.*

1. Open **02_Explosion.aep** inside the 02_Mayhem folder in Chapter_08.

2. Double-click on the **Explosion** composition. It contains two layers of stock footage, courtesy of Artbeats. The top layer is a high-contrast grayscale video copy of the bottom RGB explosion footage. You will use a track matte to create an alpha channel for this visual effect. A **track matte** is used to create transparency in one layer using another layer's alpha or luminance values.

02_Explosion

3. To set up the track matte, you need to open the Modes column in the Timeline panel. If it is not already visible, you can right-click on the **Layer Name** column header and select **Columns > Modes**.

4. Select the bottom layer, **RE222.mov**. Click on the popup menu under **TrkMat** and select **Luma Matte "RE222M.mov"** to apply the track matte (Figure 8.19). Two layers are required to set up a track matte. One layer acts as the matte that creates a hole. The second layer fills the hole with content. The layer stacking order is important. Track mattes can only be applied to the layer directly beneath it. For multiple layers, group them (precompose) inside a composition and apply a track matte to the composition.

Figure 8.19: *Apply a track matte to the bottom layer through the Modes column.*

5. In the Composition panel, click on the **Toggle Transparency Grid** button 🖾 to see the explosion on a transparent background (Figure 8.20). Similar to the alpha channel matte that you learned about in Chapter 4, luminance mattes also use pixel values to create transparency. The high-contrast matte contains black areas that become completely transparent and white areas that turn opaque. Intermediate shades appear with a certain degree of transparency.

Figure 8.20: *Anatomy of a luminance track matte.*

6. Before you render the composition, crop the Comp Window to help reduce the file size for the PNG sequence. Click on the **Region of Interest** button 🔲 at the bottom of the Composition panel.

7. Click and drag in the Comp Window to create a smaller region of interest. Scrub through the Timeline to make sure the explosion remains inside the area. Use the corner handles to resize the region if necessary.

8. Select **Composition > Crop Comp to Region of Interest**. The size of the Comp Window is reduced to the dimensions of the region of interest bounding box.

Chapter 8: Visual Effects

Figure 8.21: *Reduce the region of interest. Creating a smaller region requires less processing power and helps improve the RAM preview.*

9. Select **Composition > Make Movie**. This opens the Render Queue.

10. Click on **Best Settings** to open the Render Settings dialog box. Change the Resolution from Full to **Third** (Figure 8.22). In the Frame Rate area, set **use this frame rate** to **15** frames per second. These changes help reduce the final Flash file size by scaling down the dimensions of each PNG image and the number of images rendered from After Effects.

Figure 8.22: *Render the composition a third of its size.*

11. Click on **Lossless** next to Output Module. Set the Format to **PNG Sequence**. Under the Video Output section, set the channels to **RGB + Alpha**.

Figure 8.23: *Set the PNG files to render with an alpha channel.*

12. Click on **Output To**. In the dialog box that appears create a new folder in the 02_Mayhem folder in Chapter_08. Name it **PNG Sequence**. Click **Open**. Click **Save**. It is always a good idea to store image sequences in their own folder.

Figure 8.24: *Create a new folder to save the PNG files into.*

13. Click the **Render** button. Save your project.

14. Locate the PNG Sequence folder. It now contains over thirty PNG files each with a sequentially numbered file name. These files will be imported into a movie clip in the Flash game.

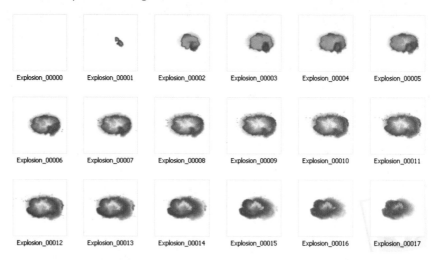

Figure 8.25: *The rendered PNG image sequence contains sequentially numbered file names that Flash can recognize.*

15. Before you import the PNG sequence into Flash, you can delete a couple of the PNG files that do not contain any pixel information. Select **Explosion_0000** and **Explosion_0024** through **Explosion_0032**. Delete the selected files or re-move them from this folder. The less you have to import into Flash, the smaller the published file size.

16. Let's move to Flash. Double-click on **MeteorBlast.fla** in the 02_Mayhem folder to open the file in Flash. It contains all the game assets minus the explosion visual effect. You will import the PNG sequence.

Flash games can be rather complex in terms of ActionScript. This game uses several ActionScript files that are linked to the main Flash FLA file. Let's first deconstruct the Flash code components. Here is the breakdown of the files:

- **MeteorBlast.fla** is the Flash document that stores all the game assets in its Library.
- **MeteorAttackClass.as** is the Document Class that initializes the game. It controls when to drop a meteor, shooting a missile, collision detection, and updating the dynamic text fields.
- **Cannon.as** is an ActionScript file that rotates the cannon.
- **Meteor.as** is an ActionScript file that controls placement and movement of each meteor on the Stage.
- **Missile.as** is an ActionScript file that controls the rotation and movement of the missiles.

02_MeteorBlast

MeteorAttackClass

Cannon

Meteor

Missile

17. In the Flash file, go to the Library and double-click on the Meteor movie clip to open its Timeline. It contains five layers. Select the blank keyframe in **Frame 2** of the **explosion** layer (Figure 8.26).

Figure 8.26: *Select the black keyframe in Frame 2 inside the Meteor movie clip.*

18. Select **File > Import > Import to Stage** to open the Import dialog box. Choose the first image in the PNG sequence (Explosion_00001). Click **Open**.

19. Flash recognizes the file naming convention as a sequence and prompts you to import the entire sequence. Click **Yes**.

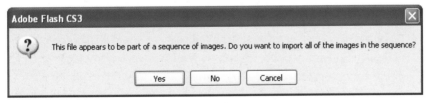

Figure 8.27: *Flash prompts you to import the entire image sequence.*

20. The PNG image sequence appears as a series of keyframes in the movie clip. Scrub through the Timeline to see the animation. Go to the Library. There is a bitmap icon for each image in the sequence.

21. Convert each bitmap image into a graphic symbol. By doing this, Flash will only store the bitmap images once in the final published file.

22. Organize the Library better. Create two new folders; one folder holds the imported PNG sequence and the other holds the graphic symbols.

23. Select **Control > Test Movie**. When a missile hits the meteor it explodes using the footage rendered out of After Effects. This adds a little bit of realism to the game. After the last PNG file is displayed on the Flash Stage, the meteor movie clip is removed. Here is the code that is triggering the explosion. The collision detection is located in the **MeteorAttackClass.as** file. Save your file.

```
// check for collisions
    if (missiles[missileNum].hitTestObject(myMeteor.target_mc)) {
            meteors[meteorNum].meteorHit();
            missiles[missileNum].deleteMissile();
            shotsHit++;
            showGameScore();
            break;
            }
        }
    }
```

There is a small movie clip with an instance name of **target_mc** inside each meteor. The code loops through all the missiles and meteors currently on the Flash Stage and checks to see if any missiles are touching any targets. If that happens, the Document Class calls a public function (meteorHit) inside the **Meteor.as** file that plays the imported PNG sequence (gotoAndPlay("explode")).

```
// meteor is hit by missile, show the explosion
    public function meteorHit() {
        removeEventListener(Event.ENTER_FRAME, moveMeteor);
        MovieClip(parent).removeMeteor(this);
        gotoAndPlay("explode");
    }
```

In this exercise you learned about track mattes and how they can define transparency in layers. They use values from either a layer's alpha channel or the luminance of its pixels. When a track matte is applied to a layer, After Effects converts the next layer above into a track matte. It turns off the video switch for the matte layer, and adds a track matte icon next to its name.

You created a luminance matte using stock footage of an explosion. Luminance mattes work best with high-contrast footage to create areas that are either completely transparent or completely opaque. Shades of gray render as partial transparency. Let's continue exploring track mattes. In the next exercise, you will use an alpha track matte to enhance a logotype for a restaurant.

Chapter 8: Visual Effects

Playing with Fire

Visual effects do not have to take up the entire Flash Stage. They can be more subtle in design, used for accenting smaller elements such as a company logo or button. In this section of the chapter, you will scale down the visual effects and bring static imagery to life using track mattes. The first exercise uses an alpha track matte to enhance a logo for a fictitious restaurant called "Brimstones."

Exercise 1: Fire and Brimstones

1. Open **01_Brimstones.aep** inside the 03_Fire folder in Chapter_08.

2. The Project panel contains all the footage you need to complete this exercise. A composition is already set up for you in a Comps folder. Double-click on the **Brimstones** composition to open its Timeline and Composition panels. It contains a logotype created in Adobe Illustrator (Figure 8.28).

01_Brimstones

Figure 8.28: *The composition contains two layers imported from Adobe Illustrator.*

3. Click and drag the **RF107.mov** footage file from the Project panel to the Timeline. Position the movie in between the two Illustrator layers (Figure 8.29).

Figure 8.29: *Add the stock footage to the Timeline.*

4. Click and drag the Artbeats footage of flames in the Comp Window. Align the bottom edge of the movie with the horizontal line in the logo (Figure 8.30).

Figure 8.30: *Reposition the stock footage layer in the Comp Window.*

5. Make sure the **RF107.mov** layer is still selected. Click on the popup menu under **TrkMat** and select **Alpha Matte "Brimstones/Brimstones.ai"** to apply the track matte (Figure 8.31).

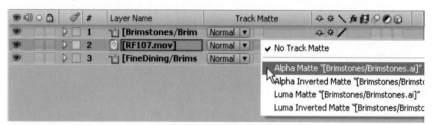

Figure 8.31: *Apply a track matte to the stock footage layer.*

6. Go to the Comp Window. The track matte uses the alpha channel information in the logo layer to mask the video. Now the flames play inside the letters, creating a unique look for the restaurant (Figure 8.32).

Figure 8.32: *The track matte uses the alpha channel information to mask the video.*

7. Click on the popup menu under **TrkMat** and select **Alpha Inverted Matte "Brimstones/Brimstones.ai"** to reverse the track matte. Now the letters punch a hole into the flames footage (Figure 8.33).

Chapter 8: Visual Effects

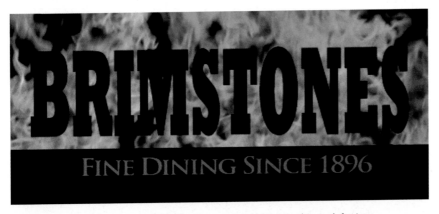

Figure 8.33: *The alpha inverted matte punches holes into the stock footage.*

8. Set the track matte back to **Alpha Matte "Brimstones/Brimstones.ai."**

9. Before you render the composition, crop the Comp Window to help reduce the file size for the Flash Video file. Click on the **Region of Interest** button ▣ at the bottom of the Composition panel.

10. Click and drag in the Comp Window to create a smaller region of interest. Select **Composition > Crop Comp to Region of Interest**. The size of the Comp Window is reduced to the dimensions of the region of interest bounding box.

Figure 8.34: *Reduce the region of interest.*

11. You now have an animated logotype that you can render out to multiple formats. Save your project. This completes the exercise. If you want to export the file to Flash, render the composition as a Flash Video (FLV) file with an encoded alpha channel. Import the video into Flash using "progressive download." At half resolution, the FLV file size will be around 350 KB. You can trim the duration of the composition to reduce the final file size.

This exercise used the alpha track matte to create transparency in a layer. When you select either alpha setting, the source layer's alpha channel is used to mask out another layer. Let's create one more quick example using stock footage and a track matte to enhance a still image.

Exercise 2: Pirate's Cove

02_Pirate

1. Open **02_Pirate.aep** inside the 03_Fire folder in Chapter_08.

2. The Project panel contains all the footage you need to complete this exercise. A composition is already set up for you in a Comps folder. Double-click on the **Pirate** composition to open its Timeline and Composition panels.

3. Select the **RE215.mov** layer. Click on the popup menu under **TrkMat** and select **Luma Matte "RE215M.mov"** to apply the track matte (Figure 8.35).

Figure 8.35: *Apply a track matte to the footage layer through the Modes column.*

4. In the Composition panel, click on the **Toggle Transparency Grid** button ▣ to see the pirate and torch on a transparent background. The black part of the torch is still visible in the stock footage.

5. Select the **Pen** tool ✑ from the Tools panel. This creates a mask that will remove unwanted areas in the Comp Window. Use the Pen tool to create a mask around the flame hiding the black torch (Figure 8.36).

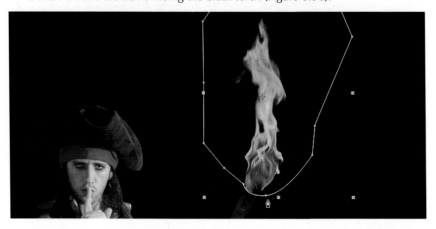

Figure 8.36: *Create a mask around the flame.*

6. Let's simulate the flickering light caused by the torch. Duplicate the **Pirate** layer. Select the layer and press **Command + D** (Mac) or **Control + D** (Windows).

Chapter 8: Visual Effects

7. With the duplicate layer still highlighted, select **Effect > Color Correction > Hue & Saturation**. Go to the Effect Controls panel and make the following changes:

   ▶ Change the **Master Hue** value to **0x +2.0**. This adds more red to the hue.

   ▶ Change the **Master Saturation** value to **50**. This increases the red saturation.

   ▶ Change the **Master Lightness** value to **−50**. This darkens the hue.

8. Type **T** on the keyboard to display the layer's Opacity property. Hold down the **Option** key (Mac) or the **Alt** key (Windows) and click on the **stopwatch** icon next to **Opacity**. This enables expressions to control the property (Figure 8.37).

Figure 8.37: *Enable expressions for the Opacity property.*

9. The code **transform.opacity** appears in the Timeline area. In the Expression layer, click on the **Expression Language Menu** arrow ⊙. Select **Random Numbers > Random(minValOrArray, maxValOrArray)** from the popup menu.

10. The code appears in the Timeline. Change the code to **random(70, 100)**. Press the Enter key on the numeric keypad to accept the expression. Scrub through the Timeline. The duplicate pirate layer randomly changes in opacity creating a flicker effect that simulates the light coming from the torch.

11. Click on the **RAM Preview** button. Save your project. If you want to export the file to Flash, render the composition as a Flash Video (FLV) file with an encoded alpha channel. Import the video into Flash using "progressive download." To see an example, launch **02_PiratesCove.swf** in the Completed folder. The video can be used as a button to launch the game.

02_PiratesCove

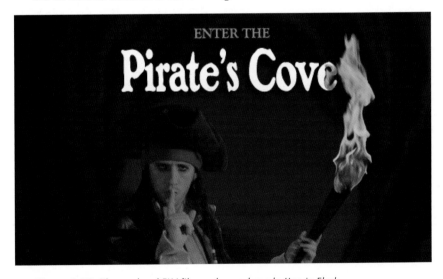

Figure 8.38: *The rendered FLV file can be used as a button in Flash.*

Fun with Fractals

Fractal Noise is a very cool effect to play around with in After Effects. It generates grayscale noise that you can use for organic-looking backgrounds, textures, or to simulate clouds or even a fireball. It has a ton of properties associated with it. The best way to learn about fractal noise is to experiment with it. Let's explore some creative applications using fractal noise.

01_DarkCity

Exercise 1: Dark City

1. Open **01_DarkCity.aep** inside the 04_Fractals folder in Chapter_08. In this exercise, you will create a smog effect using the Fractal Noise effect and add it to a 3D animation of a cityscape (Figure 8.39).

Figure 8.39: *The final composition incorporates fractal noise to create smog.*

2. The Project panel contains all the footage you need to complete this exercise. A composition is already set up for you in a Comps folder. Double-click on the **Smog** composition to open its Timeline and Composition panels. It contains a black solid layer. Select the layer.

3. Select **Effect > Noise & Grain > Fractal Noise**. The black solid layer changes to grayscale noise, similar to Abobe Photoshop's Clouds filter (Figure 8.40). Fractal noise only deals with grayscale to create the noise, not color.

Figure 8.40: *Apply the Fractal Noise effect to the black solid layer.*

4. Go to the Effect Controls panel. Fractal noise is rather complex. There are a variety of options to choose from. First, lower the **Contrast** value to **60.0**.

5. Twirl open the **Transform** properties. Make the following changes:

   ▸ Uncheck the checkbox for **Uniform Scaling**.

   ▸ Change the **Scale Height** value to **250.0**.

   ▸ Enable the **Perspective Scaling** option by clicking on its checkbox. The layers of noise now will animate moving at different depths to create a 3D look.

6. To animate the noise, use the **Offset Turbulence** property. First, click on its **stopwatch** icon to set a keyframe at the beginning of the composition.

7. Press the **End** key on the keyboard to move the CTI to the end of the composition. Change the **Offset Turbulence** value to **320.0, –1200.0**. This animates the noise vertically over the duration of the composition.

8. There is too much detail in the fractal noise. Lower the **Complexity** value to **3.0**. This controls the number of noise layers that are combined to create the fractal noise. Lowering the number softens the amount of detail.

9. Click on the **RAM Preview** button. The fractal noise slowly animates up at different depths. This completes the first part of this exercise. Save your project.

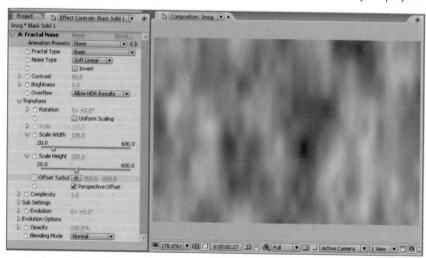

Figure 8.41: *Adjust the Fractal Noise properties to create the animated smog.*

10. With the smog ready, it is time to add it to a city. Double-click on the **CityZoom** composition to open its Timeline and Composition panels. It contains three footage layers: a foreground, middleground, and background art that create a cityscape (artwork courtesy of **www.istockphoto.com**). The layers have been converted into 3D layers and positioned in 3D space. A Camera layer animates through the space and into the cityscape (Figure 8.42). You will nest the smog composition you just created into this composition.

Figure 8.42: *The CityZoom composition contains a 3D animation using a Camera layer.*

11. Click and drag the **Smog** composition from the Project panel to the Timeline. Position the nested comp in between the foreground and Dark City logo layers (Figure 8.43). Enable the 3D Layer switch.

👁		▷ ☐	1	📷 **Camera 1**	⊕			
👁		▷ ☐	2	🎞 **foreground/bigcit**	⊕	/		▣
👁		▷ ☐	3	🖼 **Smog**	⊕	/		▣
👁		▷ ☐	4	🎞 **DarkCity.ai**	⊕ ☀	/		▣

Figure 8.43: *Add the Smog composition to the Timeline and convert it into a 3D layer.*

12. Type **P** on the keyboard to display the layer's **Position** properties. Set the layer's position to **160.0, 120.0, 400.0**.

13. Type **T** on the keyboard to display the layer's **Opacity** properties. Set the layer's opacity to **30%**.

Figure 8.44: *The final animation with the fractal noise.*

14. Click on the **RAM Preview** button. Save your project. If you want to export the file to Flash, render the composition as a Flash Video (FLV) file. Import the video into Flash using "progressive download."

Chapter 8: Visual Effects

Exercise 2: Firestorm

In this exercise you will create a seamless looping background using Fractal Noise for a Web banner ad. To see an example of what you will build, locate and launch the **02_FractalFire.swf** file in the Completed folder inside the 04_Fractals folder in Chapter_08 (Figure 8.45).

Figure 8.45: *The final Flash file integrates a seamless looping fractal noise background.*

1. Create a new project in **After Effects**. Select **Composition > New Composition**. Enter **Firestorm** as the Composition Name. Select **Web Banner, 468 x 60** from the Preset popup menu. Set the duration to **0:00:05:00**. Click **OK**.

2. Make sure the Timeline panel is highlighted. Select **Layer > New > Solid**. The Solid Settings dialog box appears. Make the following settings.

   ► Enter **FirestormFractal** for the solid name.
   ► Click on the **Make Comp Size** button.
   ► Set the color of the solid layer to **Black**.
   ► Click **OK**.

3. With the solid layer highlighted, select **Effect > Noise & Grain > Fractal Noise**.

4. Go to the Effect Controls panel. Change the **Fractal Type** to **Dynamic Progressive**. The fractal noise is created by generating a grid of random numbers for each noise layer. The Fractal Type setting determines how the grid renders the random numbers. The Dynamic Progressive setting produces cloudlike noise, perfect for a fireball. Experiment with the other settings.

5. Raise the **Contrast** value to **133.0**.

6. Twirl open the **Transform** properties and lower the **Complexity** value to **5.0**. You will use the **Evolution** property to animate the noise in this exercise. This adds progressive revolutions that continue to change the noise with each added revolution.

7. Twirl open the **Evolution** property. First, click on its **stopwatch** icon 🕐 to set a keyframe at the beginning of the composition.

8. Press the **End** key on the keyboard to move the CTI to the end of the composition. Change the **Evolution** value to **2x + 0.0**. This property now completes two revolutions based on the duration of the composition.

9. To create a looping background, twirl open the **Evolution Options** properties. Enable the **Cycle Evolution** by clicking on its checkbox. Set the **Cycle** value to **1**.

Figure 8.46: *Use the Cycle Evolution property to create a looping background.*

10. Click on the **RAM Preview** button. The evolution completes the number of revolutions you specified for Cycle for the length of the composition. Save your project. What about color? Fractal noise doesn't have any color settings.

Figure 8.47: *Evolution creates an organic-looking background.*

11. With the solid layer highlighted, select **Effect > Color Correction > Colorama**. Go to the Effect Controls panel and twirl open the **Output Cycle** properties. Select the **Fire** preset from the popup menu next to **Use Preset Palette**. Now you have a firestorm (Figure 8.48).

Figure 8.48: *Apply Colorama to create the fiery look.*

12. Before you render the composition, you have to address one small problem. The last frame of a cycle is identical to the first frame. To create a seamless loop:

  ▸ Press the **End** key to move the CTI to the end of the composition.
  ▸ Press the **Page Up** key to jump to the frame before the last frame (04:13).
  ▸ Click and drag the **Work Area End** blue tab to align with the CTI.

Figure 8.49: *Reduce the workspace by one frame to create a seamless loop.*

13. Select **Composition > Make Movie**. This opens the Render Queue.

14. Click on **Lossless** next to Output Module. Set the Format to **Adobe Flash Video**. Click on **Format Options** and select **Web Banner, 468 x 60** from the Preset popup menu (Figure 8.50).

Figure 8.50: *Render the Flash Video using the Web Banner preset.*

15. Uncheck the **Export Audio** checkbox. Click **OK**.

16. Click on **Output To** and select the Chapter_08 folder on your hard drive as the final destination for the rendered movie. Click the **Render** button.

17. Let's move to Flash. Double-click on **02_FractalFire.fla** in the 04_Fractals folder to open the file in Flash. It contains two layers: a type animation layer and a video layer. The type animation is contained in a movie clip.

02_FractalFire

18. Double-click on **mc_TitleAnimation** in the Library. It contains two layers that hold graphic symbols. Each graphic symbol tweens in over time.

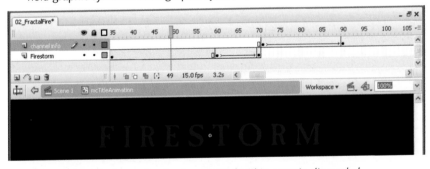

Figure 8.51: *The type animation is contained within a movie clip symbol.*

19. Return to the main Timeline. Select the blank keyframe in the **Video** layer.

20. Select **File > Import > Import Video**. The Import Video Wizard dialog box appears. To import the FLV file:

   ▸ Locate the **Firestorm.flv** file you rendered out of After Effects.
   ▸ Set the deployment to **Embedded Video in SWF and Play in Timeline**.
   ▸ Set the Embedding type to a **Movie Clip**.
   ▸ Click **Finish** to embed the video. The first frame of the video appears on the Stage and a video symbol is added to the Library.

21. Save and test your movie. The final published SWF file with the embedded video is 60 KB. If file size is a concern, you can always reduce the duration of the composition in After Effects. This completes the exercise.

Figure 8.52: *The final published SWF file is around 60 KB.*

Summary

This chapter exposed you to some of the more popular effects within After Effects and showed you how to integrate them into Flash. There are so many possible creative solutions you can come up with that it is mind-boggling. As mentioned previously, the best way to learn about the effects is to experiment.

After Effects does provide documentation that you can access directly from the application. Select **Help > Effect Reference** to open the Adobe Help Viewer. Select an effect category to find the effect you want to know more about. This completes the chapter. The next chapter explores audio and shape layers.

Figure 8.53: *Use the Effect Reference to learn more about each tool in After Effects.*

CHAPTER 9

Shapes and Sounds

Shape Layers are a new and welcomed addition to After Effects. It is like having all the drawing capabilities of Adobe Illustrator plus movement and effects. This chapter takes a look at drawing and animating shapes and how audio can impact your projects.

Shape Layers

The **Shape Layers** in Adobe After Effects are a wonder to behold. They contain vector graphic objects called, what else, shapes. The beauty of a Shape Layer lies in how it defines its vectors. You can create a shape with a stroke and a fill and scale it to any size without losing any detail or quality. Sound familiar to drawing shapes in Flash or Adobe Illustrator? It is; however, After Effects takes shapes to the next level by allowing you to apply **path operations** that can animate the shape's outlines, creating some rather interesting motion graphics.

Figure 9.1: *Path operations can manipulate the outline of Shape Layers over time.*

This chapter begins with an introduction to Shape Layers. You will start with the basics and learn how to create and modify these vector objects in the Comp Window. From there, you will apply path operations to create some interesting shape effects. Let's get started.

 Locate the Chapter_09 folder on the DVD. Copy this folder to your hard drive. The folder contains all the files needed to complete the chapter exercises.

Exercise 1: Making and Modifying Shapes

If you are familiar with drawing shapes in Adobe Illustrator, you should feel right at home in After Effects. Many of the Shape Tools are based on Illustrator's toolset. The Shape Tools are located in the Tools panel and consist of a Rectangle, Rounded Rectangle, Ellipse, Polygon, and Star Tool.

Figure 9.2: *The Shape Tools are located in the Tools panel.*

1. Create a new project in **Adobe After Effects**.

2. Select **Composition > New Composition**. Enter **myShape** as the Composition Name. Select **NTSC D1** from the Preset popup menu. Set the duration to **0:00:05:00**. Click **OK**.

3. Click and hold on the **Rectangle** tool in the Tools panel. Select the **Star Tool** from the Shape Tool popup menu (Figure 9.2).

4. Go to the Comp Window. Click and drag to scale and rotate the star as you draw it. As you drag and before you release the mouse, you can:

   ▸ Hold down the Shift key to only scale the star as you draw it.
   ▸ Hold down the Space bar to move its position in the Comp Window.
   ▸ Press the Up arrow key to add more points.
   ▸ Press the Down arrow key to remove points.

Figure 9.3: *Draw your shape in the Comp Window.*

5. When you are finished drawing, release the mouse. A Shape Layer is added to the Timeline panel. Similar to shapes in Flash, shapes in After Effects consist of a path, a stroke, and a fill. Fill and Stroke options are available for selected shapes to the right of the Toolbar.

6. With the shape still selected, click on the word **Fill** to open the Fill Options dialog box. Click on the **Radial Gradient** button. Click **OK**.

   Fills and strokes can be set to one of four modes. None performs no paint operation. Solid color paints the entire fill or stroke with one color. Linear and Radial Gradient mixes two or more colors together based on a Start and End Point in the shape.

7. Click on the Fill's **color swatch** to open the Gradient Editor dialog box. This allows you to choose the color combination for your gradient.

8. Click on the **Color Stop** icons to change the color using the color picker at the bottom of the dialog box. You can add additional Color Stops by clicking on the gradient bar. To delete a Color Stop, select it and click on the Delete button. Choose any colors you wish for your radial fill. When you are done, click **OK**.

Figure 9.4: *Adjust the colors for the gradient fill.*

9. To adjust the position of the radial gradient fill inside the shape's outline, select the **Polystar 1** layer in the Timeline. Go to the Comp Window. Using the Selection (arrow) tool, click and drag the Start and End Points to modify the gradient's position to create a faux lighting effect.

Figure 9.5: *Adjust the Start and End Point to reposition the gradient fill.*

10. Next, let's adjust the shape's stroke. Click on the Stroke's **color swatch** to open the Shape Stroke Color dialog box. Choose whatever color you want. Scrub through the **Stroke Width** value and set it to **3**.

11. In the Timeline, twirl open **Polystar 1** to display the shape's attributes. These attributes are contained within a **shape group**. Each group has its own attributes and transform properties (Figure 9.6).

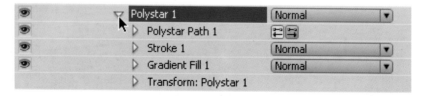

Figure 9.6: *Open the Shape Group to reveal its attributes and transform properties.*

12. Twirl open **Polystar Path 1** to reveal its attributes. Experiment with each of the values to modify the shape in the Comp Window. Notice that all of these attributes have a stop watch next to their name. This means that they can be animated over time. For this example the following changes were made:

- ► Increase the **Points** value to **24**.
- ► Increase the **Inner Radius** to **130**.
- ► Decrease the **Outer Roundness** to **–275**.

13. Twirl open **Transform: Polystar 1** to reveal its properties. These should look familiar with the addition of Skew and Skew Axis. Scrub through the Skew value to see how it affects the shape in the Comp Window (Figure 9.7).

Figure 9.7: *Skew the shape using the transform properties in the shape group.*

14. Create another shape path on the same layer. Select **Add** in the Timeline or from the Toolbar and choose another **Polystar** shape from the popup menu. A new star appears in the center of the Comp Window skewed to match the first path. As you can see, a Shape Layer can contain more than one shape path.

15. Twirl open **Polystar Path 2.** Experiment with its attributes to modify the second path. For this example, the **Outer Roundness** value was set to **260**.

16. Twirl open **Gradient Fill 1**. Change the **Fill Rule** to **Even-Odd**. This creates compound shapes. The inner shape knocks a hole out of the larger shape.

17. Save your project and keep experimenting with the Shape Layers. When you create a shape by dragging with a Shape tool in the Comp Window, you create a **parametric** shape path. These paths are defined numerically and are the basic geometric shapes you can select from the Shape Tools popup menu.

Exercise 2: Creating Bezier and Text Shapes

There are two types of shape paths: parametric shape paths and Bezier shape paths. You can create a **Bezier shape path** using the Pen tool. You have used the Pen tool to mask out unwanted areas on a selected layer. When you draw with the Pen tool in the Comp Window with no layer selected, After Effects automatically creates a shape on a new Shape Layer.

1. Create a new project. Select **Composition > New Composition**. Enter **Bezier** as the Composition Name. Select **NTSC D1** from the Preset popup menu. Set the duration to **0:00:05:00**. Click **OK**.

2. Select the **Pen** tool ![pen tool icon] from the Tools panel. Go to the Comp Window and create a Bezier shape. The shape can be anything that you want. Close the path when you are done. A new Shape Layer is added to the Timeline. Set the Fill and Stroke colors just like you did in the first exercise.

Figure 9.8: Use the Pen tool to create a Bezier shape in the Comp Window.

3. In the Timeline, twirl open **Shape 1** to display the shape's attributes. This free-form shape does not contain all of the parametric properties that the previous shapes had in the first exercise. Save your project.

4. You can also create shapes from text characters. To do this, use the Type tool to create a new text layer. With the layer highlighted select **Layer > Create Outlines**. This extracts the outlines for each character. The new Shape Layer is created at the top of the layer stacking order. The new layer contains one shape group for each selected character, plus fill and stroke properties that match those of the text (Figure 9.9).

Figure 9.9: Shape Layers can also be created from text layers in After Effects.

Exercise 3: Animating Shapes and Path Operations

Now that you have experimented with the Shape Layers and have a basic understanding of their attributes, let's create an animation using them. In this exercise, you will also apply path operations to a Shape Layer. Path operations offer distortion effects such as Pucker & Bloat, Twist, Zig Zag, and an auto-animating Wiggle Paths. Figure 9.10 shows an example of each.

Original Shape   Pucker   Bloat

Twist   Zig Zag   Wiggle Paths

Figure 9.10: *Examples of the path operations applied to a Shape Layer.*

Another path operation that you will use is the Repeater. It creates virtual copies of your shapes in the Comp Window. A project has been set up for you.

1. Open the **03_Tunnel.aep** project file located inside the 01_Shapes folder inside Chapter_09. It contains one composition labeled Tunnel.

2. There is one Shape Layer in the Timeline. The shape is a rounded rectangle with a 10-pixel stroke and no fill. Twirl open **Rectangle 1** to open the shape group. Twirl open **Transform: Rectangle 1** to view its transform properties.

Figure 9.11: *Twirl open the shape group's transform properties.*

3. Click on the **stopwatch icon** ⏱ for **Rotation** to record a keyframe at the beginning of the composition. Press the **End** key on the keyboard to move the Current Time Indicator (CTI) to the end of the composition. Change the Rotation value to **1x +0.0**. The rounded square rotates 360 degrees.

4. Select **Add** in the Timeline or from the Toolbar and choose **Repeater** from the popup menu. Three new squares appear to the right of the original shape. The Repeater is a path operation that creates virtual copies of all paths, strokes, and fills within a shape group. The virtual copies are only present in the Comp Window and do not appear as new layers in the Timeline panel.

Figure 9.12: *Add the Repeater path operation to the Shape Layer.*

5. Twirl open **Repeater 1**. Change the **Copies** value to **20**.

6. Twirl open the **Transform: Repeater 1**. You can define how each copy is transformed by modifying its position, scale and rotation values, which accumulate for each copy. Make the following changes:

   ▶ Set the **Position** values to **0.0, 0.0**. This aligns all the copies underneath the original shape.

   ▶ Change the **Scale** value to **70%**. Now you can see how the transform properties accumulate for each copy. The replicated rounded squares recede into space.

   ▶ Change the **Anchor Point** value to **0.0, –10,0**.

7. Scrub through the Timeline. Notice that the virtual copies rotate to follow the original shape. Move the CTI to the beginning of the composition.

   ▶ Set the **Rotation** value of the Repeater to **0x +10.0**. This aligns all the copies underneath the original shape. Click on the **stopwatch icon** ⏱ for **Rotation** to record a keyframe.

   ▶ Press the **End** key on the keyboard to move the CTI to the end of the composition. Change the Rotation value to **0x +90.0**.

8. Change the **End Opacity** value to **30**. This adds the illusion of depth to the rotating shapes as each copy lowers in opacity.

9. Change the **Offset** attribute under **Repeater 1** to **–2.0**. This moves the objects closer to the active camera, immersing you in the spinning vortex.

10. Click on the **RAM preview**. Save your project. Let's add a distortion effect to this animation. Select **Add** in the Timeline or from the Toolbar and choose **Twist** from the popup menu. A Twist 1 attribute appears in the Timeline. Twirl it open and change the **Angle** value to **360.0**. Let's apply some visual effects.

Figure 9.13: *Apply the Twist path operation to the Shape Layer.*

11. With the Shape Layer 1 highlighted in the Timeline, select **Effect > Generate > CC Light Burst 2.5**. In the Effect Controls panel, change the **Intensity** to **500.00** and the **Ray Length** to **150**. This creates an interesting abstract background.

Figure 9.14: *Apply the CC Light Burst 2.5 effect to create a kaleidoscope effect.*

12. Let's experiment with one more visual effect. Before you do that, disable the **CC Light Burst** effect in the Effect Controls panel by clicking on its **FX** icon *fx*.

13. Select **Effect > Distort > CC Flo Motion**. The effect is added to the Effect Controls panel underneath CC Light Burst. This effect pinches and pulls the entire layer. Change the **Knot 1** value to **275.0, 200.0**. This centers the knot in the Comp Window. Change the **Amount 1** value to **40**.

Figure 9.15: *Apply the CC Flo Motion to dramatically distort the Shape Layer.*

14. Keep experimenting with other effects and path operations to tweak the animation to whatever you want. If you want some inspiration, click on the **Brainstorm** button ⌾ at the top of the Timeline panel. This displays multiple variations of the selected property using randomized settings. To apply any of the variations, click on the check mark icon over each thumbnail image.

Figure 9.16: *Use Brainstorm to explore different possibilities for your composition.*

Flash Video

15. When you are satisfied with your composition, render it out as a Flash Video (FLV) file to use in Flash as an animated background. Why render to a FLV format instead of a Flash SWF file? Even though you are working with vector information in a Shape Layer, it will not export as vectors. All Shape Layers rasterize when exported or rendered from After Effects.

Digital Audio Basics

Let's take a detour for a moment and enter the world of digital audio. Up to this point in the book, you have been using After Effects for visual effects and animation without incorporating a lot of audio. Sound greatly enhances the user experience whether you are watching a video or interacting with elements in a Flash movie. It is important to understand a few key principles about audio to achieve great results when integrating it into Flash or After Effects.

Figure 9.17: *Vibrating objects generate waves of compressed air that we hear as sound.*

What is sound? Vibrating objects, such as guitar strings or vocal cords, generate waves of rapidly varying air pressure. Sound waves occur as repeating cycles of pressure move out and away from the vibrating object. When these vibrations reach our ears, we hear sound. The **frequency**, or pitch, refers to the number of cycles (waves) per second. The **amplitude**, or intensity, of sound is the size (height of the wave) of the variations. When you see audio waveforms in software applications, they illustrate these pressure waves.

Figure 9.18: *Audio waveforms are visually represented in Flash and After Effects.*

Electronic representations of sound waves can be recorded in either **digital** or **analog** formats. Analog recordings use audio tape, which is a very thin strip of plastic, coated with magnetic particles. A microphone converts the sound pressures into electric impulses. The electric impulses align with the magnetic particles to create a pattern on the tape that represents the sound.

Computers record audio as a series of zeroes and ones. Digital audio breaks the original waveform up into individual samples. This is referred to as digitizing or audio sampling. The **sampling rate** defines how often a sample is taken during the recording process.

When audio is recorded at a higher sampling rate, the digital waveform perfectly mimics the original analog waveform. Low sampling rates often distort the original sound because they do not capture enough of the sound frequency. The frequency of a sound is measured in Hertz (Hz), which means cycles per second. A kilohertz (kHz) is a thousand cycles per second. Table 9.1 lists some common sampling rates used in digital audio.

Table 9.1: *Common digital audio sampling rates*

Sampling Rate	Usage
8,000 Hz	Low quality with low file size used for the Web.
11,025 Hz	Good for narration only. Do not use for music.
22,050 Hz	Adequate quality and file size used in older multimedia.
44,100 Hz	Audio CD quality, used for video and music.
48,000 Hz	DVD quality, used for video and music.

The bit depth of each audio sample is equally as important as the sampling rate. In digital audio, bit depth describes the amount of data contained in each sample, measured in bits. You can compare audio bit depth to image bit depth. The lower the number, the less detail captured, resulting in poorer quality sound. Common examples of bit depth include CD audio, which is recorded at 16 bits, and DVD-Audio that records up to 24-bit audio.

Once the audio has been sampled, it can be saved out into a number of file formats. It should come as no surprise that After Effects can import a variety of these audio file formats. The imported audio works like all the other footage in the Project panel. An audio footage file is added to the Timeline as a layer. You can have multiple layers of audio to mix the sounds together. Here are some common audio file formats that can be imported into After Effects:

- ▸ **AIFF** (Audio Interchange File Format) is a standard audio format for the Mac.
- ▸ **WAV** (Waveform Audio Format) is a standard audio format on a Windows-based computer.
- ▸ **MP3** (Motion Picture Expert Group) is the file format of choice for Flash movies. It uses a compression algorithm to remove certain parts of sound that are outside the hearing range of most people. As a result, the audio still sounds great to us with a small file size.

Let's take a look at how to integrate and mix audio in a project in After Effects. A composition has already been created. You will add several sound effects and background music to an existing animation that originated in Flash. The Flash scenes were exported to After Effects to be prepared for broadcast.

Exercise: Mixing Audio in After Effects

To see an example of what you will build in this exercise, locate and play the **WizardsBlast.mov** in the Completed folder inside the 02_AudioMix folder in Chapter_09. You will add audio in After Effects to a couple of scenes from an animation. The final composition will be prepared for NTSC video.

Figure 9.19: *Sound effects greatly enhance this animation.*

1. Open the **01_SoundEffects.aep** project file located inside the 02_Audio folder inside Chapter_09. It contains three compositions in the Project panel.

2. In the Project panel, double-click on **Scene1_WizardBlast** to open its Timeline and Composition panel. The two-second composition contains an imported Flash SWF file. After Effects was used to add the visual effects of the lightning, lens flare, and sparks. Click on each solid layer and go to the Effect Controls panel to see how the visual effects were applied.

01_SoundEffects

Figure 9.20: *Effects were layered on top of the imported Flash SWF animation.*

3. In the Project panel, double-click on **Scene2_Monster** to open its Timeline and Composition panel. The three-second composition contains another imported Flash SWF file with some visual effects added to it. The **Glow** and **CC Flo Motion** effects were applied to the SWF layer to create the monster's distortion.

Figure 9.21: *Effects were applied directly to the Flash SWF animation.*

4. In the Project panel, double-click on **FinalComp** to open its Timeline and Composition panel. It contains both nested compositions and an Adjustment Layer. The Broadcast Colors effect has been applied to the Adjustment Layer to keep the composition's color space within the range allowed for NTSC broadcast video.

   Comp Markers have also been inserted to assist you with adding the sound effects. They are used to mark a point in time within the composition. These markers do not move with the layers. To create a Comp Marker, click and drag a marker icon from the top-right of the Timeline to the frame you wish to mark. They are numbered in sequential order.

Figure 9.22: *Comp Markers help label specific points in time within the composition.*

5. Now that you are aware of how the composition is set up, let's start adding the sound effects. All of the audio has already been imported into the Project panel. The footage is contained in an **Audio** folder. Click and drag **Blast.mp3** from the Project panel to the Timeline. Position the audio at the top of the layer stack. Release the mouse to create the new layer.

Chapter 9: Shapes and Sounds

6. Move the CTI to align with **Comp Marker 0**. Click and drag the audio layer's duration bar to align it with the CTI (Figure 9.23). It doesn't matter where the audio is placed within the layer stacking order. Most often, the audio layers are grouped together at either the top or bottom of the stack.

Figure 9.23: *Add the Blast.mp3 audio file to the Timeline.*

7. Click and drag **Zap.mp3** from the Project panel to the Timeline. Move the CTI to align with **Comp Marker 1**. Click and drag the audio layer's duration bar to align it with the CTI (Figure 9.24).

Figure 9.24: *Add the Zap.mp3 audio file to the Timeline.*

8. Click and drag **Creature.mp3** from the Project panel to the Timeline. Move the CTI to align with **Comp Marker 2**. Click and drag the audio layer's duration bar to align it with the CTI (Figure 9.25).

Figure 9.25: *Add the Creature.mp3 audio file to the Timeline.*

9. Click and drag **Boom.mp3** from the Project panel to the Timeline. Move the CTI to align with **Comp Marker 3**. Click and drag the audio layer's duration bar to align it with the CTI (Figure 9.26).

Figure 9.26: *Add the Boom.mp3 audio file to the Timeline.*

10. Click and drag **Music.mp3** from the Project panel to the Timeline. It should span the entire duration. With all the audio in place, click on the **RAM preview** button to hear the audio. You can also hold down the **Command** (Mac) or **Control** (Windows) key and scrub through the Timeline to hear the audio.

11. You need to tweak a couple of the audio layers to synchronize them better with the visuals. **Right-click** or **Control-click** (Mac) on the **Source Name** column header and select **Columns > Duration**.

Figure 9.27: *Open the Duration column in the Timeline.*

12. **Right-click** or **Control-click** (Mac) on the **Source Name** column header and select **Columns > Out**.

Figure 9.28: *Open the Out column in the Timeline.*

13. First, let's change the length of the **Boom.mp3** layer's duration bar. Select the layer in the Timeline. Scrub through its **Duration** value until it reads **01;05**. This change speeds up the audio, creating more of a cartoon-like sound effect.

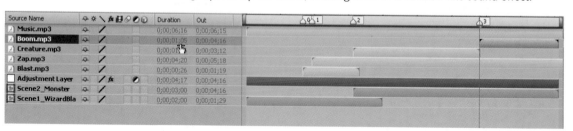

Figure 9.29: *Change the duration of the Boom.mp3 layer's duration bar.*

Chapter 9: Shapes and Sounds

14. Select the **Zap.mp3** layer in the Timeline. Scrub through its **Out** value until the end of the layer's duration bar aligns with the CTI. The value should be around **03;12**. This trims the audio, but doesn't alter the playback.

Figure 9.30: *Change the Out point of the Zap.mp3 layer's duration bar.*

15. Twirl open the **Music.mp3** layer to reveal its **Audio** property. Twirl open the **Audio** property to reveal the Audio Levels and Waveform. Twirl open the **Waveform** layer to see a visual representation of the audio file. To scale the waveform, position the cursor at the bottom of the Audio Waveform layer. When the cursor changes to a double-cursor, click and drag to scale the layer.

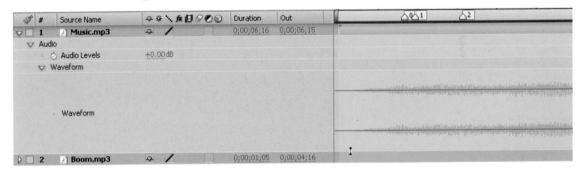

Figure 9.31: *Twirl open the Waveform layer to see a visual representation of the audio.*

16. Currently the audio's duration is longer than the composition's. You are going to fade out the audio using the Audio Levels property. Move the CTI to the four second mark (04:00). Click on the **stopwatch** icon ⏱ next to **Audio Levels** to record the current volume at that time.

17. Press the **End** key to move the CTI to the end of the composition. Lower the **Audio Levels** value to **–25.00** dB. This fades the music out at the end of the composition. The waveform also changes to illustrate the fade out.

Figure 9.32: *Fade out the Music.mp3 audio at the end of the composition.*

18. Click on the **RAM preview** to listen to the final composition. After Effects does provide some effects that can be applied to audio layers. These include:

  ▸ The **Backwards** effect reverses a layer's audio.

  ▸ The **Bass & Treble** effect increases or decreases the low frequencies (bass) or the high frequencies (treble) of the audio.

  ▸ The **Reverb** effect simulates a spacious or acoustically live interior.

  ▸ The **Stereo Mixer** effect mixes the left and right channels of audio and pans the entire signal from one channel to the other.

19. Select **Composition > Make Movie** to add the composition to the Render Queue.

20. Click on **Lossless** next to Output Module. Set the Format to **QuickTime** movie. Click on **Format Options** and set the compression setting to **MPEG-4 Video**.

21. Enable the **Audio** export for the music and sound effects. Set the sampling rate to **48.000 kHz** for DVD output. Set the bit depth to **16 Bit** and make sure the audio is exported in **Stereo**. Click **OK**.

Figure 9.33: *Export the audio in the Format Options.*

22. Click on **Output To** and select the Chapter_09 folder on your hard drive as the final destination for the rendered movie. Click the **Render** button.

This completes the exercise that focused on mixing audio in After Effects. The imported audio works like any other footage in the Project panel. Audio footage appears as its own layer in the Timeline. You can have multiple layers of audio to mix the sounds together. The **Audio Levels** property allows you to keyframe the volume of the sound over time.

Sound is an important component in digital video and Flash movies. This section of the chapter also discussed the fundamentals of audio. Some key terms to remember include sampling rate and bit depth. The sampling rate defines how often a sample is taken during the recording process. Bit depth describes the amount of data contained in each sample, measured in bits. Both work together in determining the quality of the digital sound. The higher the values, the better the sound quality and bigger the file size.

Sound Visualization

This last part of the chapter deals with visualizing audio in After Effects using the Audio Spectrum effect and converted keyframes. You will come full-circle in this chapter as you animate Shape Layers to the beat of the music.

Sound visualization is a graphic representation of an audio signal. After Effects provides a couple of methods that allow you to create this visualization at the click of a mouse. To do the same thing in Flash requires a lot of ActionScript knowledge and patience. After Effects makes it so easy and fast. Let's first explore the Audio Spectrum effect.

Exercise 1: The Audio Spectrum

1. Open a new After Effects project. Select **Composition > New Composition**. The Composition Settings dialog box appears. You will set up the composition to match the Flash file you are integrating the effect into.

2. Make the following settings and then click **OK** to create the new composition.

    ▶ Composition Name: **Spectrum**
    ▶ Width: **550**
    ▶ Height: **400**
    ▶ Pixel Aspect Ratio: **Square Pixels**
    ▶ Frame Rate: **30**
    ▶ Duration: **0:00:17:00**

3. Double-click inside the Project panel. In the Import File dialog box, locate and import the **Spectrum.wav** file in the Footage folder inside the 03_Visualize folder. Click and drag the audio file from the Project panel to the Timeline.

Figure 9.34: *Import the audio and add it to the Timeline.*

4. Make sure the Timeline panel is highlighted. Select **Layer > New > Solid**. The Solid Settings dialog box appears. Make the following settings:

    ▶ Enter **AudioSpectrum** for the solid name.
    ▶ Click on the **Make Comp Size** button.
    ▶ Set the color of the solid layer to **Black**.
    ▶ Click **OK**.

5. Make sure the solid layer is still highlighted in the Timeline. Select **Effect > Generate > Audio Spectrum**. A row of pink dots appears in the Comp Window (Figure 9.35). The effect visually displays the audio using each dot to reflect the magnitude in the sound's frequency.

Figure 9.35: *Apply the Audio Spectrum effect to the solid layer.*

6. In the Effect Controls panel, select **Spectrum.wav** from the **Audio Layer** popup menu. Click on the **RAM Preview**. As you can see, the dots swell or shrink depending upon the frequency of the audio being played.

Figure 9.36: *Set the audio layer to the Spectrum.wav in the Effect Controls panel.*

7. The effect contains a lot of properties that control the spectrum. Let's focus on a couple. You can apply the effect to a drawn path. Select the **Pen** tool in the Tools panel.

8. In the Comp Window, draw a curved path on the solid layer using the Pen tool.

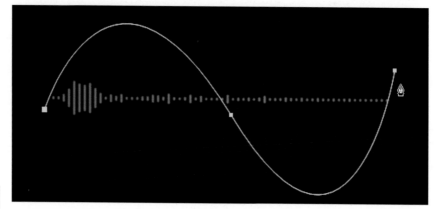

Figure 9.37: *Use the Pen tool to draw a path on the solid layer.*

9. In the Effect Controls panel, select **Mask 1** from the **Path** popup menu. The audio spectrum attaches itself to the drawn path.

10. Change the **Frequency bands** value to **100**. This generates more dots in the spectrum. Change the **Maximum Height** value to **1500**. This elongates the frequency lines that appear. Click the **RAM Preview** to see the adjustments.

Figure 9.38: *Adjust the Frequency bands and Maximum Height properties.*

11. Increase the **Thickness** value to **40**. Change the **Softness** value to **100**. This feathers the audio spectrum. Click the **RAM Preview** to see the adjustments.

Figure 9.39: *Adjust the Thickness and Softness properties of the Audio Spectrum.*

12. Use the color swatches to change the color of the audio spectrum to whatever you want. There are two swatches: the **Inside** and **Outside Color**.

13. As mentioned in Chapter 3, the Audio Spectrum effect renders as vectors. Select **File > Export > Adobe Flash (SWF)**. This opens the Save File As dialog box. Save the SWF file to the 03_Visualize folder in Chapter_09. The SWF Settings dialog box appears. In the Images area, set After Effects to **Ignore Unsupported Features**. For now, leave the Audio unchecked.

14. Locate the exported SWF file and launch it in the Flash Player. It doesn't look quite the same as it does in the Comp Window in After Effects. Certain properties, such as **Softness**, do not translate well when exported to a Flash SWF format.

Figure 9.40: *Launch the exported SWF file.*

15. Close the Flash Player and return to After Effects. In the Effect Controls panel, decrease the **Thickness** value to **5**. Change the **Softness** value to **0**.

16. Select **Analog Lines** from the **Display Options** popup menu. The other option available to you is Analog Dots. Experiment with both to see the difference.

17. Enable the **Use Polar Path** checkbox. Click the **RAM Preview** to see the results. You may need to move the solid layer over to see the audio spectrum better. You get a different effect, much like a star burst that animates to the music.

18. Save your project in After Effects. To migrate the sound visualization over to Flash, select **File > Export > Adobe Flash (SWF)**. Do not include the audio in the SWF file. It is better to keep the audio separate and import it into Flash or write some code in ActionScript to load the audio using the Sound object.

19. Don't forget that you have a ton of visual effects that you can apply to this solid layer. Figure 9.41 shows the CC Radial Fast Blur applied. If you do apply an effect, the Audio Spectrum will no longer render as vectors so you need to export the composition as a Flash Video (FLV) file to achieve a smaller file size.

Figure 9.41: *You can apply other visual effects to enhance the Audio Spectrum.*

Exercise 2: Audio Keyframes

In this exercise, you will explore how sound can be converted into keyframes using a keyframe assistant. These keyframes are then capable of manipulating other layer properties in the Timeline. You will be using an expression in After Effects to synchronize a Shape Layer's movement to the music.

1. Open **02_AudioKeyframes** in the 03_Visualize folder inside Chapter_09.

2. It contains one composition that holds a Shape Layer and an audio layer. **Right-click** or **Control-click** (Mac) on the audio layer. Select **Keyframe Assistant > Convert Audio to Keyframes** from the context popup menu.

Figure 9.42: *Convert the audio to keyframes using the Keyframe Assistant.*

3. A new null layer named **Audio Amplitude** is added to the Timeline. Twirl open the layer, and then twirl open **Effects** to reveal three Expression Controls effects: Left Channel, Right Channel, and Both Channels (Figure 9.43).

The Convert Audio To Keyframes keyframe assistant analyzes the audio amplitude within the Timeline and creates keyframes. The converted keyframes represent the audio amplitude. Each Expression Controls effect contains Slider properties that you can access and link to other layer properties such as Scale, Rotation, and Opacity.

Figure 9.43: *The keyframe assistant uses Expression Controls effects.*

4. Twirl open **Both Channels** to reveal the converted keyframes.

5. Select the **Shape Layer 1** layer in the Timeline. Twirl open the layer to reveal its attributes and transform properties. Click on **Add** in the Timeline or Toolbar and select the path operation **Pucker & Bloat**.

6. Twirl open **Pucker & Bloat 1** to reveal the **Amount** value. You are going to use the keyframes created by the keyframe assistant to link the changes in audio amplitude to this path operation's property.

7. Hold down the **Option** key (Mac) or the **Alt** key (Windows) and click on the **stopwatch** icon ⏱ next to **Amount**. This enables expressions to control the property (Figure 9.44).

Figure 9.44: *Enable expressions for the Amount property.*

8. Click on the **spiral icon** next to Expression: Amount — this is a Pick Whip tool. Drag it up to the Slider property in the Both Channels layer (Figure 9.45). This Pick Whip tool links the two properties together. Scrub through the Timeline.

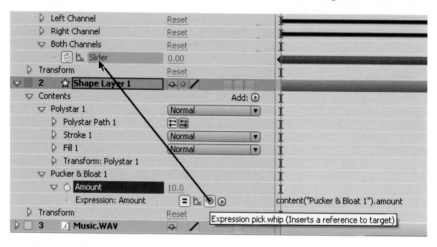

Figure 9.45: *Use the Pick Whip tool to link the two properties together.*

9. The Shape Layer deforms slightly but not enough to effectively visualize the audio. To magnify the path operation, go to the expression in the Timeline and click on it to access the code. At the very end of the expression add *** 20**. Press Enter on the numeric keypad to accept the new expression.

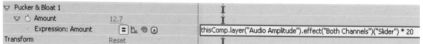

Figure 9.46: *Multiply the expression by 20 to exaggerate the Pucker & Bloat.*

10. Whatever value the audio amplitude is set to is now multiplied by 20. Click on the **RAM preview**. Save your project.

11. Experiment with other Shape Layer attributes. Link them to the Audio Amplitude layer. Multiply the expression by different numbers to create some interesting distortion effects. Have fun. Figure 9.47 shows an example of linking other properties to the Audio Amplitude.

2	☆ Shape Layer 1	⚞ ✿ /	
▽ Contents		Add: ⊙	
▽ Polystar 1		(Normal ▼)	
▽ Polystar Path 1		⊟⊞	
· Type		(Star ▼)	
· ○ Points	9.0		
· ○ Position	0.0, 0.0		
· ○ Rotation	0 x +0.0°		
· ○ Inner Radius	55.4		
· ○ Outer Radius	109.2		
▽ ○ Inner Roundness	0.5%		
· Expression: Inner ...	⊟ ⅃ ◎ ⊙		thisComp.layer("Audio Amplitude").effect("Both Channels")("Slider")
▽ ○ Outer Roundness	4.9%		
· Expression: Outer ...	⊟ ⅃ ◎ ⊙		thisComp.layer("Audio Amplitude").effect("Both Channels")("Slider") *10
▷ Stroke 1		(Normal ▼)	
▷ Fill 1		(Normal ▼)	
▷ Transform: Polystar 1			
▽ Pucker & Bloat 1			
▽ ○ Amount	9.7		
· Expression: Amount	⊟ ⅃ ◎ ⊙		thisComp.layer("Audio Amplitude").effect("Both Channels")("Slider") * 20

Figure 9.47: *Link other properties and attributes to the Audio Amplitude layer.*

12. Add a Repeater path operation to create multiple copies of the shapes all animating to the beat of the music. Figure 9.48 shows an example using the Repeater. Seven copies were replicated and rotated at different values.

Figure 9.48: *Add the Repeater path operations to create an interesting composition.*

Sound Visualization

13. Select **Composition > Make Movie**. This opens the Render Queue.

14. Click on **Lossless** next to Output Module. Set the Format to **Adobe Flash Video**. Click on **Format Options** and set the Bitrate setting to **400**.

15. Check the **Export Audio** checkbox.

Figure 9.49: *Export the audio in the Flash Video (FLV) file.*

16. Click on **Output To** and select the Chapter_09 folder on your hard drive as the final destination for the rendered movie. Click the **Render** button.

Summary

This completes the chapter on shapes and sounds. This chapter introduced you to Shape Layers and how audio can impact the final animation. You also learned how to create sound visualization using the Audio Spectrum effect and converted an audio layer into keyframes using a keyframe assistant.

Some key points to remember include:

▸ Shape Layers contain vector graphic objects that can be scaled to any size without losing any detail or quality.

▸ Shape Layers render as rasterized objects.

▸ The sampling rate defines how often a sample is taken during the recording process.

▸ Bit depth describes the amount of data contained in each sample, measured in bits.

▸ Sound visualization is a graphic representation of an audio signal.

The next, and final, chapter concludes your journey with Flash and After Effects. It focuses on optimizing your rendered compositions for Web and DVD.

CHAPTER 10

Optimization and Rendering

Your journey towards integrating Flash and After Effects comes to an end. This chapter discusses how to optimize your video renderings for Web and DVD deployment.

Understanding Compression

When you are finished with your composition in After Effects, you need to render it to a file that can be played using the QuickTime or Flash Player, imported into another software like Adobe Premiere, or transferred to another medium such as film. After Effects renders compositions for the Web, television, film, and even playback on mobile devices. The trick is knowing how to optimize the video for the final destination and still achieve great-looking video.

When integrating Flash and After Effects, obviously you want to avoid rendering uncompressed video. The resulting video files would be too large and the data rates too high to download and play back effectively on the Web. You need to compress your movies in After Effects or use the Flash Video Encoder. This chapter focuses on preparing high-quality compressed videos.

The best place to begin is in understanding why and how compression is done. Human perception is limited and compression tools take advantage of this by "losing" data that we will never miss. Compression tools and formats employ complex mathematical calculations that are way beyond the scope of this book. The concepts, however, are much easier to understand.

What is a Codec?

On a fundamental level, compression reduces the amount of transferable data, referred to as the data rate, needed to display an acceptable video image. It analyzes a sequence of images and sounds. From that, it encodes a file that removes as much data as possible while still providing a reproduction that, to our senses (sight and sound), closely retains the quality of the original source.

Figure 10.1: *Temporal compression looks for redundancy in data over a series of frames.*

There is a **co**mpressor and a **dec**ompressor, known as a **codec**, that performs the actual compression. A compressor reduces the amount of digital information required to store the video. A decompressor decodes the compressed data during playback. It's important to use the same codec for the compressor and decompressor. If the decoder can't understand the encoder's compressed data you will not be able to view the digital video.

There are two types of compression used: temporal and spatial. **Temporal compression**, also called **interframe compression**, looks for redundancy in data over a series of frames (Figure 10.1). If there is no change in the data from frame-to-frame, it copies that part of the previous frame into the next one. Temporal compression encodes only the changes from one frame to another and is used when creating a Flash Video file.

Figure 10.2: *Spatial compression looks for redundancy in only the current frame.*

Spatial compression, also referred to as **intraframe compression**, looks for redundancy within the data structure of one single frame. Since the human eye is unable to distinguish small differences in color, areas of similar color are averaged and combined using spatial compression. This works fine for static images, such as a JPEG image, but not the best choice for lots of movement.

There is a wide variety of file formats available for video and audio. Common source file formats include Apple QuickTime (MOV files), Microsoft Video for

Windows (AVI files), and MPEG files used for High Definition Video (HDV) and standard DVD. A QuickTime movie is the most common source file used in converting video into the Flash Video (FLV) format.

The Flash Player or QuickTime Player needs to have the proper codec installed in order to play back the video. Fortunately, the latest Flash Player has two specific codecs built in: **On2 VP6** and **Sorenson Spark**. Earlier versions of the Flash Player, starting with version 6, have only the Sorenson Spark codec. For the QuickTime Player, you may need to download a separate file for playback.

Figure 10.3: *Flash offers two built-in video codecs.*

Compression can also be **lossy** or **lossless**. Lossy compression loses information for good. It's gone! It can dramatically reduce a video file size up to 100:1 which is optimal for Web delivery. Similar to JPEG compression, the more you compress, the lower the quality and the more artifacts that are introduced into the image.

When it is critical that the original source and the decompressed data need to be identical, use Lossless compression. This is commonly used in the popular ZIP file format, or PNG and GIF image files. Lossless compression reduces a file anywhere from 10 to 50%. The file size still remains relatively large.

Streaming the Data

As you just learned, compression helps reduce the amount of data. On the Web, data is transferred from a Web server to your browser or Flash Player on your computer. Digital video holds a lot of data and with the limitations of storage and the Internet bandwidth, compression becomes a much needed ally. The fewer the items you have, the less you have to move. The act of transferring the video data is called streaming.

Streaming acts like a river's current, in that it moves data from a server to your Flash Player. If the current of the river remains constant and steady, you have no problem transferring the data from point A to point B. Too much water causes flooding and then you have problems. The Flash Player becomes overwhelmed by all the data being pushed its way so it creates a dam to buffer the data and then release it. If your video is constantly starting and stopping online, you may want to reconsider the data rate.

Streaming can transfer live and prerecorded audio and video. There are media server applications, such as the Adobe Flash Media Server, optimized to stream media. These server applications deliver a broad range of media experiences such as Video on Demand, live Web-event broadcasts, video blogging and video messaging. If security is a concern, these streamed files leave behind no residual copies on your computer.

Throughout this book, you have been using **progressive download** for the FLV files you created in After Effects. Why? This is a fast and effective way of playing video through the Web or locally on your hard drive. The FLV files are streamed into the Flash Player from your Web server, not a media server application. This method starts playing the video as soon as it receives enough data, before it has completed its download. It is important to note that these files are stored in the browser cache.

Figure 10.4: *The bandwidth decides how much information can stream.*

Streaming data is not the only issue you need to contend with when working with Flash Video. The **bandwidth** is the deciding factor on how much information can stream to the Flash Player. It controls the playback and the overall user experience.

Let's continue with our river metaphor. We have a school of fish, our data, moving downstream. The data rate would relate to how fast the current is moving the fish. The bandwidth would relate to the width of the river. If the river narrows, not as many fish can get through, causing a backup, or delay (Figure 10.4).

What is the best data rate to use?

Determining the Data Rate

Let's clarify what data rate is. Data rate refers to the amount of data transferred per a unit of time. Time is usually expressed in kilobits per second (Kbps). The data rate and the bandwidth work hand-in-hand. Whereas the bandwidth determines the video playback, the data rate defines the visual quality of the video.

The data rate also helps determine the bandwidth needed to play back the video smoothly. It is important to understand that the data rate contains two tracks: a video track and an audio track. The total data rate for a FLV file is the sum of the video and the audio data rates. Table 10.1 shows some suggested data rates used for different bandwidths:

Table 10.1: *Suggested data rates for different connections*

Bandwidth Connections	Suggested Data Rates
Dial-up	40–60 Kbps
DSL	100–300 Kbps
Cable	200–350 Kbps
LAN (Intranet)	384–600 Kbps

What do those number mean? Data rate is a quantity that defines the amount of information sent within a unit of time. For example, if you were using a dial-up connection (56K modem), you could effectively receive 56.6 Kbps of data every second. This occurs in a perfect world, which rarely happens. By lowering the data rate, it allows the connection to process not only the video data but other online activities that are occurring at the same time.

Data Rate Formula

How can you determine the data rate for your Flash Video? There are three components that can help you. These include the frame size, frame rate, and the codec compression used. You can determine a good starting point for a data rate using the following formula:

(Width x Height x Frame Rate x 8)/Compression = Data Rate (Kbps)

Let's take the first project you built in Chapter 1 as an example. The project in After Effects was rendered at 360 x 240 at 29.97 fps. The Flash Video codec used was On2 VP6, which compresses video at 60:1, or a compression divider of 60000. Here is what the formula would look like:

(360 x 240 x 29.97 x 8)/60000 = 345 Kbps

Where did the number eight come from? There are 8 bits to a byte. The data rate is expressed in kilo**bits** per second (Kbps). If you took that same file and rendered it using the Sorenson Spark codec, the compression divider would need to change to 48000. As you probably guessed, the On2 VP6 codec provides better compression.

$$(360 \times 240 \times 29.97 \times 8)/48000 = 432 \text{ Kbps}$$

Why do all that math when you can use the default setting for the Flash Video Encoder which encodes at 400 Kbps? This is a suggested preset data rate. It doesn't guarantee acceptable playback for everyone. Also keep in mind that the 400 Kbps is only the video track (Figure 10.5).

Figure 10.5: The default video data rate is 400 Kbps.

If your project contains audio, the default data rate for the audio encoder is 96 Kbps (Figure 10.6). This gives you a grand total of 496 Kbps, which is appropriate in a high-bandwidth situation. If you want to reduce the overall file size, choose mono instead of stereo. You will not notice too much of an audio difference from the built-in speakers on your computer.

Figure 10.6: The default audio data rate is 96 Kbps.

Even though the technology is improving and the computers are getting faster, not everyone has the latest and greatest toys. So is there a magic number to aim for? There have been many tests done and a consensus suggests a data rate less than 350 kbps for broadband situation and about 40 to 60 kbps for dial-up. There are so many variations in video clips that it is next to impossible to provide one perfect number that solves everything. You need to experiment.

Optimizing Your Video Before Encoding

Determining an appropriate data rate is not an exact science because not all video is the same. Videos that contains a lot of movement with large frame sizes are going to require a higher data rate. Figure 10.7 shows what happens if you choose a lower data rate for a video that requires much more.

Figure 10.7: *The left image has a video data rate of 400 Kbps. The right image has a video data rate of 40 Kbps. Both have the same frame size and frame rate.*

Video of a talking head doesn't require the same data rate due to the lack of movement. It all boils down to balancing the quality of the imagery and sound to the playback limitations based on user bandwidth. In addition to the video content, there are ways to optimize your video prior to encoding. If you look at the data rate formula again you will see three components that you have control over: frame size, frame rate, and codec compression.

The frame size and frame rate play important roles in determining the final data rate. You can't expect a 720 x 480 video to play back smoothly using a dial-up connection. One way to optimize your video for the Web is to reduce the frame size. Table 10.2 offers some 4:3 frame size suggestions:

Table 10.2: *Suggested frame sizes for different playbacks*

Playback	Suggested Frame Size
Dial-up	120 x 90
Broadband	240 x 180 or 320 x 240
Hard drive or CD-ROM	640 x 480

As discussed in Chapter 2, frame rate is the speed at which video plays back its frames. The NTSC format uses a frame rate of 29.97 frames per second. PAL has a frame rate of 25 frames per second. If we use our river metaphor again, both of these frame rates could flood the streaming process and overwhelm the Flash Player. One method of optimizing your frame rate is to cut it in half. If your project in After Effects is set to 29.97 or 30 frames per second, use a frame rate of 15 frames per second when creating the FLV file. For PAL, use a frame rate of 12 frames per second. You can also use equal divisions of the source frame rate such as 7.5 fps for NTSC or 6 fps for PAL.

Cutting the frame rate can produce a choppy playback. Watch your video content again. If it contains a lot of movement, it may need the higher frame rate for a smoother playback. If that is the case, you will have to reduce the frame size to compensate for the higher frame rate.

Try and match the FLV frame rate to the Flash movie's frame rate. The audio track will always remain at its original frame rate. If you create a Flash Video file at 30 fps and import it into a Flash movie set to 15 fps, the video portion will play at 15 fps, but the audio will remain at 30 fps. Proper planning done ahead of time can avoid unnecessary headaches later on.

Figure 10.8: *Try and match the FLV frame rate to the Flash movie's frame rate.*

Finally, let's focus on a video's codec compression. The most popular video codecs, such as MPEG-4, are lossy codecs. Remember, lossy compression removes information when the video is compressed in order to make the file size smaller. When you use these compressed files to create a FLV file, you are compressing a compressed file. Think of it as making a copy of a copy. The more generations you make, the lower the quality.

To create better looking FLV files, use a lossless codec on the source file before you encode it in the Flash Video Encoder. A popular lossless compression codec is **Animation**. This is the default compression codec for QuickTime movies in After Effects. If you are exporting a Flash Video file directly from After Effects, you will not need to create a lossless source file since you are exporting using the original source.

Figure 10.9: *The Animation codec is a lossless compression.*

Keep in mind that these are all just suggestions for you to follow. Nothing is cast in stone. To achieve the best results with Flash Video, you are going to have to experiment. You now have some starting points to work from. The next section of this chapter walks you through the Flash Video codec options.

Publishing for the Web

Now that you are aware of how data rates can affect your video, let's take a closer look at the Flash Video codecs. Flash Video was introduced in Flash Player 6. It used the Sorenson Spark codec that made online video an overnight sensation. You have already used the internal Flash video encoder in Chapter 3. There is another external video encoder that ships with Flash Professional CS3.

 Locate the Chapter_10 folder on the DVD. Copy this folder to your hard drive. The folder contains all the files needed to complete the chapter exercises.

1. Locate and launch the **Adobe Flash CS3 Video Encoder**. On a Mac, this application can be found inside the Flash application folder. On a Windows-based computer, you will find the encoder at C:\Program Files\Adobe\ Adobe Flash CS3 Video Encoder.

2. In the Flash Video Encoder window, click on **Add**. In the Open dialog box, locate the **3D_FlyThrough.mov** file in the Renderings folder inside Chapter_10. Select the file and click **Open**. This 3D animation was created in After Effects using a Flash SWF file and Adobe Illustrator.

Figure 10.10: *Add the QuickTime movie to the Render Queue.*

3. The file appears in the queue. Select it and click on the **Settings**. This opens the Flash Video Encoding Settings dialog box. It should look familiar to the Import Video Wizard that you used in Chapter 3.

4. A thumbnail preview of the video appears at the top of the Settings dialog box. You can scrub through the video using the scrub button (Figure 10.11). The **Encoding Profiles** tab provides a popup menu that contains a number of preset encoding options. These presets are designed for either Flash Player 7 or Flash Player 8. You will create your own custom profile. Click on the **Video** tab.

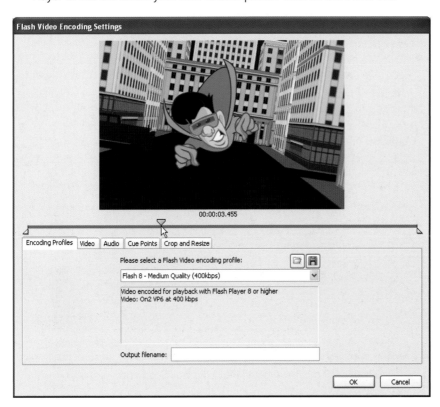

Figure 10.11: *Scrub through the video in the Encoding Settings dialog box.*

5. The Video tab presents the two built-in codecs available for Flash Video: **On2 VP6** and **Sorenson Spark**. What is the difference between the two? On2 VP6 is the newest compression codec added to Flash. It was introduced in Flash Player 8. Earlier Flash Player versions (6 and 7) do not support On2 VP6. You need to use the Sorenson Spark codec for those.

Figure 10.12: *You have two codec options to choose from.*

Before you encode your Flash Video, determine the target audience and the target software. Don't just choose the default On2 VP6 codec because it is the newest compression. Flash Player 6 and 7 have been around much longer and have a wider acceptance than the latest version.

Having worked for large corporations, I can tell you first hand that they do not have the latest plug-ins and players installed. They are usually a couple of versions behind. Make sure you have done your research.

Each video codec has its own benefits and weaknesses. Table 10.3 illustrates the differences between Sorenson Spark and On2 VP6. It also suggest when to use one over the other.

Table 10.3: *Differences between the two Flash codecs*

Sorenson Spark	On2 VP6
Supported in Flash Player 6 or higher.	Supported in Flash Player 8 or higher.
Requires less processing power than On2 VP6. It also compresses faster.	Requires up to twice as much processing power over Sorenson Spark.
Acceptable image quality.	Superior image quality.
Does not support alpha channels.	Supports alpha channels for video compositing in Flash.
Performs well on slower computer processors.	Best choice for current desktop computers on the market.

6. For this exercise, select the **On2 VP6** codec. It will produce much better results, especially with all the movement within the video content.

7. You are going to deploy this video for a cable modem connection. Enter **300** as the Max data rate. The **Quality** setting changes to **Custom**.

Figure 10.13: *Create a custom data rate of 300 Kbps.*

8. Change the **frame rate** to **15 fps**. The QuickTime movie does not contain an audio track, so there will not be a problem when it is imported into a Flash movie with the same frame rate of 15 fps.

Figure 10.14: *Change the frame rate to 15 fps.*

9. Directly underneath the Max data rate is an option for keyframe placement. Video keyframes are similar to the keyframes in Flash. They record all the information at that particular frame. The following frames only store the changes in data from the previous keyframe. You can specify the frequency of keyframes placed in your video. For now, leave the setting at **Automatic**.

10. Click on the **Audio** tab. Since this video does not contain an audio track, the options are grayed out. Audio is compressed using the **MP3 codec**. This is the best audio codec available. The compression removes certain sound data that falls outside of our hearing range. This creates a smaller file size that still sounds great to us. Its official name is MPEG-1 Audio Layer 3.

11. Click on the **Crop and Resize** button. The current frame size of the rendered video is 720 x 480 pixels. This is quite large for streaming. Check the Resize checkbox. Enter **360** in the Width field and **240** in the Height field. This scales the rendered Flash Video (FLV) file and helps improve the streaming process.

Figure 10.15: *Resize the video to 360 x 240.*

It is important to note that you are scaling down from the original source file's dimensions. Never, ever scale up. Video is pixel-based. The pixels become more noticeable as you scale larger than its normal size. It is similar to scaling any raster image in Photoshop. Avoid doing it.

12. Click **OK** to close the Flash Video Encoding Settings dialog box.

13. In the Flash Video Encoder window, click on **Start Queue**. When the encoding is done, quit out of the Flash CS3 Video Encoder. Locate the FLV file that you just created. It was saved to the same folder as the original video file — the **Renderings** folder inside Chapter_10.

Notice that the file size for the FLV file is around 395 KB compared to the QuickTime source video at 37 MB. That's a pretty impressive file reduction. Let's create a new Flash file and test the FLV file.

14. Launch **Adobe Flash CS3**. Create a new Flash file. Set the frame rate to 15 fps.

15. Select **File > Import > Import Video**. This opens the Import Video Wizard.

16. The wizard first asks you to locate the video file. Make sure **On Your Computer** is selected. Click **Browse**. In the Open dialog box, locate the 3D_FlyThrough.flv in the Renderings folder inside Chapter_10. Select it. Click **Open**.

17. Click **Next** to continue. For the deployment options, select **Progressive Download From a Web Server**. You can either embed the file or link to the file externally. Table 10.4 reviews some deployment suggestions.

Table 10.4: *Embed the video or load it externally?*

Video / Purpose	Embed	External
5 seconds or under with no audio.	X	
Used to trace frames for rotoscope animation.	X	
Used for interface interactivity (buttons, preloaders).	X	
Longer than 5 seconds with audio.		X
Used for instructional training.		X
Used in conjunction with cue points.		X

Adobe Flash Media Server

How would you like to deploy your video?

○ Progressive download from a web server
◉ Stream from Flash Video Streaming Service
○ Stream from Flash Media Server
○ As mobile device video bundled in SWF
○ Embed video in SWF and play in timeline

What about streaming video content? This deployment option lets you host video files using a Flash Media Server. This is a server solution optimized to deliver streaming, real-time media. You can host your own Flash Media Server, or use a hosted Flash Video Streaming Service (FVSS). Adobe has partnered with several content delivery network (CDN) providers that offer hosted services.

What is the benefit over using a local Web server? Flash Media Server uses bandwidth detection to deliver video or audio content based on the user's available bandwidth. You can provide different content for users based on their connection speed. For example, if your target audience tries to watch your FLV file using a dial-up modem, you can deliver an appropriately encoded file that doesn't require too much bandwidth.

When deploying streaming video the playback starts sooner than it does using other methods of incorporating video. Streaming uses less of the user's memory and disk space. For security concerns, streaming video is the way to go because the video is not saved to the user's cache when streamed. For more information about Flash Media Server, go to: **www.adobe.com/go/flash_media_server**.

18. Click **Next** to continue. The skin provides video controls such as play, stop, and seek. Select **SkinUnderPlaySeekStop.swf** from the Skin popup menu. Notice that the skin is a SWF file. Flash will save a copy of this file to the same folder it saves the FLV file to.

Chapter 10: Optimization and Rendering

19. Click **Next** to continue. Review the settings for the imported video file. Click **Finish** to import the video. Select **Control > Test Movie**.

Figure 10.16: *Import the FLV file into Flash.*

Surprisingly, the video looks pretty good for the amount of compression that took place. You have to realize that there will be some quality sacrifice on your part. How much depends on you. Figure 10.17 shows the same frame using different encoding. The last section discusses how to publish this composition in After Effects to a DVD.

On2 VP6 High Quality 700 Kbps

On2 VP6 Medium Quality 400 Kbps

Sorenson High Quality 700 Kbps

Sorenson Medium Quality 400 Kbps

Figure 10.17: *Compare the image quality using different encoding presets.*

Publishing to a DVD

You are going to use the same animation from the previous exercise to publish it onto a DVD. You cannot do this directly through After Effects. You need to use software that creates DVDs such as Adobe Encore CS3 or iDVD on the Mac.

1. Launch **Adobe After Effects**. Open the **3D_City.aep** file in Chapter_10.

3D_City

Let's quickly deconstruct the composition. The Timeline contains a lot of layers. The **SuperheroFlying.swf** layer is a 2D layer that was created in Flash. The animation consists of the superhero scaling and rotating as he flies through the city. The city is made up of nested 3D objects.

Figure 10.18: *The 3D buildings were created from three Adobe Illustrator layers.*

Similar to the 3D environment in Chapter 6, the buildings were created using five 3D layers, four for the sides and one for the roof. The artwork for the front/back, side, and roof was created in Adobe Illustrator. The vector layers are set to **Continuously Rasterize** so that they will retain their detail as the camera moves through the 3D scene.

The Camera layer animates over time. Its Position, Rotation, and Point of Interest properties all contain keyframes (Figure 10.19). Twirl open the properties to see how the animation was done.

Figure 10.19: *The 3D Camera animates over time.*

Figure 10.20: *The 3D Camera animates through the 3D scene.*

An Adjustment Layer was added. The Broadcast Colors effect has been applied to the Adjustment Layer to keep the composition's color space within the range allowed for NTSC broadcast video.

2. For this exercise, you will use **iDVD** to save your file to a DVD. It is the easiest application to use when creating a DVD. With the composition in place, select **Composition > Make Movie**.

3. Click on **Based on Lossless** next to Output Module. This opens the Output Module Settings dialog box. Set the Format to **QuickTime** movie. iDVD accepts movies in QuickTime format. Still pictures can be any QuickTime-compatible format, such as PICT, TIFF, or JPEG.

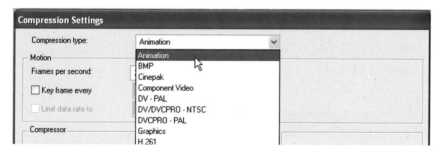

Figure 10.21: *Set the compression type to Animation.*

4. Under Format Options, set the compression setting to **Animation**. In iDVD, movies are converted into **MPEG-2** format just before they are written to the DVD disc. The Animation codec is a lossless compression. Let iDVD do all of the necessary compression.

MPEG-2 is the compression of choice for most digital television and standard DVD formats. Another popular codec is **H.264**. It is used for Blu-ray Discs and provides incredible video quality from the smallest amount of video data. H.264 delivers the same quality as MPEG-2 at a third to half the data rate.

5. Click the **Render** button. Your composition will start to render. The Render Queue provides feedback such as which frame is currently being rendered and approximately how much time is left.

iDVD

6. Launch **iDVD**. When the application loads, click on **Magic iDVD**. This is similar to the Import Video Wizard in Flash in that it walks you through the steps in creating a DVD.

Figure 10.22: *Select Magic iDVD.*

7. Next, add your movie to iDVD. To do this, the easiest way is to select the rendered movie file in Chapter_10 and drag it to the **Drop Movies Here** area.

Figure 10.23: *Add your movie to iDVD. Click and drag it from the Chapter_10 folder to the Drop Movies Here area.*

8. Enter a DVD title and choose a theme for your DVD menus. For this exercise the **Marquee** theme was used from **4.0 Themes**.

Figure 10.24: *Choose a theme.*

9. You can edit the screen text by simply clicking on it. By default, iDVD uses the file name. Click on it and change it to whatever you want.

Figure 10.25: *Change the screen text to whatever you want.*

10. Click on the **Play** button to preview your DVD playback.

Figure 10.26: *Preview the DVD playback.*

11. Insert a blank DVD into your DVD burner.

12. Click the **Burn** button . When the process is complete, iDVD ejects your DVD and you can play it on a DVD player. It is that easy! Enjoy.

Figure 10.26: *Burn the DVD.*

Summary

This completes the chapter on optimizing and rendering. You learned about compression and the popular codecs used. The next section focused on data rates and how they affect your final rendered video. Finally, you exported the same After Effects composition for the Web and DVD delivery.

Some key concepts to remember include:

▸ Compression reduces the amount of transferable data needed to display an acceptable video image.

▸ A compressor and a decompressor, known as a codec, performs the actual compression.

▸ Data rate refers to the amount of data transferred per a unit of time. Time is usually expressed in kilobits per second (Kbps).

Your journey has come full-circle. You started your quest by learning about the workspace and workflow in After Effects. In this final chapter you dug deeper into the last stage of the workflow — rendering. Along the way you created visual effects and animation using both Flash and After Effects. These two applications were made for each other. Hopefully you have been inspired to explore more uncharted possibilities using these two powerhouse applications. Thank you for taking the journey.

Index

D